*FLIGHT FROM CHILE*

*THOMAS C. WRIGHT*

*RODY OÑATE*

# Flight from Chile

VOICES OF EXILE

✢   ✢   ✢

Translations by Irene B. Hodgson

*University of New Mexico Press, Albuquerque*

*Library of Congress Cataloging-in-Publication Data*
*Flight from Chile : voices of exile / [compiled by] Thomas C. Wright,*
*Rody Oñate; translations by Irene Hodgson.*
*p. cm.*
*Includes bibliographical references (p. ) and index.*
*ISBN 0-8263-1891-6 (hardcover). — ISBN 0-8263-1957-2 (pbk.)*
*1. Chile—Politics and government—1970–1973. 2. Chile—Politics*
*and government—1973–1988. 3. Chile—Politics and government—1988–*
*4. Chileans—Foreign countries—Politics and government. 5. Social*
*adjustment. 6. Chileans—Foreign countries—Interviews.*
*7. Rufugees, Political—Chile—Interviews. I. Wright, Thomas C.*
*II. Oñate, Rody, 1948–*
*F3100.F58 1998*
*983'.065—dc21 98-13068*
*CIP*

# Contents

*El destierro es redondo:*
*un círculo, un anillo:*
*le dan vuelta tus pies, cruzas la tierra,*
*no es tu tierra,*
*te despierta la luz, y no es tu luz,*
*la noche llega: faltan tus estrellas,*
*hallas hermanos: pero no es tu sangre.*

*Exile is round:*
*a circle, a ring:*
*your feet walk around it, you cross the land,*
*it is not your land,*
*the light awakens you, and it is not your light,*
*nightfall arrives: your stars are absent,*
*you find kin: but they are not your blood.*

EPIGRAM SOURCE: "Exilo" ["Exile"] by Pablo Neruda, *Memorial de Isla Negra*, 6th edition (Buenos Aires: Editorial Losada, 1996), p. 169.

# Introduction

This book is the story of Chileans in exile. Between 1973 and 1988, an estimated 200,000 men, women, and children — nearly 2 percent of Chile's population — were forced out of their country for political reasons. In the following pages, thirty-three of those exiles recount the circumstances leading to their expatriation, the challenges they faced in adapting to life in countries around the world, and the difficulties of returning to a Chile that had changed profoundly during their absence. Their stories provide a look into the phenomenon of exile that deeply affected the lives of so many of their compatriots.

In general terms, Chilean exiles lived an experience shared by at least two million other Latin Americans over the past four decades. Beginning with the Cuban Revolution, Latin America has witnessed the new phenomenon of politically caused mass exile. While exile itself has a long history in Latin America, prior to 1959 it was the province of the few — normally political leaders on the losing side of military coups or other power struggles. All of that changed with Fidel Castro's ascension to power, as Cubans eventually numbering around a million opted for expatriation over living in the new socialist state. The military dictatorships of Brazil and the southern cone — themselves a reaction to the wave of revolutionary activity unleashed throughout Latin America by the Cuban Revolution — added to the numbers of the displaced. The military governments of Brazil (1964–1985), Uruguay (1973–1984), Chile (1973–1990), and Argentina (1976–1983) severely repressed the left in their countries, and among their strategies for destroying their opponents was the institutionalization of mass exile. Thus, for nearly twenty-five years, hundreds of thousands of individuals left their South American homelands for brief or prolonged periods of asylum abroad.

In the 1980s, the civil wars in Central America further swelled the ranks of those displaced by political conditions in their countries. In Nicaragua, the contra war drove thousands into exile. In Guatemala and El Salvador, guerrilla wars and savage government repression sent hundreds of thousands across borders and, in many cases, onward to the United States. And if one counts the far greater numbers of Latin Americans driven abroad by poverty, exacerbated by the neoliberal economic policies widely adopted in the 1970s and 1980s, the phenomenon of mass exile involves several million people from Central and South America and the Caribbean.

This book appears a quarter of a century after the military coup that launched the massive flow of exiles from Chile. It grew out of casual conversations in Santiago with returned exiles about their lives abroad and the challenges of coming back to a homeland that, for many, had become a different country from the one they were forced to leave early in the military regime. Journalist and political scientist Rody Oñate, driven out of Chile because of his political affiliation, had recently come back from fourteen years abroad. Historian Thomas Wright was trying to understand the impact of exile on those Chileans who experienced it and the role of exile in the overall politics of the Pinochet dictatorship. These initial discussions led us to the modest body of literature on exile, which, while useful and enlightening, raised as many questions as it answered. Hence the decision to undertake our own study of exile, through which we hope to contribute to a deeper understanding of a most difficult period in Chile's history.

Our goal is to present as complete a picture of exile as is possible in a single volume. Because data on exile are far from reliable, we cannot claim to have assembled a statistically representative sample of the Chilean exile experience. Nonetheless, we have sought to present a cross section of exile by interviewing women and men, members of Marxist and non-Marxist parties as well as independents, practitioners of different occupations and professions, individuals from all parts of Chile, and people who sojourned on four continents. Only a few of the testimonies are from well-known public figures; most are from ordinary people caught up in the conflagration that was Chile after the military coup of September 11, 1973.

The interviews on which this book is based were profoundly emotional experiences for those on both sides of the microphone. Since the subject of exile is largely taboo, even within families (see chapter 9), several individuals confided that our interview offered them their first opportunity to talk freely and systematically about their experience of exile and return. Despite their long silence and the passage of two decades, everyone we interviewed had retained sharply focused memories of their reactions to the 1973 coup, the traumatic events that drove them into exile, and the feelings, challenges, and routines of life in their adopted countries. Clearly, exile had made an indelible impression on its protagonists.

The interviews made equally indelible impressions on the authors. Time after time, we heard individuals say how lucky they were—lucky to have been arrested early, for example, before the military government had its intelligence apparatus honed; lucky to have gotten asylum in an embassy; lucky to have been tortured lightly. No one said the obvious: that they were lucky to be alive. We heard the most gruesome stories told matter-of-factly: stories of their torture, of their loved ones' deaths, of heart-stopping close calls with arrest or assassination. And we learned a great deal about spirit, about the incredible determination of Chileans who, believing strongly in their vision for their country's future, would not accept defeat but who fought, in any and all ways possible, to return to their homeland and reestablish Chile's disappeared democracy.

While exile is a political phenomenon that unlocks key aspects of the dictatorship, it is, much more importantly, a moving human drama. This book tells the story of exile through the exiles' own voices. It is the story of shattered dreams, broken families, and truncated careers; of psychological and physical trauma; of the struggle to adapt to strange cultures and climates. For the majority who have not returned, exile obviously continues. For those who have, the experience of repatriation is often as difficult and painful as exile itself. The Chilean diaspora and its consequences did not end, then, with the return of civilian government in 1990 or with the closing of the government's Oficina Nacional de Retorno (National Office for Return, ONR) in 1994; they will continue to affect individuals, families, and the nation for decades to come.

# Translator's Introduction

Some say that translating is the closest possible reading of a text. Translating the texts of the these testimonies has been a very interesting and rewarding experience. Since they are transcriptions of oral interviews, I have drawn on my experience of interpreting for Latin American and Spanish politicians, authors, and musicians and for Central American refugees. In an attempt to keep the flavor of the spoken language, I have tried to let the people speak to, and through, me and to follow much the same process that I do when I translate orally—even to the point of rephrasing as the thought continues and I see where it is going. I have found that my typing has slowed down and speeded up dramatically according to my own emotional response to the events I am recounting. Through the rhythm of my typing, my fingers have expressed, at times, the urgency or anguish or anger that I sometimes feel when translating orally and that sometimes creeps into my voice when I am particularly affected by the words that "I" am saying.

I have tried as much as possible to keep the flavor of the spoken Spanish. This includes contradictions in the verb tenses that exist in the original. It is striking that many of the testimonies recount past events in the present tense, or switch back and forth in the same narrative. This seems to indicate the immediacy of these events in the minds of those interviewed in spite of the intervening years. Sometimes there is also a distancing—or universalization—of the experience by the use of "one" or "you," rather than "I," which I tried to preserve whenever possible for it to still make sense and flow in English. I have also tried to use in the

English the same kind of vocabulary as in the Spanish; for example, slang and informality versus a more educated tone, and so on.

Because these are transcriptions of oral testimony, punctuation is frequently difficult. I have used dashes to indicate the parenthetical comments that we often make while speaking and have used commas, semicolons, colons, and periods where necessary to try to keep the flow of the narrative and make it clear to the reader when the speaker has changed gears in midsentence. I have also allowed myself to end thoughts with prepositions and other such things that we do when speaking and avoid when writing. In making the choices among different alternatives, as a translator always has to do, I have read and reread the Spanish paragraphs along with the English and have consulted with Rody and other Chileans on nuances and details in order to make these translations as accurate as I can. As a final step, I have even read the translations aloud and made changes where different words fit better in my mouth when speaking rather than reading.

Certain words that would never convey the same sense in English have been left in Spanish and are in italics the first time that they occur. Some explanatory material has been included in brackets: names of places, dates, and so on.

Sometimes I have had to change word order around or the grammatical function of words, for example, in the case of the adjective "solidario/a" for which we, interestingly enough, have no English equivalent, so that I have had to find a construction that would allow for the use of the noun "solidarity."

Certain words and constructions require further explanation. The words *compañero, compañera, compañeros, compañeras* can in different situations mean "friend," "colleague," "classmate," "co-worker," "comrade," "spouse," "lover/companion." Chileans often do not specify whether the man–woman relationship involves a marriage ceremony or not, using "compañero/compañera" instead of "marido y mujer" for husband and wife but also for unmarried partners. During the Unidad Popular government, it took on a special significance as an expression of the spirit of sharing an enterprise. Allende was often referred to as "*Compañero* Salvador Allende." Chileans have told me that the word was so identified with his government that its very use was forbidden during the dictatorship. When the word is clearly used to mean "colleague," "co-worker," or "classmate," I have translated it as such. For the special Unidad Popular use or for the man/woman relationship, I have left it in Spanish.

Chileans also have a special "we," the "nosotros chileno," which functions the same way as a "royal we," that is, it is really "I." In the situations in which it is clear that is what has occurred, I have used "I" rather than "we" in the translation. I have also observed the use of prepositions of place, particularly "ahí" instead of time expressions, and, in such cases, have translated them accordingly.

I want to thank Rody and Tom for involving me in this project. I have learned a great deal working on it and have only increased my love for Chile and things Chilean. I also want to thank Rody and other Chilean and Argentine friends who have generously allowed me to ask them questions about the chapter I was currently working on, and my sister and her family for waiting patiently for me to finish so that I could come visit.

# Acknowledgments

Above all, we wish to thank the exiles and former exiles who allowed us to interview them. We are very grateful to them for trusting us to listen to their stories, to understand them, and to communicate them through this book. Since repatriated exiles still face discrimination, ostracism, and the possibility of retribution, it is remarkable that only five individuals accepted our offer of anonymity. This is further testimony to the understated but very real personal courage that permeates the exiles' testimonies.

Our sincere thanks go also to numerous individuals who learned about exile and return as volunteers or as personnel of agencies involved with exiles. Their interviews offered valuable information and insights. We are deeply indebted to three individuals who welcomed us and provided expert guidance to their agencies' collections of pamphlets, newspapers and journals, hard-to-find publications, and documents dealing with human-rights issues and exile in particular: Ximena Garri of the Organización Internacional para las Migraciones (International Organization for Migration, OIM); Carmen Garretón of the Centro de Documentación (archive) of the Archbishopric of Santiago's Vicaría de la Solidaridad (Vicariate of Solidarity); and Miriam Brito of the Fundación de Ayuda Social de las Iglesias Cristianas (Social Aid Foundation of the Christian Churches, FASIC). The University Studies Abroad Consortium and its director, Carmelo Urza, provided valuable research support. Thanks to Irene Hodgson's skillful translation, the exiles' voices transcend the language barrier and remain true in meaning and content. We are grateful to David Holtby, editor and associate director of the University of New

Mexico Press, for his interest in and encouragement of our project. The many concrete contributions and the enthusiastic support of our wives, Dina Titus and Eileen Moyle, are deeply appreciated.

Many other people shared their insights, helped locate informants and sources, and encouraged us in our endeavor. The generous help of all involved made this project possible; in the truest sense, this book is a collective effort.

*FLIGHT FROM CHILE*

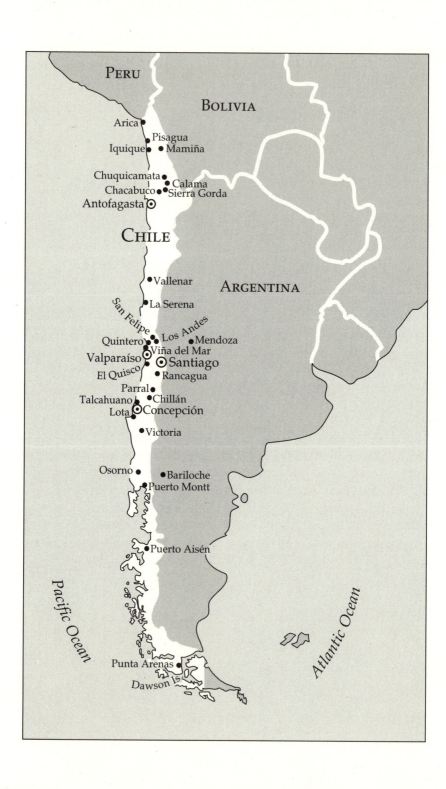

# ONE

# The Diaspora in Context

## Chilean Politics, 1970–1994

The election of Salvador Allende as president in September 1970 put Chile on center stage of world attention, for it was an event unique not only to Latin America but to the world. For the first time, a political democracy elected a Marxist on the platform of establishing socialism in his country. In contrast to the European socialist parties or the Latin American parties that belonged to the Socialist International, Allende was a traditional Marxist who believed that socialism meant state ownership of the means of production and distribution—not a welfare state or a social democracy. In contrast to the countries where socialism had been established, including the Soviet Union, Eastern Europe, China, and Cuba, Allende took power without insurrection or military conquest. Besides being a freely elected president, Allende professed allegiance to Chile's deeply rooted pluralistic political system—a further contrast to the one-party dictatorial socialist states. Thus Chile provided the laboratory test for a question that heretofore had remained hypothetical: Is there a peaceful road to socialism?

Salvador Allende had run as the candidate of Unidad Popular (UP), a coalition of the historic, middle-class Radical Party; the Movimiento de Acción Popular Unitaria (MAPU), the former left wing of the Christian Democratic Party (PDC); two small personalist parties; and the dominant Communist and Socialist parties. Allende, a medical doctor, veteran politician, and member of Chile's Socialist Party, had campaigned on the program of moving Chile as quickly and as far as possible toward socialism during the six-year term to which he was elected. He promised an acceleration of the agrarian reform launched by his predecessor, PDC President Eduardo Frei (1964–1970), extensive nationalizations, and a foreign policy free of United States–imposed restraints. Allende won with 36.5 percent of the vote, to 35.2 percent for the runner-up, conservative former president Jorge Alessandri, a narrow but not unusual margin in Chile's multiparty system whose electoral code did not require a runoff when no candidate obtained a majority. But in 1970, the stakes were far higher than usual.

Allende faced a host of problems from the outset because of his Marxism, his commitment to ending large-scale capitalism in Chile, and his quest for independence in foreign relations. His first challenge came from the Nixon administration, which, having spent millions of dollars to prevent Allende's election, moved to thwart his November inauguration by trying to subvert the process of congressional confirmation and attempting to create a climate conducive to military intervention. Once inaugurated, Allende faced the challenge of implementing his ambitious agenda while controlling only one branch of government. Lacking a congressional majority, he relied on elastic definitions of presidential powers and the creative use of existing law to push UP goals. In doing this, he faced the dogged opposition of an unsympathetic judiciary wedded to capitalist law. Finally, there was the ultimate arbiter of politics, the armed forces. Despite Chile's long history of rarely interrupted civilian government, the military was certain to face unprecedented pressure from anti-UP forces to save the nation from "communism."

Despite the obstacles facing his administration, Allende's first year in office largely measured up to his promise of "a revolution *a la chilena* with red wine and *empanadas* [meat and onion pies]"—a reference to the festive diet of the Chilean *pueblo*. The president combined old-fashioned pump priming and presidential prerogatives to redistribute income to the working and middle classes and make significant progress in agrarian reform and in nationalizing the economy. Extensive expropriations and buyouts in the banking, insurance, communications, transportation, and manufacturing sectors, combined with the complete nationalization of Chile's primary export, copper, gave the state control of the "commanding heights" of the economy within Allende's first year. Chile also reestablished diplomatic relations with Cuba, thus becoming the first Latin American nation to resume ties severed as the result of a 1964 Organization of American States (OAS) action to isolate Cuba. The April 1971 municipal elections, in which the UP received a slight majority, reflected the success of Allende's first five months as president.

By the end of his first year, mounting economic and political problems began to overshadow these successes. Expensive nationalizations and public works had consumed a large portion of Chile's foreign currency reserves, a U.S.-orchestrated credit boycott had been established, and Chile's chronic inflation had begun to accelerate. The PDC and the right-wing National Party established a formal anti-Allende alliance and used their congressional majority to block legislation and impeach cabinet ministers. The Nixon administration, firmly committed to Allende's overthrow, used the CIA and millions of dollars in pursuit of its objective.

Underlying the increasing confrontation and polarization were a growing mass mobilization and the government's ambivalent attitude toward controlling it. Throughout rural Chile, unauthorized worker occupations of estates, often organized by militants of the UP parties and the nongovernmental leftist party Movimiento de Izquierda Revolucionaria (MIR), led to chaos and frequent violence as landowners organized and armed themselves to defend their properties. In Santiago and other cities, similar extralegal expropriations proceeded apace, especially in the industrial belts of the capital, where workers seized dozens of factories. This "hypermobilization" of the rural and urban working class posed a difficult dilemma for the Allende administration. On one hand, Allende acknowledged his constitutional responsibility to enforce the law, which of course guaranteed private ownership rights until a valid expropriation order was given. On the other hand, the workers were Allende's constituency, and for ideological as well as practical reasons he was understandably loathe to use the force of a "people's" government against the people.

The inconsistency of government responses to the wave of unauthorized seizures of factories and haciendas reflected the deep division within the UP coalition and within Allende's own Socialist Party over strategy and tactics for making the revolution. A strong minority of the UP, particularly the left wing of the Socialists led by Carlos Altamirano and the MAPU, advocated pushing ahead with all speed, ignoring legal restraints, to break the back of capitalism before the opposition could regroup sufficiently to stop the process. The more conservative UP majority, consisting of the Communists, the Allende Socialists, and most of the non-Marxist groups, advocated moving vigorously toward socialism through legal means so as to avoid provoking an armed reaction against the government; they preferred consolidation of gains at a certain point, if necessary, over continual confrontation. This schism within the UP remained unresolved to the end of the Allende government.

The government's vacillation on the rule of law was a major factor in the UP's political failure. Chile's large middle class was crucial to Allende's success; he needed a share of its votes to achieve a congressional majority in the 1973 election and its tolerance was essential to keeping the military, led by a largely middle-class officer corps, on the sidelines. Yet the rising levels of violence, governmental vacillation on law enforcement, accelerating inflation, shortages of food and consumer goods, and the leveling tendencies in UP policy alienated growing segments of the middle class. This sentiment was dramatically revealed in October 1972, when a truck owners' strike, called to protest a government plan to nationalize the trucking sector, precipitated action by Chile's economic and professional associations, or *gremios*. The October strike—a full-scale business and service shutdown accompanied by housewives' "marches of the empty pots"—was settled after four weeks, but only with the incorporation of military men into the cabinet; this marked the beginning of the armed forces' overt politicization.

The March 1973 congressional elections, which gave the opposition 56 percent to the UP's 44 percent, did nothing to resolve the stalemate. Beset now by runaway inflation, declining production, shortages, decapitalization, and mounting deficits, the economy was near collapse by mid-1973. Rising street violence, open warfare in the countryside, growing incidents of assassination and sabotage by the paramilitary right-wing *Patria y Libertad*, rumors of armed worker militias, and the establishment of neighborhood vigilance patrols reflected the growing insecurity and instability that were rapidly undermining Chile's institutional foundations. An aborted military coup on June 29, 1973, forecast the breakdown of the armed forces' neutrality, and in July a second, larger gremio strike backed by CIA funding as well as reports of UP-inspired subversion in the navy put Chile into full crisis. Faced with this untenable situation, President Allende planned to announce, on the afternoon of September 11, his decision to hold a plebiscite on his continuance in office to the end of his term in 1976. The military insurrection of that morning preempted Allende's desperate attempt to preserve peace in Chile.

The coup of September 11, 1973, ended Chile's distinctive tradition of civilian, constitutional government. Given the extreme deterioration of political and economic conditions, the coup surprised few observers, but the brutality with which it was executed was shocking even to its advocates. President Allende was but one victim of the many who overwhelmed the capacities of jails, hospitals, and morgues. Soldiers rounded up thousands of suspects, conducted mass executions in soccer stadiums, burned books, and ransacked homes. The brunt of the coup's fury was directed at members of the government and the UP parties, the MIR, and at workers and peasants suspected of participating in extralegal takeovers of factories and estates. Expectations of a surgical, short-term intervention followed by new elections quickly evaporated as the military junta, led by Army General Augusto Pinochet, moved to consolidate its power by dissolving Congress, banning or recessing parties and labor unions, and establishing a curfew, strict censorship, and a state of siege.

One of the new regime's basic goals was to eradicate the left, and to accomplish this it developed a powerful apparatus of repression. Special prison camps were set up to accommodate the thousands of prisoners rounded up under the state of siege, courts-martial churned out sentences for alleged crimes, and tens of thousands of leftists went into exile. In June 1974 the government established a secret police, the Dirección Nacional de Inteligencia (DINA), to hone its intelligence and control capabilities. The DINA, along with the military's own units, detained and interrogated at will, operated torture centers, carried out assassinations and disappearances, and thoroughly intimidated potential opponents and the populace at large. Army and police sweeps of slums and indiscriminate jailings of their inhabitants were employed periodically. These massive human-rights violations earned the military government repeated condemnations by the United Nations, the Organization of American States, the World Court, and other international tribunals. Normally defiant of world opinion, the regime nonetheless engaged in occasional image polishing by periodically releasing prominent political prisoners, closing most prison camps in 1976, and in 1977 abolishing the infamous DINA, which promptly reappeared under a different name. Despite such steps, the regime never dismantled the terrorist state that it had created.

The government set forth the essence of the new order in a March 1974 "Declaration of Principles," announcing that the armed forces "do not set timetables for their management of the government, because the task of rebuilding the country morally, institutionally, and economically requires prolonged and profound actions." The moral rebuilding involved the extirpation of Marxism and its doctrine of class struggle and their replacement with the values of conservative Catholicism, class harmony, and Chilean nationalism; it entailed "changing the mentality of Chileans" by such measures as the complete revision of school curricula, strict control of the media, and strategic placement of symbols such as that of the authoritarian "founder of the nation," Diego Portales.* The reconstruction of institutions implied not only the proscription of Marxism, but the creation of a political system that, unlike liberal democracy, would guarantee its permanent exclusion.

The country's economic reconstruction was based on the neoliberal model of the Chicago school and Milton Friedman, approved by the International Monetary Fund, and largely financed by foreign private banks. The so-called "Chicago boys" set out to strip away half a century's accretion of government regulation and ownership by reducing tariffs, lifting price controls, devaluing the currency, selling off state industries, cutting government spending, guaranteeing foreign investment, and establishing good relations with U.S. lenders who had boycotted the Allende government. Through the application of this "shock" therapy, the Chilean economy was thoroughly transformed and integrated into the world economy as the state's share of total investment shrank drastically. After nurturing industry for half a century, Chile deindustrialized under competition from imports and became increasingly a raw material exporter, supplementing its traditional copper with out-of-season fruits for Northern Hemisphere markets, fishery and forestry products, and wine. After an initial contraction, the neoliberal model took hold and the economy experienced what was called a "miracle" of rapid growth between 1977 and 1981. A deep recession in 1982 forced some modifications, but the Chicago model remained largely intact throughout the life of the military government.

The poor and middle classes paid the price of the Chicago boys' radical experiment. Lacking union and political representation, they were defenseless against policies that at least tripled unemployment and cut workers' real wages by half while reducing the social welfare programs needed to survive the crisis. In the countryside, the government set out to reverse one of Latin America's most far-reaching agrarian reforms by returning much land to former owners and cutting aid to the new smallholders, forcing many to sell.

The military attempted to legitimize its rule in a 1980 plebiscite on a new constitution that essentially codified the status quo, described as a "protected democracy" based on the ongoing exclusion of political par-

* Genaro Arriagada Herrera, "The Legal and Institutional Framework of the Armed Forces in Chile," in *Military Rule in Chile: Dictatorship and Oppositions*, ed. J. Samuel Valenzuela and Arturo Valenzuela (Baltimore: Johns Hopkins University Press, 1986), 119–20.

ties and the military's "guardianship" role. The document also sanctioned
the continuation of existing dictatorial institutions until at least 1989,
with a provision for an extension of eight more years. Ratified by an announced 68 percent of the vote after a campaign in which opposition was
prohibited, the 1980 constitution legalized not only military control, but
also the personal power that Army General Augusto Pinochet had been
building over the years, first as head of the junta and later as president of
the republic.

Until the economic crash of 1982, the Pinochet dictatorship was so
firmly entrenched that almost no overt domestic opposition was possible.
The left was dead, underground, or exiled. The poor, now further impoverished and beaten down, survived through charity, a government public
works program, the invention of jobs, and an unprecedented growth of
solidarity organizations ranging from soup kitchens to cooperative production workshops. Despite these efforts, some 800,000 were driven to
neighboring Argentina in search of work.* With the left defeated and the
poor dedicated to day-to-day survival, there was little chance for a political opposition to develop.

The 1982 economic crisis, however, changed things and brought forth
an incipient civil opposition movement. The outlawed parties, including
the PDC as well as the UP parties, the church, and labor leaders issued a
"Democratic Manifesto" in March 1983 and called for monthly "national
days of protest" featuring rallies, sick-outs, boycotts, and the banging
of empty pots—the hallmark of the gremios' oppositon to Allende. By
1985 a "national dialogue" had begun as the end of hard-line military
regimes in Argentina, Uruguay, and Brazil fueled the debate on Chile's
future. Meanwhile, the MIR and the Communist Party mounted armed
operations against the regime, including a spectacular assassination attempt against Pinochet by the Communists' Frente Patriótico Manuel
Rodríguez in 1986. The regime met both the civil and the armed opposition with heightened repression reminiscent of the post-coup period, but
it also was forced to grant small but significant concessions, including
a loosening of press controls and a relaxation of restrictions on exiles'
returning.

Pinochet's 1980 constitution stipulated a 1988 plebiscite on the extension of military rule to 1997, whether by Pinochet himself or by a desig-
nated successor. As the plebiscite approached, most of the center and left
opposition united as the "Concertación por el No" and reorganized, pros-

---

* *Migrantes* 44 (August–September 1989), 17–18.

elytized, and did everything possible within the limits of the regime's tolerance to prepare for 1988. In 1987 and 1988, confident of victory, the dictatorship opened a new electoral register, legalized non-Marxist parties that could meet rigorous qualifications, loosened censorship, and finally ended forced exile. Despite the obstacles, the opposition prevailed in the plebiscite, and bowing to both domestic and international pressure, the regime grudgingly acknowledged its defeat. This led to presidential elections in 1989, in which PDC leader Patricio Aylwin, candidate of the same center–left coalition now renamed the "Concertación de Partidos por la Democracia," was victorious over the military's candidate and an independent conservative. Aylwin and a newly elected congress were inaugurated in March 1990, ending sixteen and a half years of military rule. Aylwin was succeeded in 1994 by Christian Democrat Eduardo Frei, son of the late President Eduardo Frei and candidate of the same broad center–left coalition that had won the plebiscite and elected Aylwin.

One of the hallmarks of the Pinochet dictatorship was the dispersal of Chilean exiles throughout the world: an estimated 200,000 Chileans, or nearly 2 percent of the country's population.* Exile, first and foremost, was the centerpiece of the military's strategy for gaining and retaining control of the country. While the systematic use of imprisonment, torture, assassination, and disappearance was certainly more dramatic and fearsome than exile, it would have been unthinkable to most Chileans, to world opinion, and probably to regime leaders themselves to kill, disappear, or imprison indefinitely the hundreds of thousands of people who, as party and union members or leaders or merely as voters, constituted the Chilean left. Instead, after proving its determination to establish absolute control and its willingness to use terror to that end, the regime was able to force some and induce others of the left to leave the country and pro-

---

* There is a wide range of estimates of the total number of Chileans who went into exile for political reasons. Political views certainly influenced these estimates. Another difficulty is distinguishing between political and economic considerations for exile, given the great impoverishment of many Chileans after 1973. The figure of 200,000 political exiles, offered by the Chilean Commission on Human Rights and the Organización Internacional para las Migraciones (OIM), is commonly accepted. See Mili Rodríguez Villouta, *Ya nunca me verás como me vieras: doce testimonios vivos del exilio* (Santiago: Ediciones del Ornitorrinco, 1990), 3; and Fernando Montupil I., ed., *Exilio, derechos humanos y democracia: el exilio chileno en Europa* (Brussels and Santiago: Casa de América Latina y Servicios Gráficos Caupolicán, 1993), 10.

hibit their return, presumably ridding itself of the enemy and eliminating any challenge to its authority.

Since most exiles left through normal channels, on scheduled flights with papers in order, the military and its apologists consistently portrayed exile as voluntary. Even expulsion from the country was cast as humane, as a better fate than leftist enemies of the fatherland deserved. In 1975, for example, regime mouthpiece *La Tercera de la Hora* hailed the government's decision to reduce the prison population by commuting prisoners' sentences to exile as "a clear demonstration of the humanitarian sentiment of the present administration," while *El Mercurio* proclaimed it a step toward the regime's goal of "complete liberty in Chile."* Yet, once abroad, the exiles showed their gratitude by engaging in intense and constant political activity to undermine the regime's claim to legitimacy. In response, the regime attempted to discredit the exiles by concocting the image of a "golden exile"—a comfortable, even luxurious existence that contrasted harshly with the economic hardship faced by many Chileans at home. Moreover, exiles were denounced in blanket terms as subversives, foreign agents, and anti-Chilean turncoats responsible for a campaign of calumny, not against the regime but against Chile. Interior Minister Sergio Fernández, for example, claimed that "every exiled Marxist is an agent of international subversion;" they were responsible for "the international campaign against Chile."†

In thinking that exile would disperse, silence, and thus neutralize the left, the military government underestimated the commitment and energy of its enemies. A large proportion of the exiles worked tirelessly to undermine the regime by creating literally thousands of groups—political parties, unions, human-rights organizations, and cultural associations at the local, regional, national, and international levels—to publicize the dictatorship's abuses, shape world opinion, and funnel money and support to the resistance within Chile. These activities were crucial in keeping the military government from attaining legitimacy in the international sphere and in the repeated condemnations of Pinochet and his policies in international forums. Exiles' actions also helped to keep a modicum of internal resistance alive, providing some foundation for the emergence of the organized opposition movement that appeared in the early 1980s.

---

* *La Tercera de la Hora*, May 25, 1975; *El Mercurio*, May 8, 1975).

† *Qué Pasa*, April 2–8, 1981, 7; *El Mercurio*, May 5, 1979. The regime's newspaper, *La Nación*, denounced "the jet set of exile" who "dedicate themselves full-time to anti-Chilean activism." *La Nación*, Nov. 26, 1982.

These internal and external pressures were important forces pushing the regime to make concessions, including the 1984 decision permitting most exiles to return. Following this policy shift, a large cadre of repatriated exiles risked the consequences of illegally rebuilding their parties, organizing in urban slums, and in other ways repoliticizing the population in anticipation of the scheduled 1988 plebiscite on extending military rule another eight years. Meanwhile, numbers of illegally returned exiles conducted the same types of activities while others engaged in armed resistance to the dictatorship. The efforts of these repatriated exiles were central to the victory of the "NO" in 1988 and the subsequent return to civilian rule.

Following its 1990 inauguration, the Aylwin administration launched a program for promoting the return of Chile's remaining exiles. The new Oficina Nacional de Retorno (ONR) offered moral support and financial incentives to induce exiles to come home. However, when the ONR closed its doors in 1994 it had accomplished only a small part of its mandate. Its efforts, the work of a broad spectrum of nongovernmental agencies, and the appeal of returning to a homeland liberated at last from military rule had succeeded in luring less than half of the country's political exiles back home. Thus, despite the formal, symbolic closure of Chile's experience of mass exile, for the individuals still dispersed around the globe and for their families in Chile, the diaspora begun in 1973 was, and still is, a fact of life.

TWO

# Prelude to Exile

## *The Military Coup*

When Salvador Allende was elected president, some wondered whether Chile's armed forces would intervene to prevent the enactment of Allende's revolutionary agenda. Most Chileans, however, expected the military to honor its tradition of eschewing partisan politics—a tradition that set Chile apart from the great majority of Latin American countries. Yet the spectre of a military coup haunted the UP government from the beginning, and as Allende's policies of expropriation and redistribution and the mobilization of Chile's peasants, workers, and shantytown dwellers (*pobladores*) began to polarize the country, the right came to see a military coup as its salvation. Allende supporters, on the other hand, pinned their hopes on the military's "constitutionalism" and on the notion that enlisted men, the bulk of whom were of worker and peasant backgrounds and thus presumptively loyal to Allende, would refuse to go along with a coup. By mid-1973, when polarization had given way to incessant confrontation and street battles, speculation centered on the timing and nature of a coup that almost everyone expected.

The kind of intervention that most anticipated was a version of the standard Latin American coup in which the armed forces remove an offending government with little or no bloodshed, jail or exile a few fallen leaders, hold power a year or two, and, after overseeing elections, turn power back to the civilians. Instead, the coup of September 11, 1973, was the first step toward a long-term military dictatorship with the ambitious agenda of cleansing Chile of all leftist influence, dismantling the liberal democratic state, and recasting the country's economy. The most public drama of September 11 was the bombing of the seat of government, the historic Moneda Palace in downtown Santiago; after President Allende refused military orders to surrender, he took his own life during the attack. Simultaneously, under cover of a declared state of war and an around-the-clock curfew, the military launched a reign of terror against government officials, leftist activists, union leaders, intellectuals, and the poor, using mass arrests, beatings, torture, summary executions, and military sweeps of industrial zones and shantytowns (*poblaciones*). The military-controlled radio and television network repeatedly broadcast military edicts (*bandos*) naming individuals required to turn themselves in immediately to the new authorities. Santiago's major soccer arenas, the *Estadio Nacional* and the *Estadio Chile*, filled up with prisoners, the hospitals with wounded, and the morgues with bodies. This massive show of military force met little opposition outside of a few isolated pockets of resistance.

During the two days of continuous curfew, the military rebels succeeded in capturing most ranking UP government and party leaders and driving the rest underground. The newly constituted junta then turned to the systematic search for lower-ranking party, government, and union leaders, visible Allende supporters such as media personalities and student leaders, and the few thousand foreign leftists who had come to Chile to escape persecution at home and collaborate in constructing socialism. Despite the massive arrests and indiscriminate use of state terror, during the early months following the coup the military's inexperience in its new mission and the lack of coordination among its branches allowed some of its targets to go underground, escape into foreign embassies, or elude controls on international transportation. It was these deficiencies in the regime's intelligence and control capabilities that led to the establishment of the DINA, the secret police that reported directly to Pinochet, nine months after the coup.

# María Elena Carrera

*María Elena Carrera was born in the capital in 1929 to a middle-class family. The daughter of an employee of the Ministry of Public Works, whose job took him around the country, she studied in the public schools in Santiago, Concepción, and Osorno. She graduated from the medical school of the University of Concepción as a surgeon, but soon chose the practice of politics over a medical career. In 1973 she was a senator and a member of the central committee of the Socialist Party. After an absence of twenty years, she returned to the Chilean Senate as the replacement for President-elect Eduardo Frei, having been the runner-up in his district, and served the balance of his term through 1997.*

*Carrera's reflections on the coup reveal Chileans' common feeling that a coup was coming, but like almost everyone else, the Socialists were not anticipating the force and brutality that the armed forces used to overthrow the government and take control. On September 11, she was one of the high-profile UP officials named in the bandos and was required to turn herself in. That brought up a terrible decision for many, including Socialist Deputy Carmen Lazo, who initially intended to turn herself in to clear her name: "My first impulse, because one is naive, was to turn myself in. I told my husband: 'I haven't done anything wrong, so I'm going to turn myself in.' That's what some of us said, that's what José Tohá [Allende's former Interior and Defense Minister, who died in March 1974 of maltreatment following his imprisonment on Dawson Island in the Strait of Magellan] said, and he's dead because of it."\* Luckily for them, both she and Senator Carrera opted for clandestinity and asylum.*

I think that many people in the Chilean left sensed that a coup was coming. The president himself—I was with him many times before the coup—announced to us that something big was in the works and many times he said: "but I am not going to resign because of this." It seems to me that I can hear him: "and I am not going to resign; they will have to carry me out of the Moneda dead." And the phrase that he said with a certain black humor: "they will have to take me out of here feet first." The political commission of the Socialist Party predicted that a coup was coming. Two or three months before the coup we had evidence that a coup

---

\* Mili Rodríguez Villouta, *Ya nunca me verás como me vieras,* 78.

was coming; however, we never really thought about what the coup would be like. We never thought — at least the majority of people didn't — that it would be so brutal.

All of our preparations were more plans than realities, and the little that was done was very tentative, very inadequate, and had no chance of succeeding. What I thought was the following: I thought, the logical thing here is that these people will kill the leaders, not the masses. We thought that naturally we leaders were going to die. It seemed logical to me, I didn't have any desire to die, but this was the state of mind — I think, of the president too and many of us — of the leaders.

I even talked to one of my children with whom I had problems. I thought, since they are going to kill me, this little girl will certainly be left with guilt feelings. So I looked for any way I could to get close to her, to be reconciled with her. I even said to her at one point, look, if they kill me don't feel guilty because these things are natural — this kind of precautions, with nothing military about them, rather they are completely domestic and human matters.

I also thought that in the case of a coup I should go stay in a *población* because I didn't think that they would traffic in the way that they did with the deaths of the poor people. It would have been a terrible mistake because they would have bombed me as they did with some of the poor neighborhoods. So that, at the end, I didn't take any more precautions than those that the party came up with, that I don't think were effective at all and the day of the coup a group of young *compañeros*, men of action, let's say, were going to stay at my house, but it seemed to me to be too much trouble, so that I made them leave, and there was no one to take care of me or anything the day of the coup. We didn't think that it would be that day either but things were moved up, it seems.

The day of the coup human beings reacted in the strangest ways that you can imagine. At six o'clock in the morning a friend of mine, who was married to the daughter of a general in the *carabineros* [national police], called and told me, "María Elena, the coup has begun, the navy has left Valparaíso. It is at sea — there is no communication at all with Valparaíso. The coup has begun and I am going right now to such and such a place." He was an economist, an *interventor* in a factory [a manager appointed by the Allende government to run a factory or business; such appointments were often preludes to expropriation]. "And I wish you good luck. Take the necessary precautions." Then my friend went to the factory and they killed him that day. His name was Sócrates Ponce; he was an economist of

Ecuadorian origin but had settled in Chile and was very Chilean – he died there.

We had a plan, with the central committee of my party, to gather in a certain place if there was a coup. So I didn't have a car that day but I did have what we had called in my family the "coup bag," and in the coup bag were the essentials you need when you go on a picnic or when you are going to camp out on the mountain. My coup bag was pretty funny, but this meant that all the children had their bags for the coup and my mother-in-law also, so we all took our bags, but we didn't have a car.

My elder son belonged to the party youth group and he was already staying somewhere else in anticipation of what was to come. My son at that time was eighteen, my daughter fifteen and my younger son was thirteen; my mother-in-law must have been seventy. An economist lived next door to me who was a member of the party and we had been working together. So I went and told him that I didn't have a car and that the coup was coming, and he got my children, we took them to my parents' house, and my mother-in-law too, and I went with him downtown, to look for my central committee, which I couldn't find.

I was on the first list [or *bando*, the list of people required to turn themselves in to the new authorities] that the military read on the radio. I must have been fourth or something like that. I was, it seemed, extremely dangerous.

I went first to the headquarters and there was nobody there. Then I went to the party office on Londres Street, number 33 or 38, that later was used as a torture chamber – it was a torture center of the DINA. Well, the central committee wasn't there either and they told me that the central committee was in what was called the *monja* of the Housing Ministry [a meeting place for the Socialist Party in moments of crisis], there on Portugal Street. So this man who was worried because he had his own responsibilities – and I felt bad that he was taking me all over Santiago – took me to the monja, and the central committee wasn't there either but I found many of the leaders there. So they said to me, "Go call and let them know," and they called and they told me not to go to the municipal level of the party, but to one of the offices of the Ministry of Housing, I'm not sure if it was CORMU [Corporación de Mejoramiento Urbano, or Corporation for Urban Improvement, under the Housing Ministry], but they weren't there either. Later I learned that they had been somewhere else and, it seems that, really, they didn't want me there, because I couldn't find them.

When I was in the monja, I saw the bombing of the Moneda because the balconies of that building allowed me to see the Hawker Hunters when they bombed the Moneda, from which we immediately deduced that the president was dead and afterward when I got to the CORMU office — it was around three in the afternoon, then, when my friend left me there — I was there a long time and I heard on the radio there that the president had died. I didn't hear Allende's last words; I heard them later in the recordings that have become famous all over the world.

Two people came up to me there and said "we can hide you." I had a pistol that was completely legal, that the Senate had bought me and that was part of what every senator had, but they said on the radio that "those who are armed will be shot immediately." So I threw away the pistol where it wouldn't be found and I got into an old *Citroneta* [a two cylinder mini-Citroën, popular in Chile because of its low price], with the compañero who suggested what I thought was the safest option. One said to me, "I will take you to Las Condes [an upper-class neighborhood of Santiago] and hide you at my father-in-law's house," and another said, "I will take you to a house that is empty but people go there, no one will notice you, it's in Lo Espejo." Since Lo Espejo was more proletarian, I went to Lo Espejo, but everything went well. It was a good choice — nobody realized who I was. I entered the house. Since Lo Espejo is very close to El Bosque [site of an air force base], the area was full of air force people with hand-held machine guns on all sides, but I didn't have any problems.

Afterward, I made contact through the same person that took me to that house and then messengers came, and the messages were that I should seek asylum quickly. I had not really cultivated relationships with the embassies — something which I will certainly never let happen again. I will always be near an embassy and I will look at the size of the walls, in whatever country I am, but at that time we had a kind of intellectual arrogance that did not allow me to associate much with the embassies. But I did have contacts with the Peruvian embassy, the Chinese embassy, and two or three more. Fortunately, I didn't try to go to the Chinese embassy because the Chinese shut their doors completely to all the people on the left and wouldn't let in even their closest friends, which was really strange and amusing.

I was friends with the Peruvian ambassador who always invited me to things and I always went to these events. So I said to the messengers that the party sent me, that I thought that the only embassy that was a possibility was the Peruvian embassy, and, in fact, the ambassador, who was not on the left — on the contrary, he was a gentleman on the right, but a gentleman — came to get me in his car and took me out of the población and took me to his embassy. This was some five days after the coup. My central committee ordered me to seek asylum.

## José (Pepe) Silva

*Born in Greater Santiago in 1951, José Silva was one of thirteen children of working-class parents. He grew up in the industrial suburb of San Miguel, where he attended but did not graduate from a commercial high school and joined the Communist Party's youth organization, the Juventudes Comunistas. He began working in the shipping department at the Sumar nylon factory, one of Chile's largest textile plants, in 1970; the following year Sumar became one of the first large industries to be expropriated during the Allende administration. Silva left for Canada in May 1974 with his wife and daughter and, following a divorce, returned to Chile in 1983. He currently works as administrator of service personnel in the presidential palace, La Moneda.*

*Santiago's cordones industriales, or factory districts, were at the center of conflict during the UP government. From early in the Allende administration, unionized workers occupied factories to press for their expropriation. It was in the cordones that workers responded to the "bosses' strikes" of October 1972 and August 1973, in which Chile's entrepreneurial and professional associations tried to shut down the national economy and bring down the government, by seizing dozens of both state- and privately owned factories. Allende's opponents alleged that factory workers, aided by MIR and Socialist Party operatives, were arming and training for a seizure of power, and in the months before the coup the military vigorously enforced a new arms-control law in the cordones, regularly surrounding and searching factories and intimidating workers.\* Pepe Silva's experience reflects the vigorous repression applied to the industrial belts and adjacent poblaciones, where many of the workers lived, during and after the coup.*

The day of the coup we went to the factory. The factory was taken over in the sense that there were meetings at the last minute to see what was to be done. The military were already hovering in helicopters, and at noon it was decided that each political party would make its own decisions inde-

---

\* Peter Winn, *Weavers of Revolution: The Yarur Workers and Chile's Road to Socialism* (New York: Oxford University Press, 1986), is a study of another of Chile's largest textile plants during the UP government, when it was seized and run by its workers.

pendently of the company. The company would be turned over to the military because there was no way to defend it—there were arms, but the people left. The order was given for people to leave, that the people who wanted to leave go home, and a large percentage—let's say some 90 percent of the workers—left. This was another reason it was decided we would turn over the company.

Only a few days before, on September 7, there was a search of the company during which many workers were arrested. The FACh [Fuerza Aerea de Chile, the Chilean air force] was in charge of arms control in our sector. When they searched on the seventh, they found absolutely nothing. The truth is that the arms arrived later; on the seventh, there weren't any.

On the eleventh, the company was turned over. The military arrived to occupy it and they ordered us, I think, I am not really sure, sometime between four and five o'clock to assemble, just to assemble. They had an assembly in the patio. A young soldier spoke, an official, and said "we have called you here to talk to you a little. In your case, we have a list of people who have worked politically and been involved with arms and everything," and this list was presented by this man. The guy who had made the list was an engineer who worked in the office. Then he said "all of the people whose names I am going to read have to raise their left hands with their identity cards and those who are beside them and know them and, if they don't raise their hands, have to denounce them. If not they are also going to be loaded into the trucks." Then, in general, it was the people best known for political activity within the company. They took out a hundred or so people—the trucks came. We were in the middle of a población and all the people were shouting because also the majority of the people who worked in this company lived in the same sector and those people were shouting outside and threw fruit or things to the people who were detained and the trucks left and drove around for about an hour and a half. They didn't go to the Estadio Chile nor to the Estadio Nacional and the same official that was in charge came back and said "there are too many of them." So they brought them back to the company. I wasn't part of this, I wasn't on the list.

All of us workers who had stayed were gathered outside the factory to see how we could communicate with those who had left, and the trucks returned with the same people and the guy made a new check, not according to the list but personally. Then the guy summoned them, and—according to the testimony of the people who stayed later—he asked them what party they were active in, what they did, and, finally, they kept around twelve of the hundred or so that they had detained. There were around twelve to fourteen that ended up at the Estadio Chile and the rest were able to go home. The house of the guy that gave the information was fired on that same night.

After people went back to work the new persecution started, more selective, more precise, and then they waited for people when their shifts ended. They used the company vehicles and this was how two of my fellow workers were shot at the company itself. I remember well—it was after September 18, the twentieth or the twenty-first. We didn't know and, in the morning, their innards were still there. These two compañeros were Socialists and the charges against them said that they were involved with arms, in preparations for military action. Besides this being completely false because what preparation there was—and that I helped with—was for personal defense, the people were never prepared militarily. It is true, and I even witnessed it, that on the eleventh, arms arrived. When this happened, our trucks arrived loaded and left loaded with the people leaving the company. At this time there was a Revolutionary Worker's Front (Frente de Trabajadores Revolucionarios, FTR) of the MIR. Several compañeros from their group, when they left the company, went to the other one because the Sumar Company is divided into three parts. The other two resisted, there were confrontations with the military and with the carabineros, and at the end, the people from there died, as did some eight to twelve other people from the factory where they worked.

We found the bullet-riddled bodies of several of our compañeros in the road. One guy who was also a co-worker of ours at the company—he was a Socialist—fired a bazooka at a bus. We got on the bus and the ponchos that the carabineros had been wearing were still there, their gunbelts were there, we saw blood. But it wasn't true—like they said—that all the carabineros died. I think that there were two or three that died. There was a carabinero hung from a post, so that when the repressive forces came in it would have an impact on them. I think this was one of the cases of greatest resistance there was and was used to justify the repression later—that the members of the armed forces were being attacked.

The next day the Hawker Hunters flew over in the early morning, but they didn't drop bombs—they flew over very low. The noise was atrocious and broke a good deal of glass; they flew low over the poblaciones of La Legua and El Pinar—where I lived—but they didn't drop any bombs. They passed the word that they were going to drop bombs, then you saw on both sides the people who went out toward Vicuña Mackenna Street to leave. It was like seeing the movies of the Second World War when the people fled. It was like that, a mass of people with their bags, with the little kids hanging on them, moving toward Santa Rosa, to get transportation to the south and on Vicuña Mackenna, too. The Hawker Hunters went by at 6:30 A.M., from 7:00 to about 11:00 A.M.

The first days after the coup the repression in the poor neighborhoods was in the form of sweeps, like it was at the company. Later it was more selective — later they came with names, with addresses. We kept working secretly but more in finding people, finding out about those who had been arrested, figuring out how to help them, passing out homemade fliers, but it was all on this level until several of them, several of the young people of the neighborhood, were arrested and along with all that, later, I was arrested. Then the people at the *Jota* level [Juventudes Comunistas — the Communist Youth] really scattered because there was terrible fear. The early days of October, November, there was enormous repression in the poblaciones.

I continued working until approximately September 30, and after that they threw us all out. There was a list and they threw us all out.

I was arrested at home. I realized then that there were also several of the neighbors and they took us away. They threw us on top of a jeep, head first, about seven or eight people, among them two women. From there they took us to different police stations. It was because someone had reported that there were secret meetings. We were tortured but nothing else happened. They held us some ten to twelve days, first in one police station, then in another, but all of us were released without any problem.

## Sergio Buschmann

*Born in Santiago in 1942, Sergio Buschmann grew up in Mendoza, Argentina, where his father, a member of a family of wealthy southern landowners and businessmen, had bought agricultural land. He studied in a private German school in Buenos Aires, where he rejected his family's conservative politics by joining the Peronist youth movement. Returning to Santiago in 1959, he entered the University of Chile's school of theatre, joined the Communist Youth and, later, the Communist Party. He became a professional actor in 1965, was a founding member of the actors' union, and during the UP government represented the unions of Chilean artists in the national labor organization, the Central Unica de Trabajadores (CUT).*

*Thousands of suspected UP sympathizers were rounded up during and following the coup and taken to the two large soccer stadiums, the Estadio Nacional and the Estadio Chile. These stadiums, where many of the prisoners were beaten, tortured, and assassinated, became symbols of the brutality of the coup. Sergio Buschmann's experiences in the Estadio Chile as well as in another makeshift prison confirm the excesses as well as the confusion of the first months of military rule. After inexplicably being freed in December 1973, he worked in the underground resistance until he was arrested again three years later. He went into exile in 1977.*

I was taken prisoner the Friday after the coup and I ended up in the Estadio Chile. They were looking for me to kill me. I was on the list of the *Cordón Santiago Centro*, a union list. They came to the union office and they took us all prisoners and they took us all away and at the police station they got mixed up and I ended up at the stadium. I was there for around ten days. There was a lot of confusion at the Estadio Chile. No one knew who was there and why they were there. People arrived and they packed everybody in.

I am there with Víctor Jara [one of Chile's most popular singers of folk and protest music]. I was good friends with Víctor Jara besides our having worked together in several plays, but we were very close personal friends. I got to the stadium that Friday and I saw him sitting in a chair in the hallway where they put me. His face looked awful and his right eye was swollen shut. So then I asked him: "What happened? Did they hit you?"

"Yes," he said, "when I was coming into the stadium they hit me, they kicked me, they threw me on the ground, and on the ground, I got kicked in the face. They were shouting at me, 'you son of a bitch, we'll see if you'll be able to sing again.'" From then on, we sat together—he, Bartulin [Dr. Danilo Bartulin, Allende's doctor], and I. And then, around Monday, I go stand in a very long line to be able to urinate and when I come back, Víctor isn't there. So then I ask Bartulin and the people that are nearby, "What happened to Víctor? Where is he?" "They took him down to the dressing rooms," they told me.

When I don't find Víctor, I go crazy looking for him. I try to get down to the dressing rooms, which were torture chambers. At one point, they took me to the dressing rooms. That was where they were killing the foreigners, principally Argentines and Uruguayans—I saw some terrible things. But, later, they sent me back up, when they realized that I was a Chilean. I have an Argentine accent and they got confused.

When they let me go, I know that Víctor had already turned up dead. He was found dead in the garbage area behind the stadium. Joan Jara had gotten his body from the Instituto Médico Legal.*

They arrested me again in the *Remodelación San Borja* [a sprawling high-rise urban renewal project on the edge of downtown], then they released me. But in November they kidnapped me and I ended up at Cerro Chena [a temporary prison camp near the Santiago suburb of San Bernardo], which was part of the San Bernardo Infantry School, where I saw an incredibly barbarous series of murders and tortures in a single day. I witnessed massive killings by firing squad, for example, of all the leaders of the San Bernardo association of state railroad workers. Then I talked with their relatives and thanks to my testimony they were able to form a committee on the assassination of these compañeros, the labor leaders of the railroads.

But, in that place, they were killing people day and night. They killed them during torture or they shot them at dawn. I was also sentenced to die there. But I never knew why — perhaps someday I will — I was saved, they didn't shoot me. I was at Cerro Chena for about a month and in December of 1973 they released me.

I go into hiding and begin my underground struggle. The task we face is enormous, the formation of an entire underground network working against the dictatorship. They are looking for me and it is three years before I am taken. With my wife, I am kidnapped by the *comando conjunto* [an anti-left vigilante group comprised of air force and naval personnel and members of the terrorist group Patria y Libertad] in December of 1976 and taken to the air force base of Colina. I am savagely tortured in front of my wife. There was great international solidarity trying to save me since they knew my work as a labor leader, as founder of the actors' union in Chile, and the torturers, then, began to take care of me so that I would not die under torture.

---

* The arrest and execution of Víctor Jara are described in Chile, Comisión Nacional de Verdad y Reconciliación, *Report of the Chilean National Commission on Truth and Reconciliation*, trans. Phillip E. Berryman (Notre Dame: Notre Dame University Press, 1993), 1:165–66 (hereafter cited as Comisión Nacional de Verdad y Reconciliación). The autopsy report on Víctor Jara listed forty-four bullet wounds.

Then they decide to turn me loose and follow me. I remain in hiding until 1977 and, at the end of that year, I leave for Sweden, which grants me political asylum.

## María Inés Ruz

*María Inés Ruz was twenty-three years of age in September 1973. Her artisan mother had died when María Inés was three years old, and her father was a teacher in the public system of commercial schools. She attended public schools in the cities where her father taught: La Serena, Santiago, and Chillán. At the University of Concepción she studied sociology and journalism, joined the MIR, and became the compañera of MIR leader Fernando Krauss. After leaving Chile in 1975, she spent sixteen years in Cuba.*

*The experience of María Inés Ruz during and following the coup illustrates two dangers: being a member of MIR and living in a provincial city. MIRistas were seen as dangerous because they were thought to be armed and prepared to resist the imposition of military control. Leftists in the provinces were especially vulnerable in the coup's aftermath, for outside greater Santiago only the Valparaíso-Viña del Mar and Concepción-Talcahuano metropolitan areas, each with populations of nearly half a million, offered any possibility of prolonged underground sanctuary. By seizing control of communications and transportation from outlying areas, the military gained a free hand in dealing with its enemies in the provinces. The recollections of María Inés Ruz about September 11 and the following month illustrate the precarious situation of MIRistas in a small city and the brutality of the military effort to snuff out potential resistance. They also reveal the MIR's lack of preparation to resist the coup.*

We knew about the coup. The party was ready. We were on the highest degree of alert—the sociopolitical atmosphere in Valdivia was very eloquent. Only a few days before the coup, a bookstore in Valdivia was attacked by a group of rightists. The bookstore belonged to a leftist, and there was a demonstration, and Fernando was going by and he was the regional secretary of MIR—he couldn't be getting involved and exposed—but he couldn't just do nothing, and he came home very disturbed by the degree to which the carabineros intervened in favor of the rightist demonstrators. In Valdivia, then, we were already breathing the atmosphere of the coup. They had even thrown stones at our house one day—the stone fell right in the room where our little girl slept—and we were already in a state of fear. It was a serious situation, but we never thought about exile.

We were prepared in the sense that we knew that something was going to happen and we had thought that I would have to go to Concepción with our little girl—we were in Valdivia—and that was the extent of our "preparation," in quotation marks. It was incredibly precarious. Looking back now, you realize that it was really very irresponsible because we were involved in a tremendous mess, except for some things which were pretty flimsy—so much so that the day after the coup, Fernando, who was the regional secretary of the MIR in Valdivia, didn't have anywhere to hide. And I—who wasn't part of the [party] structure, who was working openly with the masses and was his compañera—the days right after the coup I had to spend my time looking for a place for him to hide and what I found was the house of the mother of a compañera from the party. She was a very poor person who lived in a población where the houses were two-family, very small. She took Fernando into her house and he couldn't come out of the room where he was because, if he went out to the patio, the neighbors would see him. He had to stay shut inside the room in order to remain more or less hidden. So we really hadn't made preparations for the coup, besides having cleared out some of the papers at the house, but even the day of the coup itself, Fernando went out very early in the morning and, once he knew that the coup d'état had taken place, came home to get rid of the last of the papers that were left at the house. Even so, the military later found a box of mine that had letters from Fernando from when he was in Valdivia and I was still in Concepción. And, well, you don't want to get rid of these things. I don't know if they could have gotten any information from them. I don't think that really, as a party or on a personal level, we were prepared for the magnitude of a coup d'état.

They got Fernando on September 22. Fernando was very easy to recognize. We didn't have a way to change his appearance, but we dyed his hair, he wore some glasses and a beret—this was his only camouflage. And we had agreed that he would go to Osorno because the entrance to the route to Osorno was less controlled than the route to the north. I was going to take a train the next day that would connect with the train that he was going to take in Osorno. This was our plan to escape from Valdivia, but this plan was never put into action because, the night before he was to leave, they got him. They got him because of a statement someone made under torture.

Fernando and I had always said that if anything happened, I should leave with our little girl so that they would not get me and use that to put more pressure on him. Well, when I went to Concepción, I traveled to Chillán; I left Camila at my father's house and returned to Concepción to go with *señora* Teresa, Fernando's mother, to Valdivia. There, I began to go around with her trying to find out where he was, from the very first. Later it was the same story as always, that of course they denied having him . . .

I returned to Valdivia something like the twenty-fourth and I managed to locate him the day before he was shot, which was October 4. October 3, I was standing in line at the jail to take him some food because we knew that he was incommunicado all those days, from September 22 to October 3. And there they gave me the clothes Fernando had been wearing, and his belongings — I don't know for sure — my memories are somewhat confused because after they shot him I went to the jail too, and then they gave me everything, the photos that he was carrying, his ring — I don't remember exactly.

They shot Fernando and another group of compañeros on the fourth.[*] I don't know if you have heard the story that Fernando sang a lot in jail — there is a poem by a Valdivian poet, Omar Lara, which is about all these things that happened and there is a poem that tells how he said goodbye singing the International, etc. Omar Lara is a Valdivian poet who won the Casa de las Américas prize [a prestigious award offered by Cuba's Casa de las Américas] specifically for this little book which is called *Oh Buenas Maneras*, in the year 1977 — then this poem has a little part which says that in the last few days of his life, Fernando Krauss sang to his daughter Camila, someday she will sing to her father in the free streets of Chile.[†]

Well, since Fernando sang and sang and, when he went before the prosecutor, he talked, they broke his jaw and the day that they were to shoot them, Fernando spoke to the firing squad and got them to stop, so that they didn't shoot them then. They had to get a different firing squad, they brought in some black berets or green berets because the people of the regiment that were to have carried out the order of execution disobeyed orders. Fernando gave them the standard speech we used at that

---

[*] The execution of Fernando Krauss and eleven other MIRistas, mostly members of the MIR's peasant branch, is described in *Comisión Nacional de Verdad y Reconciliación*, 1:417–18.

[†] Omar Lara, *Oh Buenas Maneras* (Havana: Casa de las Américas, 1975).

time — which was that they shouldn't fire against their own people. I heard
this story from people who were on our side, but I also heard it later, because, a month or so later, when I came back to Valdivia to move Fernando's remains, since they had put them in a common grave, the grave
diggers told me the story.

The same day that they killed him, they went to get his mother and me
at the house so that we could say goodbye to Fernando. He was the only
person that they did this with — with the other people it would have been
impossible since they were all people from the country — and Fernando
talked to his mother. His mother even today thinks that was worse — it was
terrible for her — seeing Fernando with his hands behind him because they
didn't want to untie him and with his jaw broken and he saying that he was
a good man, that they were committing an injustice and trying to be sure
that his mother's image of him was absolutely clear and clean — his mother
has never forgotten, she cannot get beyond this memory.

During those moments, Fernando asked them to look for me. He asked
his mother to take care of me, to take care of Camila and Fernandito. I
was expecting little Fernando and he named him. So they went to look for
me and, at that time, I had gone to talk to a lawyer, because in that period
everything was still very recent so that we didn't know what we could
do — there were no organizations to turn to. With his mother, in the pre-
ceding days, I had gone to talk with the bishop of Valdivia, to see if he
could intercede for Fernando. The bishop received us and said, "Fernando
Krauss, a very violent man" and he didn't hold out any hope.

So then I was doing that — out of desperation going to talk with this
lawyer — so that when they went to the house to get me so that I could say
goodbye to Fernando, I wasn't there. And they tried to find me but they
didn't know where I was. When they finally found me — this part is rather
dramatic and I have to stay calm to be able to tell it, because they took me
to where Fernando's mother had gone to say goodbye to him, which was
to the police station. And there they told me that he wasn't there, to go to
the regiment. We went to the regiment, and they told me that he wasn't
there, to go to the Fourth Division. So I went to the Fourth Division and
they told me, no, to go back to the police station. And when I got back to
the police station, they told me to go pick him up at the morgue, that they
had already shot him. This was, of course, when I went to pieces. I went
in — I pushed the carabineros aside and ran to the back of the station
shouting, of course, all the things one shouts, and they took me out of
there, and I didn't have anywhere to go any more — without realizing that
at that time they couldn't have shot him yet, because the execution had

had to be postponed until eight o'clock at night and it was somewhere far from Valdivia where there was a firing range.

The next day I went to the Fourth Division to get them to give me his body, but they wouldn't. There was no way to get them to turn him over to me, and they told everyone to go in the afternoon to the cemetery where the funerals were to take place. In the cemetery only two people could go in for each of the dead compañeros. I went with my sister-in-law, Fernando's younger sister — his mother stayed at home. It was a really terrible thing because the whole zone was cordoned off by the military, by soldiers who searched us, pointed their guns at us, and we went in. Then we saw the boxes of pine wood, the wood was white, with blood-stained shoes — as if in order to nail the boxes shut they had hammered them with the boots so the blood-stained boots were on top of the boxes — they were really blood-stained. Afterward they explained to me that when they shoot people this phenomenon occurs. The truth is that it was a really awful situation. I don't know how all the people had gathered there. In spite of the fact that there were already two for each of the compañeros, people were gathered there who were from the polyclinic where I took Camila and from the day-care center where Camila went every day — I don't know how they got into the cemetery. So there was a group of people; they were putting the boxes in the eleven holes, and the army chaplain who was going to give the blessing was there. In the morning, I had talked to the chaplain to try to get him to let me have Fernando's body and it hadn't done any good, so that for me, at that moment, he represented all the negative replies I had gotten; so that when he began to say his prayer it seemed to me that it was the last straw, that, at the very least, something should be said. So, then, I spoke and shouted the slogans of the MIR, and the people who were there, who were not from the MIR — who were the people that I told you that I don't know how they got in — answered — and even though it was cordoned off by the military — and the people answered the slogans of the MIR. Immediately, the soldiers grabbed me and took me to a place away from where this was happening, and they took away my identity card, and my sister-in-law's too. They took us away from there and, at that point, I realized that my father was there. I had notified my father the day before about the execution, and he came immediately and managed to get to the cemetery, and I met up with him there. My father was very scared by all of this — he asked me not to do anything else. He said that I was not going to accomplish anything in those circumstances. That is what happened in the cemetery.

## Miriam Casanova

*Miriam Casanova was born in the beach resort city of Viña del Mar in
1935. The only child of a middle-class family, she attended Catholic schools
in Viña and the neighboring port city of Valparaíso. While studying ped-
agogy in Valparaíso, she discovered her vocation in theater and finished her
studies in a university-affiliated theater school. She first joined the Communist Youth and later the Communist Party, but dropped out of active
membership for a long period. At the time of the coup she was married
with two children and had resumed an active role in the party.*

*For a sizable contingent of Chileans, exile began as well as ended on
foreign soil. Thousands of Chileans were traveling or living abroad at the
time of the coup: tourists, delegates to international conferences, embassy
personnel, students, and professionals and workers employed outside the
country. Among these was the folk group Inti Illimani, which turned its
music into a weapon against the Pinochet government during fifteen
years of exile. The early days following the coup were an agonizing time
during which communication with home was difficult and most information was rumor. As the picture became clearer, Chileans abroad had to
determine whether they were permitted to return and, if so, the degree of
risk involved for themselves, their families, and their associates. Miriam
Casanova's story provides insights into the experience of those Chileans
whose exile began without the usual sad goodbyes or the final glimpse of
the Andes.*

I left a month before the coup. Times were hard, but we never anticipated
how hard they would be. At that time I was no longer young and I was
part of a group of Chilean artists who were accompanying the official delegation invited to the festival—"The World Youth Festival," that was held
every six months in different countries, especially in socialist countries,
and that one was in Berlin in 1973. We were planning to return in mid-
September, but then, because some returned they got here a day before
the coup took place. However, I stayed because I was going to go to Spain
and I went to see some friends in Paris and, the night that I was going to
Spain by train from Paris to Madrid, the coup took place—Tuesday the
eleventh.

I didn't even get on the train, because the news had already been announced on TV and on the radio in the afternoon, more or less, and the
coup had taken place in the morning. The news was chilling because I was

very afraid for my family, for my small children and for my husband—for my husband because he was a university professor and, besides, was a leader in the university. He was more visible publicly, in Valparaíso, and he was active in the Communist Party.

We began to try to get through by telephone and the lines were cut; there was no way to get through to Chile. There were five or six terrible days in which we tried to get through. In Paris, we got together with other Chileans who were there—we needed to see what could be done, how to get in touch—and the only news that we had was what we got from the newspapers, from radio and TV. There was no personal news—the telephone lines were cut for at least three days—and, later, you could only get through to Santiago. It was impossible to get through to the provinces.

I continued to be in a terrible state of desperation, and my first impulse was to go back. We knew that the airport was closed, all the borders, but even so I decided to go to Lima, to go to Peru to see if there was any way to get through anywhere, or to wait there for the borders to be opened so that I could get into Chile. This must have been about September 16, and from Lima we began to try to get through. Finally, from Lima I was able to reach my parents, who had not been able to get to Valparaíso to see what had happened to my husband and my children because the roads had been blocked. But I got through several times and I was calmer when I found out that they were all right. My husband had had to hide and my children had been taken somewhere else. There had at first been a situation of waiting that was like an impasse, with the people in Chile not knowing what was going on. They didn't know how long it was going to last, what the situation was going to be, and while they were waiting, Allende had already committed suicide, so that the news about that was very dramatic. I was in Peru when news started to appear in the newspapers, and I began to learn of the deaths of different people that I knew. It was very dramatic in Peru; that was where I had the greatest sense of what was happening, but it began to happen about the second week after the coup—firing squads, people who were found dead.

I was in very bad shape in Lima, very depressed. I had very little money with me, and suddenly it occurred to me to get in touch with a relative of my husband's whom I had met some time before, an Italian who lived in Lima. And, well, I got in touch with him and I asked him for help, and he came to get me at the hotel where I was, and he took me to his house. And those days were very black, very bitter. On the one hand, I got together with other Chileans to see what the possibilities were for getting into Chile. The truth is that almost none of us had any idea—I don't mean of

the seriousness of the situation, because we all understood the seriousness
. . . But all of us wanted to go back to Chile — we all had the idea of getting
back in and that I think was a common thing. Everyone was worried about
their loved ones and we all thought that nothing would happen to us —
that was the idea we had. So I began to call and insist that I needed to go,
to go by land or to go as soon as the borders were opened, but later they
called me from Chile. I never knew who called me. An anonymous call
to tell me to calm down, that my family was fine and that I shouldn't
come back to Chile at all. Later I learned that all this was because of the
situation that existed in Valparaíso, that they were looking for many of my
friends — my husband perhaps less so — and they had arrested many
friends of some of the members of Congress, of some people especially.
So there was great pressure through families and friends to try to find the
people they wanted, so they recommended that I not come back, that my
husband would try to get in touch with me to see if we could meet outside
the country. So I had to wait, but later I decided that the atmosphere in
Peru, the climate, everything, was depressing me and I had friends in
Buenos Aires. So I got in touch with Buenos Aires and I decided to go to
Buenos Aires. This was at the beginning of October — I remember perfectly because it was during that period that Perón was to be inaugurated — so I got there, and I went to the home of some Argentine friends.
And there in Buenos Aires I was better, because I was with friends. On a
personal level, I felt better in Buenos Aires: I knew it better, I was at the
home of a couple who lived very comfortably, let's say, and this also meant
that they treated me very well: they took me out, they entertained me,
they took me to the theater, in order to distract me.

  We even met General Prats [General Carlos Prats, commander of the
army under Allende, who resigned his position shortly before the coup,
went into exile in Buenos Aires, and was assassinated there in September
1974]. I think that he arrived in Buenos Aires around November. We met
once in a group of people at a social event, where he talked to us. It was
very short, but we had the chance to meet him. He was trying — he was
very bitter — but he was trying to move ahead. He had looked for work;
they had gotten him a job in a company, and, well, we knew about him. I
was not in Argentina when they assassinated him; I had already gone to
Poland.

  Well, more and more news reached Buenos Aires. There were also
large demonstrations in Argentina in solidarity with Chile. And on the
one hand, the news was ever more hair-raising, but also, on the other,
there was more contact than in Lima because people went there, they

came to Argentina, they went to Chile to help people. There was much more rapid and more obvious contact with Buenos Aires—with the Argentine press, with the newspapers, with the radio, etc. I was there with them for four months—four months that at the beginning were pretty nice because, you could say, I was calmer. But after that, the last two months were very complicated because the situation was more complicated in Chile. My husband had not been able to leave legally as he had wished, and in January he went to an embassy with the children and went in without knowing anything, because, since we lived in Valparaíso, we were more provincial. Some friends helped him get into an embassy—it was the Polish embassy, but it was under the Swiss flag, because all the socialist countries had to be under another country's flag. He went there and then was there for about a month, until they gave him permission to leave. Well, when I learned that he was there, that also made me feel better, because then I knew what our path would be, more or less, that we would have to return to Europe, that there wasn't anything else to do.

## Mario González

*Mario González was born in 1937, in the southern coal-mining town of Lota, the youngest of five children of a housewife and an administrative employee of the coal company. After pursuing studies in a government technical school, he enlisted in the Chilean air force at age seventeen. He trained as a flight mechanic and was approaching retirement age at the time of the overthrow of Allende. González did not affiliate with any party, either as a youth or as a member of the air force, but was sympathetic to the left and to the UP government*

*The coup was carried out by a military that had been considered one of Latin America's least politically involved. However, from González's viewpoint the officer corps had become increasingly politicized during the 1960s, under the influence of U.S.-promoted national security doctrine. During the UP government, he recalls, "those of us who supported the government—as we had always done with any government—suffered discrimination: they marginalized us from certain commands, certain trips abroad and specialized training courses." The country's polarization after 1970 was reflected in a growing split within the armed forces, but, as González explains, when the orders finally came on September 11 the internal opposition to a coup was insufficient to overcome the strength of the military command structure. After being summarily removed from*

*military ranks and losing his accumulated benefits, Mario González left for
exile in England.*

*Chile's new military masters could not permit a public funeral for
President Allende without risking massive protests, nor could they allow his
burial in Santiago's Cementerio General [General Cemetery], where most
of the country's presidents and other political leaders are buried, without
inviting a permanent pilgrimage to the fallen martyr's tomb. Thus they
allowed only the immediate family to attend a private service at the small,
easily guarded Santa Inés cemetery in Viña del Mar, where the president
was buried in an unmarked grave in a family-owned plot. It was Mario
González's sad plight to be the flight mechanic on the air force plane that
flew the president's body and family to the burial. This was a duty he has
not forgotten. Salvador Allende was reburied in Santiago's Cementerio
General following a state funeral on September 4, 1990, exactly twenty
years after winning the presidential election.*

Well, all this uncertainty, this uneasiness, this insecurity within the units
led me to make some pretty extreme decisions. I had already told my family that I was going to resign from the air force. The situation there was
so intolerable and my personal situation was very serious, very risky. I resigned from the air force September 10, 1973, at four o'clock in the afternoon.

I knew that it was a matter of hours, days, weeks, a month, until the
coup, but I didn't have the exact information. We tried to get information
about messages, about the coup, from people we were friendly with who
worked in communications. We asked them if there were any serious messages, important ones. No, nothing, nothing's going on, nothing has come
in — because all the messages were in code then. Obviously, if we didn't
have the code, we couldn't know what they really said.

I began the morning of the tenth, following the regular channels, the
normal procedure. Then I appeared at 8:30 A.M. before the appropriate
officer to ask, according to regular procedure, to sign my resignation papers. They were very surprised, they told me. "Agreed, it's accepted," and,
by four o'clock in the afternoon, I was already at the personnel office asking for the application for discharge and signing it, effective in three
months. The man who was there, who was a civilian, told me, "Look, I
have never seen this in the air force. You are going to lose your pension,
you are going to lose everything, everything. Go home, sleep on it and tell
me tomorrow." "No," I said, "it is decided. I have already done it; I have

already thought about it; everything is decided. I don't want to be here when something happens, because I am going to be used to do something very bad. I am going to lose everything." I had been in for eighteen years; at twenty, you get your pension. "I am leaving. I'll lose everything, it doesn't matter. I don't want to stain myself with the blood of my countrymen. I resign."

It was rumored that if there were a coup order, maybe the majority of the armed forces, who were common people themselves, would not fire on the people, and that a coup would not be possible because there would be massive disobedience. I think that, in part, this is true, but also, there was strong influence of the verticality of the command and obedience. The discipline influenced greatly, but there were cases of people who didn't fire on other people or, if they did, they fired into the air, and many people were saved by our people who were there. But the day of the coup itself, people came to me: "What should we do now? Are we going to take action or not?" I think that we would have done something, but the alliance of parties and movements outside did not have a specific and detailed plan of how to react to an attempted coup, so there was no way for us to have acted on our own, without any coordinated plan. We realized that there wasn't any.

The day before the coup, well, I signed my resignation and turned in the papers; I went home as usual. And the next day, I go back at 8:30 A.M. Immediately, they tell us that there is a state of emergency, an alert. They have us get our weapons and occupy combat positions, like the anti-riot troops. I had my plane, a C47 transport, and it was armed with a 50-caliber machine gun and I was waiting for orders. When it is time for the bombing of the Moneda, I see the Hawker Hunter planes fly over the Moneda. I get into my plane, into the cabin, observing the bombing of the Moneda from some six meters of altitude. That day, in the afternoon, my plane is used to go to El Bosque, from Cerrillos [El Bosque is an air force base, Cerrillos a civilian airport, both in greater Santiago]. We took off from Cerrillos at around 2:30 or 3:00 P.M. and we flew over Santiago. We flew over the Moneda. It was still in flames, but they were almost out, and you could see that only the walls were left.

That day, except for this flight, we spent the whole day inside, and we spent the night in the unit. That night many people arrived in army transport planes from La Serena [a city with an air force base some 475 kilometers north of Santiago]. They used them to replace people from Santiago—who were taken to La Serena or Concepción and from Concepción to La Serena. It was all prearranged. It was night, everything was dark, and they were recruits. They replaced them, to send them somewhere else. This was the most critical night, because those of us who knew who our people were got together and said "What are we going to do?" And we almost set up a plan for self-defense, more than for attack. And it was a plan for self-protection because the situation was so serious; there was incredible tension in there, and the pro-coup officers were really terrified, because they knew that we could have reacted – they were terrified. In the units, I think that there were around fifteen to twenty of us.

We sensed that we were being watched and we slept in combat bunks, and I with my rifle under my bed with a bullet in the chamber and the safety off in order to defend myself from them. And I also asked for a revolver, a Colt, to have it under my flight jacket, in case of emergency – not to use against the people but against them.

So we managed to survive that night and the next day was when I had to go on an awful mission. At about ten in the morning, they told me that I was on duty and I could be asked to go on any of the flights. I was told: "González, there is a flight with passengers and freight." It turned out that the freight was President Allende's casket and the passengers were his relatives and the air force attaché, and I had to go from Group 10, that I was in at that time, to Group 7, where I had been before for fifteen years. I knew everyone.

The army ambulance arrived with the president's casket inside, and they moved it from there to the bed of the plane. I was alone with him for about twenty minutes and I was trying at that moment to think of some way to strike a blow against the dictatorship. Well, I almost decided to hijack the plane, to fly it to Argentina, but I was alone and I couldn't do it. So then an assistant came, a young kid, with all this tension. He was one of our boys. I told him that the president was there. At that point, the group arrived, which consisted of his wife, the attaché, two nephews, and a godchild – a boy. Laura Allende [Salvador Allende's sister, who committed suicide in exile] was also inside. I didn't know how to let them know who I was, because it wasn't possible.

The kid got behind me, we were surrounded by people, and he was so tense, so tense that his rifle went off. He had it pointed down and a chunk of pavement hit the plane, and everyone threw themselves on the ground. Only the two of us remained standing. I turn around; I take his rifle away from him; I take out the bullet – he was new – I take out the bullet, and I give him the shell, and I say to him, "Go on, get out of here." I knew that he was one of ours and that I had to protect him. And then an officer arrived, and he asked me who had fired. "It was a young kid," I told him. "I don't know who he is." This officer didn't know me — didn't know that I had been there for fifteen years — so he couldn't say to me: "Yes, you do know who he is." "I don't know him," I told him. And he left.

We got in the plane and took off toward Quintero [a town north of Viña del Mar]. During the flight I tried to make contact with them, but it was impossible because of the level of tension in there. And I sat down next to his nephews and one of them said to me: "You aren't going to believe me, but President Allende received ovations from the people in Mexico and today he is here on the floor. But one thing I can tell you is that history is not written in two days," he told me. I will never forget those words. We arrived at Quintero and the casket was taken by people from the navy and the air force and taken to Viña del Mar. I don't know why it happened, that spring day in September — I was wearing gloves and a flight helmet, a flight suit — and I took the back of the casket; I began to lower it. As the casket came out, a piece of the plastic from the handle came off in my hand. I tried to put the piece back on and I couldn't, and I put it in my pocket and then the casket was gone. I have always kept that piece — I put it away and I even took it to England. When I was in jail, I said to my wife: "You have to get what is most valuable from the house, get that piece of plastic and we'll take it to England. Don't leave it." It went with us to England and came back with us.

Later, at about four o'clock in the afternoon, the family came back to return to Santiago again, bringing some of the president's belongings, some photographs and personal things from Cerro Castillo [the summer residence of Chile's presidents in Viña del Mar].

It was a nightmare. It was really terrible and I don't know how I made it through all that. My family had no idea what I was doing because we stayed inside the unit for four days and I couldn't see my family.

I spent the other days inside the unit and I saw when they brought the ministers and deputies from the Unidad Popular government, and those leaders were also removed by plane, a DC6 passenger transport to Dawson Island [a cold, windswept island in the Strait of Magellan where captured UP leaders were imprisoned, most of them for approximately a year before being exiled]. There were people that they treated roughly. The defense minister was there, don José Tohá. All the people that they took to Dawson Island at that time were there. They arrived in buses with all the emergency doors and windows sealed against a possible attempt at sabotage. I was crossing the runway from Cerrillos. I was with a pilot, a reactionary. When he saw that we had all the ministers there, members of Congress, he said to me in a very disagreeable way: "Why use so much fuel taking these people to Punta Arenas? Why not shoot them in the back of the neck, period?" In front of me. This made me want to say to him, to take out my revolver and say to him: "Then why don't you start with me?" But it was really crazy, like he was trying one way or another to provoke me to act. I had to remain very calm, be very patient to endure all of that.

In our unit there were scarcely any casualties or confrontations, rather it was all searches and shooting and robbing and looting. There was a psychosis within the unit directed toward the other side of the barriers where the civilian population was. All of them gathered along the perimeter of the barriers looking out toward the civilian population, which was subject to a curfew—everyone in their homes. A dog moved and there was a blast of firing. It was practically a psychosis. Getting them to stop firing was hard. But I didn't hear of any casualties. It was really an abuse—coming in with things, things that had been stolen. After the second day, get off the buses, go to a newsstand and ask the employee for cigarettes or a newspaper, and get back on the bus without paying. Aboard, we asked ourselves: "Why do they have to do that, that is robbery. All of them are doing it, why don't I do it?" This was the experience that we had during those days.

On September 22, they called eight of us to the unit command to tell us that we were relieved from duty, expelled from the institution. We could have done something crazy there because we were all armed. It was ridiculous, why summon us to the unit command, to present ourselves before the commander—with my rifle there, loaded, I could have reacted any way. But rather than that, when they tell me that I am expelled from the armed forces, I ask why. "Because of a lack of confidence on the part of the high command." I felt very relieved and very calm and happy to be able to take off my uniform and get out of the unit.

I was arrested here at home on December 12, by air force special forces. Oddly enough, a pilot with whom I had flown missions in the south of Chile was one of the ones who came to arrest me at home. I was expecting this arrest. Other compañeros had already been taken and were already in the public jail, and others—I had information that they were in the Aerial War Academy. So I was expecting this arrest. I couldn't notify my family, I didn't want them to be worried, but I knew that sooner or later they would arrest me.

# José Muñoz

*José Muñoz was born into a military family in 1938. His father was an army officer stationed in Antofagasta, and his mother a housewife. Muñoz attended public schools in Antofagasta and Santiago, entered the military school but dropped out to finish high school in the humanities curriculum. After graduation he entered the School of Carabineros, Chile's national police force. At the time of the coup he was the thirty-five-year-old chief of the carabineros' special presidential guard unit.*

*Unlike the leadership of the three military branches, the upper echelons of the carabineros' officer corps did not support the overthrow of Allende. Even after pro-coup General César Mendoza was elevated to the command of the carabineros, the presidential guard defied orders to surrender and defended the government on September 11 until dismissed by President Allende. Muñoz's commitment to defending the constitutional government was based on a personal and political empathy with Allende and a deeply ingrained sense of duty. His memories of the coup from inside the Moneda provide an unusual view of the battle of wills, bullets, and bombs that changed the course of Chilean history on September 11, 1973. Shortly after the coup he was sacked from the carabineros and exiled to East Germany.*

In the carabineros there was a break in the command that didn't occur in the other [military] institutions, through which the seventh general of the carabineros, César Mendoza, was self-appointed as director general in circumstances during which the constitutionally legitimate high command was at the Moneda. General Sepúlveda and General Urrutia, who was second-in-command, demonstrated their loyalty until the very end.

I can verify the calls attempted on the radio from the Moneda to try to keep the carabineros a cohesive group. The palace guard of some thirty men stayed until 10:30 a.m., when they were ordered through other channels to withdraw — even though the director general was there and our service maintained its presence there until the president arranged for its withdrawal fifteen minutes before the bombing and the order to withdraw came from the director general. Also, we stayed with him until he left the palace; after that, I arranged for the withdrawal of our people. I think that in the first moments of the coup, when, at six o'clock in the morning, we headed toward the Moneda Palace, an occurrence of this kind never entered our heads. Even when the planes were flying overhead and the bullets hit the windowpanes and the noise of the tanks was deafening and all the rest, we did not think that there would be violence of such magnitude. Answering the fire — the Moneda Palace was being attacked — without taking the offensive — I am referring more to our efforts to defend ourselves without causing more serious occurrences, because we didn't consider such a thing possible. We never thought that our colleagues would carry out such a terrifying and savage mission like bombing the Moneda Palace in these conditions.

The great magnitude of firepower that the coup perpetrators had, that they so bravely showed, demonstrated fear, not the fear of the force that those of us inside the Moneda might have, but rather the moral and ethical fear produced by their action — as a result, they had the Moneda surrounded from 8:00 A.M. until 1:30 P.M. and were never able to enter, in circumstances that with the firepower they had, the tanks they had — if it had been a brilliant military action, it would have been over in half an hour. This shows their lack of coordination, the lack of basic knowledge with which this undertaking was begun.

Being near President Allende, I could see his serenity with respect to the coup, which was, I would say, admirable. In his last words, he tells us in advance everything that is going to happen — something which those of us hearing him didn't believe could happen. With great concern he personally directed the defense of the Moneda, his concern for each one of the people who were in the Moneda, as regards their safety, and later, in his farewell he thanks us for our loyalty and asks us to withdraw.

That day, the longest day of my life, is something that I will never forget because of what the presence of the president meant in that situation.

Well, a day later I was part of a unit with no commander and no personnel, and later I was notified of my dismissal from the institution, citing a lack of confidence on the part of the new command, in spite of my having passed all the tests and always having been rated on the top list. Compared to other officers of the carabineros who had problems as a result of the coup, I was one of the most fortunate in the sense that besides some psychological pressures, psychological mistreatment, there was very little of a physical nature. I was not tortured like some more senior colleagues who were arrested, tortured, and sent to prison. I did not suffer this kind of abuse.

# THREE

# Paths to Exile

Chile, in effect, became a huge concentration camp on September 11, 1973. Stretching twenty-six hundred miles in a narrow strip between the Andes and the Pacific Ocean, Chile is defined by natural boundaries on every side except its short border with Peru in the north and a stretch of Patagonia it shares with Argentina. Symbol of Chile's independence and its insularity, the Andes, with their passes closed by winter snow, were transformed into a massive wall imprisoning the country's people. Thus when the junta sealed Chile's borders on the day of the coup, suspending all international transit for the next eleven days, escape became virtually impossible. For UP officials, militants, and sympathizers in small cities and towns from Arica to Punta Arenas, where they were known and vulnerable, Santiago, with its three million inhabitants, its sprawl, and its embassies, became the only viable refuge. But given the ease of controlling the single highway and single rail line linking north and south, reaching the capital was very difficult.

For those named in the bandos and the thousands more whose positions defined them as important enemies of the new regime, avoiding detention became the first priority. Some went underground to hide or try to forge a resistance movement. Many opted for asylum on the foreign soil of embassies and ambassadors' residences. Asylum was a common form of refuge well established in international law and in Latin American regional agreements, but one rarely used in Chile, where civil wars, coups, and repressive governments had been exceptional in the country's history. From early on September 11, individuals who realized their vulnerability began entering those embassies that allowed them in; after the continuous curfew was lifted on September 13, embassies began filling up. The Mexican, Italian, Argentine, French, Swedish, Venezuelan, and other embassies took in thousands of asylum seekers, both Chilean and foreign, until the junta reacted by deploying beefed-up patrols and limiting access to the embassies' environs. The military junta expelled Swedish Ambassador Harald Edelstam in December 1973 for his exceptionally active role in providing asylum for the persecuted. Ultimately, some thirty-five hundred Chileans used asylum as their first step toward exile.*

In addition to those whose exile began with asylum, others got out of the country in the months following the coup by irregular means, such as using false documents and fleeing across obscure Andean passes or northern desert trails. Around four thousand Chileans were formally expelled from the country.[†] Some of these expulsions were conducted under Decree Law 81 of November 1973, which gave the regime virtually unconditional authority to expel citizens. Two measures were adopted to reduce the prison population without the inconvenience of having potentially dangerous leftists at liberty inside Chile: A December 1974 agreement allowed unsentenced detainees held under the state of siege to petition for their freedom on condition of immediate expulsion, and Decree Law 504 of April 1975 extended the same policy to sentenced prisoners. In attempting to improve its international image following the 1976 assassination of former UP leader Orlando Letelier in Washington and the elec-

---

* Patricio Orellana, "Exilio y desexilio" (1991, unpublished), Vicaría de la Solidaridad (1991), 217. See the same author's Master's thesis, "El exilio chileno" (Institute of Development Studies, University of Sussex, 1981). Faride Zerán Chelech, *O el asilo contra la opresión: 23 historias para recordar* (Santiago: Paradox, 1991), 229–91, describes the asylum network; Tomaso de Vergottini, *Miguel Claro 1359: Recuerdos de un diplomático italiano en Chile (1973–1975)* (Santiago: Atena, 1991), tells the story of asylum from a host's perspective.

[†] Orellana, "Exilio y desexilio," 218–21.

tion of Jimmy Carter, the dictatorship used these policies on a large scale to enable it to close most of its prison camps.

For most of Chile's exiles, departure was somewhat less precipitous and dramatic: The majority left the country legally, using their passports, most commonly on scheduled flights. Many of these exiles had suffered repression in one or more of the standard methods used by the dictatorship to encourage its enemies to leave: firing and blacklisting; short-term incarceration, sometimes repeated, often accompanied by torture; arrests of family members; home searches; and general harassment. As they observed the constantly widening cast of the repressive net during the dictatorship's first three years or so, with crackdowns on low-profile party members, bureaucrats, students, journalists, professionals, intellectuals, and others whose crime was mere association with the left, many others realized that they were members of an endangered category and that their safety required them to leave.

Of the tens of thousands of Chileans who left under these circumstances as well as the thousands who left via asylum and expulsion, a large proportion did so with the aid of a remarkable network of religious and secular, Chilean and international organizations that arose to aid the families of the dictatorship's victims and, for the several years when leaving the country was the only certain way of avoiding prison or death, to assist the persecuted into exile. Within weeks of the coup, an ecumenical Comité Pro Paz (Committee for Peace) had formed under the leadership of Catholic Bishop Fernando Ariztía and Lutheran Bishop Helmut Frenz, with support from the World Council of Churches. Constantly harassed by the regime, the Comité Pro Paz dissolved in late 1975, to be replaced by two complementary organizations that continue to function to the present day: the Archbishopric of Santiago's Vicaría de la Solidaridad (Vicariate of Solidarity), headed for many years by Father Cristián Precht; and the ecumenical Fundación de Ayuda Social de las Iglesias Cristianas (Social Aid Foundation of the Christian Churches, FASIC). Besides facilitating exile for those leaving the country, the Vicaría and FASIC worked in all aspects of human rights and supported numerous other organizations set up to deal with specific issues and groups such as families of the disappeared, the tortured, and political prisoners.*

In addition to the Chilean groups, several international agencies played key roles in aiding exiles. The Chilean office of the Comité Intergubernamental para las Migraciones Europeas (Intergovernmental Committee for European Migration, CIME), later renamed the Organización Internacional para las Migraciones (International Organization for Migration, OIM), was very active and effective. Under the direction of Roberto Kozak, the agency located host countries and obtained visas, safe conducts, and discounted or free flights for those en route to exile, and connected exiles with support services after their arrival abroad. CIME personnel went to great lengths to assure the safety of their wards; after some ugly incidents involving government violations of safe conducts it had granted, Kozak and his staff routinely accompanied people leaving the embassies to the international airport and literally into waiting airplanes in order to discourage regime operatives from snatching them.[†]

The International Red Cross and the United Nations' High Commission on Refugees (UNHCR) played major roles in the mass exodus of Chileans, and the World University Service (WUS) provided scholarships for exiles to study abroad as well as offering a variety of other services. The tireless work of these Chilean and international organizations not only saved many lives, but made the traumatic process of going into exile as smooth as possible for those forced to leave their country.

Many of those who left in the first few months after September 11 believed that their exile would be brief because the military government would not last. As a result, thousands of refugees went to neighboring Argentina and Peru, expecting to return before long. The passage of time erased the illusion of a brief dictatorship, but even earlier, Argentina and

---

* Pamela Lowden, *Moral Opposition to Authoritarian Rule in Chile, 1973–90* (London: MacMillan Press, 1996), focuses on the Vicaría de la Solidaridad and related organizations. FASIC is discussed in Patricio Orellana and Elizabeth Quay Hutchison, *El movimiento de derechos humanos en Chile, 1973–1990* (Santiago: CEPLA, 1991), 143–98.

[†] CIME aided in the resettlement abroad of some thirty-five thousand Chileans. Roberto Kozak, interview, Sept. 10, 1994.

Peru proved to be reluctant hosts. While accepting the Chileans arriving in Peru, the military government of General Juan Velasco Alvarado (1968–1975) made it clear that their stay was to be temporary. This position reflected the historic enmity stemming from Peru's defeat by and territorial loss to Chile in the War of the Pacific (1879–1884), the government's concern for security, and the inability of Peru's weak economy to provide jobs for refugees. In Argentina it was a changing political climate that drove most Chileans on to more secure places of exile. With Peronists in control, the Argentine government welcomed the Chileans at first; but the climate turned hostile following Peron's death in July 1974, and sometimes lethal after the military government of General Jorge Rafael Videla unleashed its "dirty war" against the left in 1976. Moreover, the Chilean junta could easily infiltrate and harass the exile community in Argentina; the September 1974 assassination of retired pro-Allende army commander Carlos Prats and his wife, Sofía Cuthbert, in Buenos Aires was a clear warning that exiles in Argentina were not beyond the regime's reach.

Peru and Argentina were not the only stops along the road to stable resettlement abroad. Chileans found their options determined largely by foreign governments' disposition toward the Chilean situation and by their refugee and immigration policies. If they were under relatively mild pressure to leave Chile, individuals could take the time to apply for scholarships, to consult about work opportunities, or even to apply for visas from several countries. Those under greater pressure to leave normally accepted any offer of sanctuary or sometimes fled without documentation, as did a woman who, denied entry at several European airports, in desperation broke a window in the Helsinki airport and threatened to kill her baby with a shard of its glass; Finnish authorities granted her asylum on the spot.

For those desperate to leave, it was quite common to be received by a host country that turned out to be unsuitable, or less attractive than others, for reasons of culture, politics, or economic opportunity. As a result, many Chileans experienced transitory exile in Latin America — beyond Peru and Argentina — as well as in Europe and around the globe before finding a long-term solution to their needs. Perhaps the most notable case of a short-term European host country is Romania, which generously opened its doors to hundreds of desperate Chileans who, once there, found adaptation to the country very difficult and moved on as soon as possible.

Going into exile, then, was not a simple process. For many, the period between deciding to leave Chile and arriving in a definitive exile location was traumatic, dangerous, and long. Following this was the tremendous challenge of adapting to foreign cultures, climates, and peoples that awaited the exiles in their host countries.

## Francisco Ruiz

*Francisco (Pancho) Ruiz was born in Santiago in 1949. The son of a small businessman and a housewife, he grew up and attended public schools in the working-class district of Quinta Normal. Later he pursued religious studies in a seminary in Santiago and, attracted to liberation theology and Catholic political activism, joined the Izquierda Cristiana (Christian Left), a small faction that left the Christian Democratic Party in 1971 to support the UP government.*

*Francisco Ruiz was a volunteer with the Comité Pro Paz from its beginnings, and as such worked in the varied, improvised programs of assistance to early victims of the dictatorship. Among his coworkers were several clerics and lay persons acknowledged as heroes of the effort to save the persecuted. He was arrested for his involvement, tortured extensively, and freed after nine months of detention. After resuming his volunteer work despite the warnings he had received, he was advised by members of the Comité Pro Paz to leave the country. He went to Canada in December 1975 and remained thirteen years.*

I have always been closely linked to the work of the church, so I knew the bishop well, the priests. I participated in a movement that was called Christians for Socialism, that was a group of priests, nuns, and laity that were studying liberation theology. After the coup, the Comité Pro Paz was formed and I didn't know what to do to help in this effort and I approached the priest who was directing it, Salas, a Jesuit. I told him that I wanted to participate in it. "What do I do?" He accepted me immediately and the work that I did, that had also been my suggestion, was to organize the relatives of the political prisoners who had limited financial means; that is, I could organize trips to northern Chile, to Chacabuco, to Pisagua, etc. Organize these relatives and travel with them and meet the prisoners for the first time [since their arrest]. They are people that didn't have money to go by plane, or by bus or any other way—this was the purpose.

The first time was in a regular city bus. It took us four days to reach the north. Chacabuco is a camp that is in Antofagasta more to the north, an old nitrate plant that they turned into a concentration camp. So we organized this trip with people who had not seen their relatives since they had been imprisoned, because these were people who went to the National Stadium and from the National Stadium were taken directly there. The first trip was in early December 1973, because I remember that we took up a collection thinking of Christmas, of taking things to these people, nonperishable goods. So we did it with thirty-five people the first time. It was an incredible experience, first the uncertainty of whether or not we would be able to see the prisoners. We didn't know if they would let us in to see the prisoners because everything depended on Antofagasta.

Then, these were people who had never been outside of Santiago—they were people from the poblaciones. There were many people who had never seen the sea, so they made these trips with a certain excitement too. It wasn't just sit on the bus and go; rather, we had to stop, encourage people, make it more pleasant. It's one of the most incredible things you have experienced—crossing the desert, stopping, talking, seeing how people were, crying together, singing—it was fantastic. On the first trip, we got to Antofagasta, we got the necessary authorization and after almost five days we were able to go there. They gave us half an hour.

This was very good because it created the possibility of at least seeing every person in the camp. They said, "Please, let them know that I am here," so that this broke down their isolation a little. They gave us many letters, notes, on this first trip. There was a priest who was an army chaplain there, who wore military garb, but he gave us the letters so that we could bring them to people's relatives. That's how this work started. Later, I think that, in total, we made five trips, until eventually there were four buses, five buses, filled with two hundred people. Later there were people who came from Concepción with Bishop Camilo Vial. We met here [in Santiago] and continued north.

This is what the work was, and parallel to this there was a group of the same priests that I mentioned before that began to form a kind of network to help the people who were most important or who were most wanted, who desired to seek asylum. Because there were people who were very desperate, they didn't know how nor to whom they could turn. So this was very strange too, because all of a sudden very important people arrived, you didn't know what to do, where to put them, where to hide them. Usually there were houses of priests or nuns, but to get someone who is super-militant there is very difficult because the repression was so fierce.

So, this is how it began. After some reflection, whether it was moral or not, because also the political parties were a factor. All the agonizing began about whether to go into exile or not. People came to you who weren't very well known and presented themselves to you, saying they were Che Guevara's first cousin, or Miguel Enríquez's [leader of the MIR], people like that. So this committee of priests began to develop contacts with the political leaders of the moment, to determine whether such and such a person really was who he or she said. Because there were so many people who wanted to leave, we had to find a way to know that if they caught this one, they would kill him or her. There was this part with the political leaders and also diplomatic work with the embassies.

The role played by the foreign religious that worked there—they were fantastic—the support of the foreign priests was stronger than that of many Chileans, except for the group like Mariano Puga, Roberto Bolton, Aldunate, Rafael Marot, all those people who were important in the effort.

Getting people asylum was done in the most primitive way that you can imagine, because they didn't have any experience; my God, people had never sought asylum before. So there were some very amusing situations, people trying to disguise themselves by putting a little dye in their hair, pushing others over the wall, others when the ambassador was more approachable . . . trustworthy, with cars from the embassy—every kind of trick to get the work done. With great fear—and fear also because none of us had immunity or anything.

I remember a case that was tragicomic. It involved a priest friend, Roberto Bolton, who was somewhat up in years. The idea was to go by car to a certain place, and then, I with someone who needed asylum and he with another, to the Italian embassy. I was to walk along, but passing by the walls—now the walls are higher—the idea was that I go ahead, put out my hand, the person would put his foot in it and jump, but without look-ing back—something very quick and natural, without looking at the priest behind me, nothing. Well, I do what I am supposed to and this person from nerves and everything flew over to the other side, jumped with no problem. But, with this strange thing that we have, I looked back, even though I shouldn't have, and I see my poor friend who had the opposite reaction; that is, instead of jumping, he panicked. Then the poor fellow jumped, he was falling, they caught him, they pushed his rear end up but it was useless. I had to go back and with two people helping, throw him to the other side and careful that the guards don't catch you.

Among the most receptive embassies were the Italian, the Canadian. The nunciature was very difficult, of course. The Mexican embassy was receptive; France was very cooperative; Sweden too. Argentina—many people left through its embassy; Germany. There were a couple of embassies that even called the police to come take people out, they closed up completely. There were people who behaved very badly, who were completely closed to anything. Even after you had done everything, the person was in, and you had to go get them because there was a threat from the ambassador that "if you don't come get this person, I will let the police in"—it was to that point.

Within the network that we had, nobody was taken by the police except one person who unfortunately we had convinced to go—because all indications were that he could leave from the airport. With other priests, we took him, got him through the police and everything. We left him there, and when we see him again, they are taking him back off the plane. It is the only case that was that dramatic that I remember having experienced, but in general, in spite of the primitiveness of the system, the contacts were made, the time fixed, the O.K. of the ambassador or the consul given. Then there weren't dramatic situations to regret. Unfortunately, the police barricades around the embassies got progressively worse. We could only use this method for a few months, because afterward all the embassies were surrounded by military personnel in plain clothes. Also, there began to be infiltrators, who were government people who wanted you to get them in. So they started coming to ask for asylum, trying to see who were the people who arranged for asylum, how you got asylum, and many times they passed themselves off as asylum-seekers, were there for a time, and then they left.

There was a great deal of pressure on the Comité Pro Paz. Fortunately, the committee was composed of Lutherans, Jews, Anglicans, Catholics, and some Evangelicals. It was as if all religions were represented on the committee and it was respected. It wasn't possible to strike a heavy blow against all the churches and dissolve it, but the government regularly and systematically put heavy pressure on the church hierarchy. Later, there was a systematic effort with the members to discover who was who. All of them were on the left or committed priests and clergy. They began to denounce personally this member, that member, and later in November of

1975 when the Comité Pro Paz dissolved and the Vicariate of Solidarity was formed, only the Catholic Church was left, and then the church had some weak moments. For different reasons, several officials were imprisoned and then they began to expel foreign clergy. They no longer respected the Catholic Church.

## Ximena González

*Ximena González was twenty-nine years old when the UP government was overthrown. Born in Santiago, she grew up in a middle-class family, studied in an experimental school and the University of Chile's School of Journalism, and took her first job in the university's television station. During the UP government, she worked in the Information Office of the Presidency of the Republic. As a member of the Socialist Party and a known collaborator of the Allende government, she realized her vulnerability in the coup's aftermath. After learning of the arrests, deaths, and disappearances of several fellow workers, she opted for asylum.*

*González took refuge with her husband and three small children in the Mexican embassy two days after the coup. Her experience reveals the anxiety, the hardship, and the ad hoc nature of asylum in the earliest days of military rule. It also demonstrates the relative ease of obtaining asylum in the early post-coup period, before the junta reacted to the entry of thousands of Chileans into embassies and embassy residences by surrounding their grounds with police to impede access. The decisive actions of the Mexican embassy and government were symptomatic of the humanitarian efforts of several governments whose efforts saved many Chileans from prison, torture, and death. Ximena González spent twelve years in Mexico. Today, she edits a supplement for children for the Santiago newspaper* La Tercera.

We took advantage of the first hours after the curfew was lifted on the thirteenth so that people could buy food. The Mexican chancellery was in the *barrio alto* [upper-class neighborhood] of Santiago. At this time there was not yet any police presence around the chancellery. Thirty or forty people had already gone there, many of them officials of Salvador Allende's government.

The personnel in the embassy didn't have any experience in this type of situation and were worried about how to determine who had serious problems and who didn't. This was the first thing that they thought of—

of course, it was at the instigation of some of the Chileans who feared that if many people got in, the right to asylum could be in danger. They wanted to set up selection criteria such that they would be the ones making the decisions.

This attitude made fear and insecurity increase as the hours passed. It was necessary for a military attaché from the embassy to assure people that no one would be left unprotected.

The first night we slept on the floor with no covering except the clothes we were wearing. It was a long night, anxious, full of fears. People kept coming—by the fifteenth, there were more than a hundred of us. There were also a large number in the ambassador's house.

The Mexican ambassador got us together and told us that his government had given the express order to protect everyone and that we shouldn't be afraid. He added that he was to return to Mexico to report on the situation and that Salvador Allende's family and those who worked most closely with him who had sought asylum in the embassy, as well as his security guards—all of them considered to be Chileans at high risk at that moment—would travel in the plane sent by his government.

The ambassador got a tourist bus and put the Mexican flag on it to take the first group of exiles and some Mexicans to the airport. A series of automobiles from other diplomatic delegations followed in caravan. In the airport, one of the safe conducts was revoked and the director of the state publishing house [Quimantú], Sergio Maurín, was not allowed to leave. The bus was supposed to return to the embassy with Maurín on board, without the ambassador, without the diplomatic caravan, and in violation of the curfew. That was a night of terror. No one knew what was happening. The embassy office remained dark. Gunfire on the skirts of San Cristóbal hill lighted the night. In the entrance, the bus was waiting with the motor on. Two policemen were blocking the passenger's entry while an official from the embassy tried to change their minds. Inside, some perverse person had been spreading the rumor that the police were going to break into the embassy—that Mexican officials had gotten "the word" that some people were armed and there would be a search.

Some people who kept their heads decided to do something to make the situation less explosive. They organized shifts for cleaning up, cooking, and entertaining the children. A pobladora, who was there with her husband, her small children, and was pregnant, announced that she was about to give birth. Two or three doctors improvised an operating room, and after an arduous effort a boy was born.

On the other hand, meals became more infrequent. An airplane with medicine and food, sent by the Mexican government, had been prevented, by the military government, from delivering its cargo. People began to get their possessions, clothes, work materials, and something to eat from outside. On the outskirts, there was a great deal of movement—the relatives of those in asylum wanted to know what was going on and were ready to help. Also, there were groups that came to insult the Mexican government and those of us who were in the embassy.

September 19, a week after we got there, couples with children were able to leave the country to make the embassy less congested. We went to Mexico in one of the many flights that the Mexican government provided to get out of the country the people in asylum who had come to their embassy in search of protection.

## Eduardo Olivares

*Eduardo Olivares was born in Valparaíso in 1948, the son of a housewife and a worker at Cemento Melón, one of Chile's largest cement companies, located nearby in La Calera. He studied at the company school and later at Catholic boarding schools before entering the University of Concepción, where he pursued a degree in journalism between 1966 and 1972. Although he was not persuaded to join the MIR, founded by Concepción students in 1966, he became sufficiently radicalized in the ferment of the university scene to break with the Christian Democratic Party and join the MAPU when it split off in 1969. The MAPU joined the UP coalition and formed part of the Allende administration.*

*A member of the MAPU central committee, Olivares was charged after the coup with protecting the party's secretary general and only congressman, Oscar Garretón, a special target of the military for his alleged role in fomenting subversion among the ranks of naval enlisted men. After Garretón took asylum in an embassy, Olivares went underground to wait out the fall of the regime, which, he recalls, "our analysis indicated would be no later than March 1974." Upon being discovered, he opted for asylum for himself and his pregnant wife. His wife's uncle, a former ambassador to Austria, facilitated their entry into the Hungarian embassy, which was under Austrian protection after the Hungarian government broke relations with the junta. His wife quickly obtained a safe conduct, and after nearly six months of asylum, Olivares joined her in Austria. They later settled in Paris.*

We entered during the night and the next day, in the morning, the people in charge went to the Ministry of Foreign Affairs and told them: "Look, we want to notify you that this location is under Austrian diplomatic protection." They only said this, and people continued to come. And then, after several days, the Austrian embassy communicated to the Chilean government that they had granted asylum to several people, I don't know the details, and the truth of the matter is that there never really was a police presence there.

So, there we were. Well, my wife came with me and as we were so unsure about the idea of leaving, I hadn't worried about whether they would take wives or not. But we had just gotten married. We were expecting our first baby, and we didn't want to be separated. So we went into the embassy together, which meant that since she personally did not have any great political problems, they gave her a safe conduct at the end of December and made her leave in mid-February. It was very difficult for the people with safe conducts to continue to be at the embassy, because this would seem to verify the military government's accusation that the embassies were protecting people who wanted to stay here and cause problems. So as to not complicate the situation further and not jeopardize the possibility of asylum for other people, she went alone. Well, it was hard, but we finally accepted it. The Austrians said: "Don't worry—you will be taken in there and it will be great," and she went.

The majority of the people who were in that embassy had come at the same time. We all arrived on December 8, during the night, because that was the day that it opened. There was a Communist group related to the security apparatus and protection for the secretary general, who by then didn't need it because he was a prisoner. We were a small group, thirty people, which meant a relatively easy coexistence, and, in general, rather harmonious and with a good deal of solidarity, brotherhood—similar to what you would expect when normal and well-brought up people live in a situation like that. There was a good deal of discussion of politics—of course it was of the kind, it was your fault, no, it was your fault—but always in a brotherly spirit, that is, fighting but like members of the same family, let's say. There were some nice gestures. I remember especially the actions of a boy named Carlos, who was with the Communist Party in finance, who was of Arab heritage. And since he saw that a great many of the people who were there had taken asylum in very poor conditions, without clothes, he arranged things and got in touch with the Arab community, and one day a truck arrived with underwear, shirts, a lot of clothes. That was a nice gesture. The parties for Christmas, New Year's, were very interesting.

There is no doubt that because the people at the embassy were Hungarians, one supposed that they were from a Socialist country and they themselves *a priori* were Communists. There was a different attitude, great solidarity, great friendliness.

I remember something very special. There was a person in charge of security at the embassy, a Hungarian peasant, a very simple fellow who struggled with Spanish, scarcely spoke it, but he was basically a fellow with a really good heart. One day he comes and says: "We not be in Chile for long, the cave of wine not use so eat and drink." He was saying that it wouldn't be of any use because they wouldn't have receptions. There was salami, which is a delicacy, Tokay wine, bull's blood wine [both typical Hungarian wines], a palinka [cherry schnaps], brandy—all very good. Every day he came and showed us how the Hungarian peasant eats. Around eleven o'clock in the morning he would arrive with black bread, a salami, onions, barely peeled, and paprika—which is always an ingredient of their food. He would cut a piece of salami, put paprika on the onion, and put this on the bread, and then it was eaten. This with wine at eleven o'clock in the morning.

We ate a great deal, people who weren't doing anything...what can you do in an embassy? At one moment there were thirty of us, at the beginning, and very quickly there were some who left. Because, well, it was chaotic. The Red Cross never even knew. Later, there were five of us and thirty portions would come and we ate a great deal. I gained twenty-five kilos in six months. When I got to Austria, I had been separated from my wife for four months and she didn't recognize me. "No," she said to me, "you aren't my husband."

Life inside the embassy was rather strange. We received visitors, almost regularly; it was quite unique because there was never a presence of carabineros outside. One day the visits began, so then this was organized so that not too many people would come, so that there would not be a parade of people, and it worked well. We had contact with neighboring houses as well, with the servants. They would bring us gifts over the wall; some love relationships occurred with the neighboring houses. So this part worked that way. The visitors, the people getting to know each other. We were meeting their relatives. It was a very good experience for me, having more contact with people.

We got word that they had attacked such and such an embassy, that they had attacked another, that they had fired from outside, that this or that had happened. And these things caused an increase in anguish. And there isn't anyone to ask if it is true or not, because you suffer from a certain degree of isolation, so we became a bit neurotic. People got up rather late; they watched soap operas: *"La señora joven"* [the young wife], *"Muchachita italiana viene a casarse"* [Italian girl comes to get married] were those which had the top ratings in that period. The physical space included a small garden, and we could play soccer there, three against three.

We received daily newspapers and everyone tried to interpret them, because, of course, we were starting from the premise that they were telling lies. The problem is that once you get into a paranoid state, to try to figure out which of the shit is true is supercomplicated. I think that the idea of the news — the effect that it produced, the effect produced by each news item — was like a small psychodrama that took place, according to who was affected by it; for example, "Listen, they gave a safe conduct to such and such a Communist," and then the Communists, "Oh! Listen, such and such a Socialist or such and such a Radical was taken prisoner."

There were many arguments inside the embassy. The most serious ones were the conflicts that were characteristic of that political moment, and, obviously, at that time there were confrontations between the Christian Democrats and the MIR or the Communist Party and the MIR or between the Communist Party and the Socialist Party. This was also present, but it wasn't really dramatic. In the embassy, the people were mostly Communists. There was also a small number of Socialists; there were three or four young people from the MIR and some from MAPU. However, the Communists were somewhat withdrawn. They were a homogeneous group, like a task force — the group that had been in charge of the security for the secretary general. So they spent a lot of time together as a group. Not that they didn't interact with the rest of us, but, let's say, they spent the majority of their time in long meetings.

There were certain advantages to having been in that place: one, quantitative, is that there weren't many of us, and because the embassy wasn't functioning as such, there was plenty of space and the hygienic conditions were good. Qualitatively, the people who lived there were really rather nice, they were friends. It wasn't always easy, considering the circumstances. It was possible to relax in our daily situation. The tensions came from other things. It wasn't like in other embassies where there were also tensions as a result of just living together; nobody stole anyone else's wife — oh, what do I know?

I finally left on May 27. I was able to go because my wife's brother, who had friends connected with the regime, agreed to run the risk of admitting that he had a "communist" brother-in-law, and he said, "My sister just had her baby alone in Austria and he is still shut up here." Because of that, a sentimental official speeded things up and I left a week after my daughter was born. At the moment that you leave the country, you feel like the president of the republic, because, at that time, you left in an embassy car and with a motorcycle policeman who opened the way for the car. At the airport, someone from CIME [OIM] went with the exile, someone from the Ministry of Foreign Affairs and someone from the embassy. Of course, these three came.

## Julio Pérez

*Julio Pérez was born in Victoria, some six hundred kilometers south of Santiago, in the heart of Chile's Mapuche Indian region. The son of a railroad worker and a teacher, he grew up under the influence of grandparents who introduced him to literature and the history of Chile's labor struggles. Observing the conditions of the impoverished and largely landless indigenous population, Pérez early on developed a social conscience and progressive political views. After attending public schools in Victoria, he enrolled at the University of Concepción during the period when the MIR was founded. He joined the MIR and graduated with a degree in journalism in 1972.*

*In 1972 Pérez found a job with the Agrarian Reform Corporation (CORA) as coordinator of communications for the southern zone. In that position he was witness to the extreme mobilization of the rural labor force in the south, where the accelerated pace of land reform, extralegal land occupations, and landowners' armed resistance created a climate of extreme tension. Throughout rural Chile, CORA employees were special targets after the coup. Living in Puerto Montt, a city of some eighty thousand population, exacerbated Pérez's vulnerability to the repression, leading him to opt for refuge in Santiago. His five months in the capital provided a temporary respite, but facing destitution and increasing persecution, he took advantage of a contact with the Canadian embassy to arrange for exile in Quebec.*

Those of us government officials who were working in agrarian reform projects suffered constant harassment from armed groups of landowners, armed attacks on government vehicles. It was almost impossible to use the rural roads. We did our work secretly and at night to avoid these confrontations. Already some days prior to the coup, in the region of Fresia, near Puerto Montt, the armed forces had made incursions with helicopters and commandos into the lands under peasant control, under the pretext of looking for weapons. On more than one occasion, the armed forces detained peasant leaders, who were hung by their feet and suspended over the peasant villages as a way to create a climate of terror.

So in this atmosphere we were caught by September 11, 1973. At five o'clock in the morning, I was notified by a friend who worked at the telephone company, who had overheard conversations, messages in code, and an unusual amount of telephone traffic among the different armed groups. Obviously, it was time to take the minimum security measures of which we had spoken, but they gained control of a small city like Puerto Montt quickly. Besides, there was an air base there, an important regiment, a naval base, carabineros, and a strong paramilitary organization of sectors of the right, which had many weapons and was well trained.

The repressive forces already had control of the city at seven o'clock in the morning. Those of us who were so lucky as to have a telephone at home were able to escape in time. Many of our compañeros were detained, several shot or killed under torture during the first forty-eight hours when the curfew was in effect. Those of us who reached a safe house lived like rats for several days, only going out with a crude disguise or at dusk before the curfew began.

The orders were to take refuge in the country, because the resistance was to be organized starting from the peasant base. However, our first trips into the rural zones with the greatest leftist influence showed us that there was nothing to be done there. The armed forces, the carabineros, and with particular violence, the owners of the lands which had been expropriated, supported by the paramilitary groups, did away with all of those who were leaders in the expropriation process. Many were murdered, among them a Socialist congressman well known in the region, to whom the *"ley de fuga"* was applied [the "fugitive law" refers to the military or police "right" to shoot an allegedly "fleeing" prisoner, often used to justify prisoner deaths].

My organization [MIR] decided to send a message to the capital to get information and help for those families who from one day to the next found themselves without any way to live. This responsibility fell on me. It was a long and dangerous journey because of the multiple checkpoints that existed along the route, the only route to get to the capital. I traveled on buses that had short runs, getting off a few kilometers before each checkpoint, and taking the long way around to avoid them — one week to cover one thousand kilómeters. Later we copied the bourgeoisie of the region, traveling in a train with a sleeping car, where passengers were not bothered.

During two and a half months, we tried to organize the small groups of active party members dispersed through the southern zone of the country, but the cordon around us grew ever smaller. There wasn't much space left anymore to live peacefully even for a single night. More than once, we slept in the street, in sewers under construction in the city of Puerto Montt, because we hadn't had time to get to a safe house or because someone who had promised us a place to stay wouldn't open the door to us just a few minutes before the curfew began. So it was that at the beginning of December we received orders to leave the zone.

In Santiago, a city unknown to a southerner like me, it wasn't easy. With great good luck, I met up on the street with a university classmate and good friend, who invited me to stay at his house. However, his parents didn't share his opinion. Then we met another friend from Concepción. We were three journalists in the same situation, and from then on, we were always together.

I also managed to get in touch with Miguel Rivas Rachitoff, who had been my immediate supervisor, an active member of the Socialist Party. He had organized an underground press agency to send information out of the country. We met in the capital city's parks to turn in our material every so often. One morning I arrived late at the meeting place because of a military sweep in the area where I was staying. When I didn't see my contacts, after walking around the park, I stopped to buy a newspaper and the vendor mentioned to me that a little before there had been a roundup and they had taken a number of people away. From that moment, I lost contact with two of my colleagues, Juan Pérez and Miguel Rivas. Today they are on the lists of those disappeared.

At that moment, I felt that the world was falling down around my ears. The feeling of impotence of knowing that they had been arrested; I was angry that I wasn't with them, for having gotten there late. I was afraid they would suspect that I had betrayed them. Those were perhaps the bitterest, saddest, most desolate days after the coup.

At any rate, I had to find a way to survive. The three of us had no possibility of finding work in our profession, of course, nor did we want to risk applying for any regular job for fear that when we gave our personal data we would be revealed as "subversives." For this reason, we decided to devote ourselves to the buying and selling of antiques. This was an unknown area for us, so we went to libraries and museums in order to study up on it. But we soon realized that given the economic situation, many people were having to sell items of value in order to survive, but no one was buying. Then we decided to sell eggs in the poblaciones. Everything went very well until we found an ad in the newspaper offering eggs at very low prices. We bought all we could, we made our deliveries, and the next week, when we went to collect and deliver a new batch, our clients greeted us by throwing the eggs at us. The reason for the low prices had been the state of decomposition of the eggs. And this meant the end of our business.

At the same time, we were writing journalistic materials for a press agency directed by Sister Denisse, a Canadian nun who worked in the committees aiding those being sought by the police, in the Comité Pro Paz. She gave us a small amount of money for this work. We also produced materials analyzing the situation of different sectors for the media that the MIR circulated on microfilm.

That was a very hard period, sleeping here, there, in the home of someone in solidarity, some Trotskyites, at the house of a colleague's brother, or wherever night found us. Our poverty was such that on more than one occasion we shared a hot dog and a beer among the three of us. On one occasion, a Sunday, it occurred to one of my colleagues that we should go to the race track and bet the little money we had. Our surprise was great when the horse we had chosen won. We spent an unforgettable afternoon. We were able to have a decent meal and drink *vino con frutillas* [wine with strawberries, a popular warm-weather drink] and we still had money left over for several days.

The time went by with doubts and arguments over whether to leave or stay. None of us planned to leave. We still had faith in the political organizations. This couldn't last long. Seeking asylum was seen, in the first months of 1974, as cowardice. Besides, our organization's order was not to seek asylum.

However, the cordon was closing in on us more and more. On one occasion, we arrived at a friend's house only minutes after the police had searched it. Then, at the end of March of 1974, Sister Denisse was ordered to leave the country within twenty-four hours. She had been caught helping people being sought by the military get asylum and with material from her press agency. She managed to get in touch with us. She gave us the name of an official in the Canadian embassy so that if we decided to leave the country we could go see him. At that point, we still planned to stay in the country, but arrests and killings of our contacts with the MIR, plus the difficulty of making ends meet, made us change our minds.

My parents came to the capital and I managed to see them. My mother, worried, brought me some clothing and some delicacies that, obviously, shared with my friends, didn't last more than a few hours. My ex-wife came so that I could see my two-year-old daughter—this at great risk.

Finally, we decided to go to the Canadian embassy. We saw the contact person, and from the very beginning we knew that this was our man. His way of conducting himself, his caution in dealing with the bureaucracy, his biting humor about the Chilean situation made us feel safe. Medical exams, interviews, and a thousand kinds of checks. At the end of April, he told us that only two of our applications had been accepted. One of my colleagues was rejected because, it seems, the Royal Canadian Mounted Police discovered something in his record which was communicated to the dictatorship's police force and his visa was denied. He left clandestinely for Argentina. The other left for Canada without any problem.

As for me, the government denied my request for a passport, so I had to turn to the United Nations High Commission for Refugees. After three tries, they got me a passport and a safe conduct, and they took me to the airport and they put me on the plane. Once on the plane, I began to relax until a military patrol came on board, advancing slowly, looking for someone. Three or four meters away, they fixed their eyes on me—at least, that's what I thought—but they were looking at the passenger behind me. It was a tense moment that cost me what little energy I had left after spending eight months in a state of permanent stress. Once we were airborne, I drank two whiskeys, something I had never drunk before in my life. This put me into such a deep sleep that it would have taken an earthquake to wake me. This happened again, sleeping for several days, upon my arrival in la belle province, Quebec.

## Gabriel Fernández

*Gabriel Fernández, son of a medical doctor and a housewife, was born in 1946 and raised in the middle-class Santiago neighborhood of Ñuñoa. As a student at the University of Chile, he developed leftist sympathies, but remained independent of parties. After finishing medical school, he went to work with the National Health Service in a provincial city.*

*Fernández was detained in January 1974 at the hospital while performing an operation, and charged with being one of the intellectual authors of Plan Zeta (Plan Z), an alleged secret UP plan to assassinate leading military men and rightist politicians and install a Marxist dictatorship; this fabricated plot, purportedly discovered by the military, was offered as one of the justifications for the coup. After torture, Fernández was tried in a court-martial and sentenced to three years of relegation (relegación, or internal exile) in a small, poor, isolated provincial town. Compared with a prison sentence, internal exile was preferable in every way but one: It carried no salary or means of subsistence, and in Dr. Fernández's case, he was banned from working in any public institution, including the National Health Service's clinic. He left Chile for the United States in 1976, sponsored by Amnesty International, and, after passing the required exams, practiced medicine in southern California until 1994. After returning to Chile, he resumed his career as a surgeon with the National Health Service.*

The sentence was handed down in a trial in which we were assigned a lawyer from the Comité Pro Paz, and he talked with us the day before the trial, in the evening. In this war council, I was sentenced to 541 days of relegación. But about a month went by after this, and we found to our surprise when we left jail that the sentences had been doubled.

I was freed from jail in April or May of 1974 and I had to report to a city in the provinces within a week. I went to the town to figure out where I was going to stay and evidently everything was taken, including the houses — they were rented — the inns, the residential hotels — everything was rented to foreigners, at exorbitant prices because they were just then building a huge factory. I was married with two children, who were two and three years old. Fortunately, a friend who had relatives in Santiago, who had just been operated on for a stomach problem, told me that she had a house in that town that had a couple of rooms that she could let me use — also so that I could take care of her. I took it as a gift from heaven that this person could offer me a couple of rooms, one of which I used as an "office" and the other which was very small with my wife and one of the children, the older one. My younger daughter had to stay in Santiago because of the limited space.

Since there was no salary or assistance, I had to make a living as best I could, and for me this meant that I had to have patients. This was not as difficult as I had thought, because in that town there had been a very famous doctor some years back, some thirty years ago, who had lived there and who had gone back to the city where I had been in practice before the coup, and everyone found out that I had trained with this doctor. I had performed numerous operations with him, so it seemed that the fact that I had trained with someone this famous gave me a certain status. It was a

town of some three thousand people. The fact that a doctor had been rel-
egated there became known in two days, so I think that, as a result, it was
a gesture of solidarity to consult me on certain things — besides I was
available all day long. I was forbidden to hold a public post, that is, I
couldn't work at the clinic, and that allowed me to be available all day.

Another of the factors that allowed us to survive, let's say, without having a salary was what happened one day some two months after arriving in
town. They knock on the door where I was living and the ambulance from
the clinic tells me that they need me at the clinic, and I say to the driver
of the ambulance, "How can I go if I can't set foot in the clinic?" "Doctor, the doctor on duty told me that you can come in." I leave for the
clinic, the ambulance takes me, and I meet the young doctor who tells me
that he has a serious problem with a birth, and that he can't send the patient to the hospital in the nearest city because she is in shock, she has lost
a great deal of blood, and that he knows that I had some surgical experience and if I could help him . . . Obviously, the first thing that occurs to
me is "I shouldn't be here," but I saw that he was desperate and I thought
about the patient that I could probably help, knowing the risks that there
were, that usually there are risks. At this moment I thought about the fact
that I was a doctor in internal exile and that I might not be successful in
an operation that was urgent in a critical situation, and at that moment I
decided in favor of the patient — in spite of everything, I took the risk. I
ended up operating, I think with the chief nurse, and he gave the anesthe-
sia and, well, the patient . . . had a hysterectomy due to a uterine hemor-
rhage and, well, she survived. I think that within a couple of days, in a
small town, this was talked about, and that the doctor who was there had
gone to the clinic and had solved these problems. I think that all of this
helped the people to trust me and come to see me in the room that I had
for this purpose.

I was in that town for over two years. Then, due to some very extraordinary circumstances, I leave for the United States. The story begins with
my being released from jail, on my way to internal exile. You had a week
after you were released from jail to report to the relegation site. During
that week someone approached me to give me some eighty to one hundred letters that had arrived from the United States. A person in the post
office, where these letters had arrived, saved them for me and gave them
to me when she met me in the street. An interesting gesture. Very nice.

They were written in English and asked if I was in jail there — they were
addressed to the *cárcel presidio* [a prison that mixed regular and political
prisoners] in the city where I was arrested. Obviously I never got those

letters because, in fact, no one could get a letter inside and it seems that this lady with good intentions saved them, hoping to give them to me at some time. I knew very little about Amnesty International. Afterward I was able to verify that it was an organization that had taken my case, what they call a "prisoner of conscience," which is someone who has not used violence, but rather is imprisoned because of his or her ideas. The letters were clearly not asking anything other than how I was, how I felt; they mentioned this kind of thing. The letters didn't try to go beyond letting it be known that someone was asking about me. For reasons at the time, I never thought that those letters could take me to the United States, that someone would know me by name, so I never answered them. Later I had the opportunity to become a member of Amnesty International, and obviously I had the opportunity to meet the people who had sent the letters; I participated in this organization and I was able to see the documents, how I was an Amnesty case.

A year and a half after I went into internal exile, someone from the church in a nearby city approached me and brought me a letter, which was a letter from Amnesty International, which said again that they had finally been able to find out where I was, that they wanted me to write to them, that they were aware of my situation. They seemed to be well informed, because they asked about my children, my family. They had much more information about who I was, or what I had done, than I had about Amnesty International.

The contacts to go to the United States were made after the same person came and brought me another letter from Amnesty International, which said that if I wished to immigrate to the United States that I should write and that they could probably help me. I wrote and, obviously, the people in Los Angeles were interested, and later I received a couple more letters which said that the United States embassy had an immigration program for two hundred families, to which I should apply, but, in fact, the program was for people who were in jail, and, since I was in internal exile, I wasn't eligible. I told Amnesty International this in a letter in which I thanked them for giving me this information, but said that I wasn't eligible for the reasons that I have already mentioned. The truth is that Amnesty International seems to have contact with senators in the United States, especially Kennedy, and it seems that some way they managed to get the number increased so that I could qualify and, in fact, I received an answer from the consulate that I should report there sometime soon because I was eligible to immigrate.

## Ana Laura Cataldo

*In September 1973 Ana Laura Cataldo was a twenty-eight-year-old radio and television journalist with a degree from the University of Chile. She was raised in a middle-class Santiago family; her mother was a housewife, her father a public employee in the Ministry of Public Works and a member of the Radical Party. Her university experience during the 1960s made her a leftist, but she did not join any party. Elected treasurer of the radio journalists' union of Santiago during the Allende government, Cataldo was fired two months before the coup from the private, anti-government Radio Chilena.*

*Like many of the exiles, Ana Laura Cataldo left Chile legally, under no threat of imminent arrest, but unemployed and without prospects of finding work. Sharing the common belief that the military government would be brief, she went to Peru expecting to return shortly. According to Anthony Vassiliadis, who worked with the United Nations High Commission for Refugees (UNHCR) in Peru, there were between three thousand and four thousand Chileans in Lima in 1974. His greatest challenge was not finding countries to accept the refugees, but getting the refugees to leave Peru for long-term exile in distant lands.\* Along with these thousands, Ana Laura Cataldo experienced transitory exile in Peru before leaving for definitive exile in Canada. She now works in public relations for the Santiago Department of Sanitation.*

We met at Lucho's apartment and began to talk about which of our friends were still free, which of our friends were already prisoners, and which of our friends were dead. Then we began to realize that the circle was closing in on us and that was the first time I thought I might leave the country. I said, "Well, I'll go to Peru for six months and come back." I didn't really understand what sin I had committed for which I had to go into exile.

Obviously, the idea was to go to Peru to be there six months, a year, because we supposed that this wouldn't last any longer, and so why go any farther away? I had no desire to leave this country, I had no plan to do so, that is, to make my life somewhere else.

I bought my ticket and I left for Lima on February 6, 1974. Apparently there were still people in the International Police that helped people leave

* Interview, June 28, 1994.

and didn't give you too much trouble. My friend Marcelo, who had left in January, was waiting for me there.

I spent seven months in Lima. I arrived the first night and they sent me to a big house, with lots of rooms, with lots of people, lots of bedrooms, and it was the first time in my life that I slept on a mattress of leaves, in a large group of people, with people who were in rather bad shape emotionally. There was one woman, Juanita, who was with her son who was about two years old — she was from Concepción — who had had to leave urgently because they had her husband in Quiriquina [a naval base–turned-prison on an island in the Bay of Concepción] and they were looking for her. So she left through the church. I must have been at this boarding house for four or five days, and afterward they moved us to another boarding house somewhere else. There, I was in a room that was not that of a five-star hotel but rather one that had no stars, with a widow with her two daughters whose son had been taken prisoner in Concepción. Well, we were in this boarding house about two months, and after that, they moved us again to another one, where I stayed until I left for Canada.

There must have been at least fifteen or twenty places lodging Chileans, where, suddenly, there was a big jump in numbers, because there were places where there were more than one hundred people, where there was room for thirty, and with children, with everything.

The majority of us left without money, thinking that we would be able to work at something, but, since the situation got worse — the government of Velasco Alvarado began to have problems — we were not able to work, they wouldn't let us. So I did something having to do with public relations in the pastoral work of the Catholic Church, but this had to be concealed. If the police caught you, they would take you prisoner and they would also throw you out of the country. They wouldn't send you somewhere else, they would only send you back to Chile. We were never able to really do any kind of paid work.

I remember that in the last boarding house where we were, we weren't so piled up, because there they were six or seven per room. Imagine what it is to not be doing anything. That is, without money, because then you can't go out. Actually, we went out for walks, of course. We went out to explore the city, but you don't have money. So what could we do? We played cards. And we sat down suddenly at two o'clock in the afternoon to play cards and we would play until two o'clock in the morning, because we didn't have anything else to do. When someone got money from their relatives, we bought two roasted chickens for about thirty people and we each ate a little of the chicken. But we had a party, because, well, it was entertaining. Besides, the Peruvian food is very different—imagine that the UNHCR was paying a lady and suddenly she gave you a soup with rice, a second course with white rice, and for dessert they gave us rice pudding. And that's what happened.

Then, when the political situation in Peru, some two months after we got there, began to get worse for the Peruvians themselves, they came often to the boarding houses, and they took us to make statements to the political police. "What were you doing? What did you do in Chile?" They thought that all of us must walk around with submachine guns and they looked at us as if we were just lying.

We all depended on the UNHCR. The UNHCR got you all your documents, the papers that you hadn't brought from Chile. Besides your upkeep—they paid your room and gave you food—they put you in contact with the various embassies, they introduced you to people and they helped you go to other countries.

I spent three months trying to stay, to get a job and even through some friends of my mother's cousin who worked in the National Bank of Peru. I tried to get work at the bank as a secretary or whatever, and there was no way. I was Chilean and they didn't have an opening. The fact of being Chilean, and under the protection of the United Nations . . . you were a pariah. So you didn't have any chance of finding a job that would allow you to stay. So I said then, they haven't beat me yet—I have to start the paperwork.

The Chileans preferred some countries over others because of political contacts; for example, Romania, Cuba. Others had relatives who had gone to a particular country or had a friend or had someone who had written to them and told them: "Look, it's like this here, there are possibilities. You can come," I don't know exactly. And many people probably were thinking about studying somewhere, because that was what the countries of the Socialist bloc offered most often, that is, they gave you a chance to study.

I put in applications at several embassies and had my visa ready to go to Australia and, can you believe it, I imagined Australia to be a really faraway island in the Pacific. The next day I had an interview with Mrs. Ashton, who was the business representative for the British embassy, and she said to me: "I can put a visa stamp in your passport right away so that you can go to Great Britain, but what other possibilities do you have?" So I told her that I had possibilities in Australia, Canada, and Luxembourg. And she told me: "You know what? Go to Canada—it's a young country where since you are traveling alone, you are a young professional woman, you are going to have many more opportunities to develop yourself than you would have in my country, in Great Britain." She said to me: "The economy is more depressed. I would advise you to go to Canada." She was the one who advised me to go there, can you believe it? So I went to Canada.

## Gabriel Sanhueza

*Gabriel Sanhueza, the son of a housewife and a shipyard worker in the southern port of Talcahuano, was born in nearby Concepción in 1947. He studied journalism at the University of Concepción and joined the MIR in its early days. A separated father of a three-year-old child, at the time of the coup he was pursuing a second degree in sociology, teaching journalism, and working in the MIR's propaganda apparatus. He was arrested in a sweep of the university on the day of the coup and taken to the naval base at Quiriquina Island, a major detention center for the Concepción region. He was released after three weeks owing to the confusion and lack of coordination among the diverse military and police units which had yet to learn to work together. As he remembers, "It was a good thing to have been arrested that first day. It was incredible luck that they didn't have information."*

*Too well known to remain in Concepción, Sanhueza went to Santiago to hide out and work in the MIR's underground network. Feeling the noose tighten around him, he soon left for Mendoza, the Argentine city closest to Santiago, where he joined several thousand other Chilean refugees. His feelings about leaving reflect the dilemma facing MIR members torn between obedience to the party order forbidding members to leave and a will to survive. His experience in transitory exile reveals both the attractions of relocating in Argentina during Perón's presidency and the dangers posed by Chilean agents infiltrating the refugee community. After Perón's death in July 1974, both government and paramilitary anticommunist forces made life increasingly difficult for Chileans as well as for Uruguayan and Brazilian political refugees who had fled dictatorships in their own countries. Sanhueza left after six months for West Germany. Back in Santiago, he is manager of a firm that installs exhibitions at special events.*

At first, we thought that there would be great resistance to the coup, that because of the very nature of Chile, because of the way the working class was organized, because the parties were so strong, and so forth, the military wasn't going to be able to remain in power very long. But when the first months went by and you began to talk to people, you realized the terror that they felt. People were terrified, and soon we realized that this would last for a long time.

It was very hard for me to leave Chile because even if I was convinced on a rational level that I had to leave, my heart, our feelings, said the opposite. "It doesn't make any sense to stay — they will kill me, we aren't doing anything important." But there is a part of you that says, "Shit, you are running out on your compañeros, you are leaving." Ethics tell you to sacrifice your personal considerations and accept, let's say, what's best for the group as a whole. So then, this was very hard. I remember, before I left, talking with compañeros from the MIR who thought the same way I did, but who stayed and later they were killed. So they also had doubts, but they stayed anyway. So it was really shitty.

I left in May of 1974, on the bus, with a false ID card. At that time, when you bought a ticket to leave the country on an airplane, train, or bus, the company was obliged to send the list of passengers twenty-four hours in advance, with their names and their ID numbers, to the police. I bought my ticket in San Felipe [a small town north of Santiago, in the Andean foothills, on the route to Argentina] thinking that if you buy it there — since, in spite of so many months having passed, the coordination wasn't all that good — it was unlikely that San Felipe would have all the information. At this time, they didn't have computers. In the bus I took, two or three people were detained at the border, but I didn't have any problems.

I spent about four days in Mendoza, and from there we went directly to Buenos Aires. I found work, with the help of some friends of Peronists, in a publishing house correcting proofs of books. There was a great solidarity in the Peronist sectors regarding the Chilean situation, and they treated us very well, they helped us. The state of the Argentine economy was also very favorable for us. We made contact with old friends from Concepción. We didn't live in luxurious conditions: family hotels, meals, sometimes a movie, but there were weeks that we were rather badly off. But there was great solidarity among the exiles who knew each other, among friends; the ones who had work helped the others, and there was really a fraternal spirit.

The United Nations had arranged for a group of hotels to house the people who fled — old hotels in which there were one hundred people. The order those of us in the MIR had gotten was to not live in those hotels, rather to try to lose ourselves in greater Buenos Aires and not be with the mass of refugees because we knew that the dictatorship had sent many people—military—to infiltrate the refugees to know what they were doing in exile. In that sense, we were very careful. The assassination of Prats had a great impact on people.

I had the impression that we were being watched, in spite of our efforts to mix with the Argentines. I remember that one time I was detained because I made a statement in defense of the Chilean journalists who were imprisoned, at a meeting organized by all of us journalists who were there. They took us to the police station and they explained to us that this was interference in Argentine politics and was not allowed. So we changed hotels, we didn't go back to certain places. But during the six months that I was there, the harassment of Chileans wasn't very strong yet. At this time, the Chileans weren't very important within the Argentine political panorama. After the coup [March 1976], yes. They were killing the Uruguayans especially. I was greatly impacted by the death of some members of Congress who were exiled, who were murdered in cold blood by the Uruguayan military acting in Buenos Aires.

At first, we thought that the military would not be able to stay in power for very long. I'll go to Argentina because this won't last long, so then I'll be able to get back faster being practically next door. But as seen from Argentina, the military seemed to be very strong and there was absolutely no sign of resistance. I became convinced that it would be at least five years. So, in November of 1974, I went to Germany, at the instigation of the MIR.

## Miriam Casanova

*Miriam Casanova (introduced in chapter 2) did not find a home in exile until two years after the coup. After four anxious months in Peru and Argentina, she joined her husband and children in Poland, which had offered them sanctuary. There, the family spent a year and a half, from early 1974 to September 1975, in considerable material comfort and economic security. While the children seemed to adapt readily, Miriam and her husband were unable to overcome linguistic and cultural barriers to integration and moved to Italy, where her husband, a Chilean of Italian background, had family and connections.*

I managed to join my husband and my children in Poland. Those who were exiled there were a rather small number of Chileans, some twenty-five families. We were housed in a vacation retreat for the military, beautiful, with an artificial lake where people skated. They taught the children to skate on the ice. It was all very nice.

We were treated very well; we were always rather privileged. They gave us an apartment. It was a little uncomfortable to have all the Chileans living together in the same part of Warsaw. They offered us good jobs. My husband was a translator of Italian and Spanish in an official translation company, and I went to work at the Polish radio station. I was doing Latin American musical programs as part of their Spanish-language programming.

But in general, we realized that we had little in common with the Polish world. First, there was the problem of the language—which was a terrible language. My husband had had the opportunity to study a little Polish at the embassy while they were in asylum, but I went directly from Argentina to Poland without even knowing how to say "Good morning." When I arrived, they weren't even there to meet me because there had been a problem with the plane, and so I had to make myself understood by the people at the airport with what little English I knew—a little French and a little English.

The Polish world had many very interesting things. There was a cultural world—the movies, the theater—the level was unimaginable, it was sensational. But they knew absolutely nothing about Latin America—they had absolutely no idea nor any interest either—a language like Spanish, a fifth-rate language in Poland. Well, and we realized that there was nothing for us there.

We thought that the Polish period wouldn't last very long, because we thought that we would be going back to Chile. We spent a good deal of time there thinking and trying to get news. We listened to Radio Moscow in Spanish, which was the one that gave news that was supposed to be more or less recent, and then we learned that it didn't have any relationship to what was really happening. But several French newspapers and some English daily papers reached Warsaw, so we were continually reading the foreign press and a news item or two that appeared in the Polish papers. But from Poland we were able to get in touch with relatives. Letters were sent through Argentina; we corresponded with my relatives, with my family. We wrote half in code, not saying things clearly so as not to cause problems.

There were acts of solidarity, but with very little participation on the part of the Polish people. Things were done at the institutional level, tributes to Neruda [Pablo Neruda, Chile's Nobel laureate poet and prominent member of the Communist Party, who died within days of the coup], cultural tributes or political ones, but only with the participation of what the people there called the "intelligentsia"—the political world at a certain level, the university people, the intellectual world. There was no participation by the masses of the people, no one was very interested. The Polish people understood little about our history or weren't very interested in it.

As far as food, we never had much problem with respect to that. The problems were with the meat. Meat was rather scarce, they often ran out of it, but there were other kinds of food. I think that Poland never had the problems that existed in the USSR. In Poland, there was plenty of everything. So we cooked in the apartment. On the other hand, they had no authentic cuisine; they had a cuisine somewhere between the Russian and the German, that is, with no character of its own. The typical dish was a horrible thing: a piece of potato, shredded cooked cabbage, and a kind of sausage. And the Poles ate this almost every day. They had a tremendous lack of imagination, because you could make other things, but the Poles eat their dish.

My children were fine. After six months, both of them spoke Polish. They were very involved, they went to school. My daughter entered the school of dance—they were fine. But very soon after we got there, we began to think about the possibility of going to Italy, because my husband is the son of Italians and thinking that they might recognize his citizenship. It was terrible when we told them that we were leaving; it was terrible politically. They were really upset, they practically called us ungrateful, everything they could think of. They didn't want us to go; it was an insult to them for us to leave and, even more so, that we would go to Italy. But the truth is that we were decided and my husband had the possibility of getting citizenship, and besides, he had the immediate possibility of work in Ferrara, which was the city we went to.

*FOUR*

# Resistance and Exile

The speed, efficiency, and relative ease with which the military took control on September 11 and during the following days surprised most observers. Armed resistance on the day of the coup, limited to isolated pockets in Santiago's industrial zones and poblaciones, was easily broken and the possibility of effective popular resistance was eliminated from the start. Stunned by the overwhelming display of force and perhaps convinced by President Allende's radio message from the Moneda that resistance was futile, the great bulk of union and UP party members who might have been inclined to fight for their government succumbed to a mood of resignation and bitterness. As Gladys Díaz remembers, making her way toward downtown on the morning of September 11: "The workers were already coming back very bitter. The most pathetic image that I remember was that of people who were leaving the downtown area with their work clothes, their hard hats, and they said to me, 'Don't go downtown because they are going to bomb the Moneda.'"* The swift capture of government and party leaders, and the broadcast of numerous bandos listing persons required to turn themselves in, placed most potential resistance leaders in a defensive position, driving them underground. In addi-

* Interview, June 16, 1994.

tion, the two days of uninterrupted curfew made it very difficult to gather for organizing any resistance.

In the months following the coup, the effectiveness of the repression and the apparent hopelessness of resisting inside the country led a major share of the left's as yet uncaptured leaders to opt for asylum or clandestine escape from Chile. All UP parties attempted to reorganize underground; of them, the Socialists and the Communists were most successful. The Communists had an advantage, both in their cell organizational structure and in their experience in clandestinity between 1948 and 1958, when the party had been illegal. By 1975 the regime's security forces began to capture and kill the parties' underground leadership after extracting information from partisans under torture. The assassination of the Communist Party's underground central committee in May 1976 effectively destroyed the UP parties' resistance. While skeletal units remained, they were incapable of any significant anti-regime activity until the climate began to change in the early 1980s.

The MIR took a harder line on resisting the military. Established at the University of Concepción in 1966 as a group dedicated to achieving socialism through armed revolution, the MIR had suspended its guerrilla actions during the 1970 presidential campaign to avoid creating a climate unfavorable to Allende's candidacy. During the UP administration, the MIR collaborated in some areas without holding any government posts; it simultaneously worked intensely with peasants, workers, and pobladores to build organizations and to apply pressure from below to deepen and hasten Allende's revolution. Always convinced that there was no peaceful, legal path to socialism, the MIR preserved its commitment to armed struggle whenever conditions should dictate. The combination of its commitment to armed struggle, its organizational strength among the poor, and its control of unknown quantities of arms presaged a fierce resistance to a coup. But the morning of September 11 revealed that the MIR was no better prepared for armed defense of the Allende government than were the UP parties.

Despite the initial setback, the MIR vowed to resist. While the UP parties placed a premium on saving their leaders' lives by getting them out of the country, the MIR called on all its leaders and members to form an underground resistance; it adopted the slogan "el MIR no se asila" (the MIR does not seek asylum) to define its position and rally its membership. This hard line split the MIR's ranks from the beginning: Numerous militants opted for personal safety and that of their families over obedience to the party line, while others calculated that they could work more effectively against military rule from abroad. As the junta honed its intelligence capability and improved its coordination after the coup, particularly after the DINA's founding in June 1974, other MIRistas abandoned their initial commitment to resistance as hopeless.

Those who persisted in resisting dedicated themselves initially to surviving, keeping a skeletal organization going in the face of repeated losses of leadership, and smuggling news of the repression and human-rights violations out of Chile. Given the MIR's presumptive power and hard line, the regime targeted it immediately. These efforts paid off in the shooting deaths of several leaders, including MIR founder and secretary general Miguel Enríquez in October 1974. In February 1975, four captured MIRistas were forced to make a televised plea to their comrades to abandon the resistance. A major turning point came in October 1975, when MIR leaders Andrés Pascal Allende and Nelson Gutiérrez and their compañeras were ambushed and, with Gutiérrez seriously wounded, took asylum and subsequently left the country. After these setbacks shattered the MIR's domestic organization, the party's surviving leadership regrouped abroad. Nonetheless, a small MIR underground persisted and became more active in the 1980s, when it was joined by the Communist Party's Frente Patriótico Manuel Rodríguez in the armed struggle against the dictatorship.*

The testimonies that follow are the stories of MIRistas who resisted and survived, although not without severe physical and/or psychological trauma. Yet as survivors they are the fortunate ones of the MIR resistance.

---

* The MIR's resistance through 1977 is chronicled in Carmen Rojas, *Recuerdos de una MIRista* (Montevideo: Ediciones del Taller, 1988). The incident involving Pascal Allende and Gutiérrez is described by a protagonist in Sheila Cassidy, *Audacity to Believe* (London: Collins, 1977), 156–64.

## Patricio Rivas

*Born in 1953, Patricio Rivas was brought up in the middle-class Santiago
neighborhood of Ñuñoa. He was one of four children of a businessman
trained in theoretical mathematics and a Jewish housewife who painted
and played music. He attended Catholic schools and in 1968 joined the
MIR, which recruited heavily among secondary-school students. After
entering the University of Chile in 1970, Rivas abandoned his studies to
dedicate his full time to the MIR, recruiting and organizing students
and coordinating strikes and related activities for the party. In 1973 he
was a member of the MIR's central committee.*

*Rivas's recollections provide insights into the MIR leadership's reactions
to the coup, its attempt to mount a resistance, its strategy of building international support for the internal resistance, and the dangers of participating in the underground opposition to the military government. After his
capture, he was tortured, sentenced to prison, and expelled from the country
in 1976. He subsequently worked for the MIR in France and Cuba, and in
the 1980s operated clandestinely in Chile as a MIR agent.*

The night of the eleventh there was already a lot of discussion among the
members of the political commission. Early on the morning of the
eleventh, with a group of people we had gone to the house of a classmate
from the university who was the compañera of Bautista Van Schouwen, a
member of the political commission of the MIR. I meet with Bautista
there, and then he tells me that it is necessary to resist at all cost—in
whatever way possible. So then I am left with this order—it was a definite
order—he wasn't asking for any discussion. It was an order. So we tried to
get people reorganized. I remember that the Socialist Party, if you can believe it, gave us a huge quantity of arms because they didn't know what to
do with them. The Izquierda Cristiana [Christian Left] also had arms;
they gave us arms. So, suddenly, we had more arms than people by the
evening of that day.

So we planned to resist; we said that on the twelfth we would go out
into the streets and at least harass them to keep them from coming into
the working-class neighborhoods. That is, we would defend this territory,
counting on the political support of the international community. If we
could hold out for three days, we had the Peronists in the Argentine government, and Peronism was clearly pro-Allende. We had the progressive
military in Peru, and they were clearly pro-Allende. There was a meeting

going on in Algeria that Fidel [Castro] was attending. . . . It was a question of gaining time so that the international community could isolate the attempted coup, that is, change the coup into an attempted coup, but in order for this to happen, you have to show strength, that is, to hold out for two, three days. Comforted by this reasoning, we got ready for the twelfth. And the twelfth, the whole morning, we were holding out, but it was really pathetic. I mean, it was us, those of us who were in the streets — there were little groups of MIR, little groups of Socialists and the military. There was no concentration of people. I mean, clearly, this was conquered territory.

Now, the afternoon of the twelfth, I meet with Miguel [Miguel Enríquez, MIR leader], and Miguel gives me another order. He tells me, "We have to fall back, we have to recognize that they caught us by surprise." He was yelling at me, no, mad at me. "If you keep on doing this, they are going to kill all our people, now we have to fall back." I tell him that I talked to Bautista Van Schouwen and that he told me the opposite. And I remember that he said, "No, Bausha is reacting at the gut level and we have to use our heads," since it was Bausha and he is passion itself. So we fell back the twelfth and I will tell you, whatever armed resistance there was, was over by the afternoon of the twelfth, that was the end of it. That's what happened the day of the coup.

By the end of September, we had realized several things. The first was that the coup was in place and then strong arguments took place, because there were two different points of view on how to conceptualize the period politically. One that was put forth was that it was a time of revolutionary crisis and that, therefore, we had to forge ahead with Leninist logic, and the other suggested that it was a time for resistance. Well, there was an argument, and the thesis that it was a period of resistance won out.

We were intact until December, organically dismembered, but the leadership not broken up. The Communist Party's secretary general was a prisoner and a significant part of its leaders were in asylum in embassies; the Socialist Party was almost totally dismembered and in asylum, and Altamirano [Carlos Altamirano, secretary-general of the Socialist Party] disappeared; and the MIR with its central committee intact, the forty-eight members of the central committee were alive and we knew where they were, and the political commission was intact. The MIR, between September and October, made all the structure of its leadership secret, that is, we were able to make false identity documents for anyone who needed them, sometimes up to four or five different fake IDs, that were good enough to pass at the checkpoints in the street. We received tremendously important financial support at that time; we must have gotten between three and four million dollars from the ERP [the Ejército Revolucionario del Pueblo, the People's Revolutionary Army, one of the largest of several Argentine guerrilla groups that raised money by kidnappings for ransom and robbing banks] in Argentina. This means we had financial resources, we had our leadership, and we had IDs. And our arms stores were intact. In other words, in the balance of things, our situation wasn't so bad.

And so it was decided to put into effect a plan that was called the "law of three." It was a very old conspiracy scheme, from the French resistance, that consists of each member of the political commission taking responsibility for three members of the central committee. Each member of the central committee takes responsibility for three structures, and, thus, successively. This means that it is like a woven fabric, woven in such a way that if one is taken, two more may fall if that one talks, but not everyone. Of course, that is in theory. But, at any rate, by December we were organized in that way.

The Cubans had left a large number of arms at their embassy and the embassy was in the hands of the Swedes, and we got the arms out of the embassy right under the soldiers' noses, and we got them out using gas containers. These forty-five kilo gas containers from Gasco [the bottled gas distributing company], were cut in half and fixed to screw back together. Three gas trucks entered the embassy, the arms were put inside, the gas containers were closed, and it just looked like the Swedish embassy used a lot of gas.

So we had everything worked out. In December, it was decided to send Pollo Enríquez out of the country. So Edgardo [Pollo] Enríquez, Miguel's brother, goes to Argentina, meets with the Peronists, with the PRT [Partido Revolucionario de los Trabajadores, or Workers' Revolutionary Party, a small leftist group, originally Trotskyist, which had formed the ERP in 1970]; he goes to Cuba, he goes to Europe. I'll tell you that, at that time, the MIR—and this has been said to me by high-level members of the French Socialist Party—seemed to be the only functioning organization left in Chile. The motto at the time was "the MIR does not seek asylum." We began to receive, through the international work that Edgardo was doing, support from the French Socialists, the Italian Socialists— which means that we got more support from the Socialist parties than from the Communist parties because they were supporting the [Chilean]

Communist Party. Almost all the social democratic world, the German social democratic youth movement, gave us an extraordinary amount of aid. So we had a lot of support.

In December, that was our situation. . . .Well, we were a little bloodied, but in good shape. But then what happened? I remember that on December 22, I went to a contact and was told that Van Schouwen had been taken. And I couldn't believe it. We had fake IDs and a thousand things, and not one cell had been captured. And then, at the end of December, January perhaps, the following begins to happen. Fifteen of us came to a meeting; it was on a Monday. We met the next Monday and ten of us came. The next Monday we were five. There were fewer left, fewer and fewer of us.

A factor here that was important is the rivalry between the air force and the army, that is, between Leigh [General Gustavo Leigh, air force commander and junta member] and Pinochet, which is the same thing. The air force didn't turn over the information about the MIR to the army, which kept the coup from being efficient, because if they had gotten together they would have decimated us in those months. There wouldn't be anyone left. But since there was infighting, they kept the information to themselves.

We were more or less taking advantage of this and we tried to restructure ourselves, but we were already really hurting. It was really pathetic, and I tell you, the decision made at the time represented a total commitment, that is, that we would stay here.

I was taken in June of 1974.

## Patricio Jorquera

*Patricio Jorquera was two months short of his twenty-third birthday when the Allende government fell. Born into a middle-class Santiago family, he attended public schools, joined the MIR, and was a student of chemistry at the University of Chile in 1973. He completed a doctorate at the University of Paris while in exile, and today is a professor of chemistry at the University of Chile.*

*Jorquera's story illustrates the high risks involved in underground resistance activities as well as the continuation of interbranch rivalry within the military. Even though he was captured in January 1975, some seven months after the DINA's founding, he fell to the Air Force Intelligence Service (Servicio de Inteligencia de la Fuerza Aerea, SIFA) and was held*

*at the air force hospital. There, he came under the control of the SIFA
head, Colonel Edgardo Ceballos, a man with the air of a gentleman who
had his prisoners tortured but liked to take them out to lunch at elegant
restaurants. After partially recovering from his wound in prison, Jorquera
applied for the commutation of his sentence in exchange for expulsion from
the country. He left for Sweden in 1976 and proceeded to Paris, where he
resumed working for the MIR at its headquarters in exile.*

Let's say the process of detention, actually the security forces closing in,
started, I would say, around November of 1974. I was taken in January of
1975. By November of 1974 there were a series of tensions very close to
the structure of my work. A number of things began to happen . . . in fact,
around those same dates, there were searches of my house, of my parents'
house, there were searches at a couple of our locales . . . the structure, that
is, the situation, made it rather clear that the repression was closing in on
our units.

Those who were watching us most closely were the SIFA and the
searches and even the arrest of Coño Aguilar were carried out by the commander of the SIFA at that time, Edgardo Ceballos. And well, a series of
things more or less linked to my getting caught and then finally in January of 1975, I have a contact set up with a compañero who was working
with me. By this time, there was a series of complicated mechanisms set
up to see whether there were security problems or not. In this case, the
plan was the following: I was to see him at lunchtime between 12:30 and
1:30 in the place where he had lunch. I would go there to eat and he, from
where he was seated, would give a series of signals to tell me whether to
make or not make contact with him.

I get there — it is the canteen of a firehouse. I am at Plaza Brazil. I arrive there; I go up to the second floor where the canteen was; I sit down;
I see that this person is there and he gives the signals that there is no danger. This means also that he would in turn leave and that an hour later I
could go to his place, to where he worked.

Well, they were the normal signals and when I go downstairs and am
leaving the canteen of the fire company, someone is coming toward me.
This person seems to be coming in, I am leaving, and when both of us
reach the door, he hits me. At that moment . . . warning or not, I realize
that this could be the person who is going to arrest me. So the blow
knocks me to the ground and then two more guys come out. One of them
is a fireman who goes on the fire truck and the other works at the reception desk and answers the phone.

That is the first part of the story. So they restrain me. Then one of them asks, "What happened to the commander?" and the other who was there tells him that he had left a few minutes earlier, that they have to communicate the information. Then two of them go up to the second floor. I am left with only one of them. At that moment, I tried to escape, and so they fired because of the attempted escape. In this exchange, they fire at me. At this point, I didn't have a weapon, I didn't have anything and I take off. They shoot me and I fall wounded at the corner of Cathedral Street and Brazil. Two shots hit me and I fell in the street. The traffic stopped – Cathedral is a very narrow street with a lot of vehicle traffic and public transportation.

Well, a crowd gathered and the people who were there dragged me off toward the fire station. Of course, many people who were in the canteen at the fire station came out. It was a confused situation at first because I had been shot but nobody knew who had shot me. They had seemingly disappeared, but those guys were still there, waiting. People asked what's going on here and they call the first-aid station and for public assistance to come check since there is someone wounded here.

I was conscious through all of this, conscious but bleeding a lot. I knew that the situation was critical for me, but . . . and then the first to arrive is the ambulance from Emergency Post 3 that is six or seven blocks away, on Matucana. When the ambulance arrives, during all of this, people come over to me and ask me, "What do you want me to do?" and I gave them my parents' telephone number to let them know that I am wounded. And the ambulance comes and then these guys appear again – who until then hadn't taken any active role and say that the wounded person is under arrest, and they say that I can't be taken to the emergency post, that they are waiting for the FACh [Fuerza Aérea de Chile; Chilean air force] ambulance. The doctor in charge of the ambulance says no, if there is someone wounded, they have orders to take them and, well, there is an argument. And it ends up with these guys letting them take me to the Central Emergency Clinic, not to Emergency Post 3, and they are going to follow in their car and wait for the FACh ambulance. They put me on the stretcher. Besides my being wounded, a fireman – I don't know if at that moment he was arriving or leaving – was wounded in the hand, and his wife or girlfriend had hysterics, and they put all three of us in the ambulance. And then I lost consciousness. When they put me in the ambulance I exchanged a few words with the fireman. Anyway, he was very scared and they didn't respond to what I asked . . . I also gave them my phone number, a number of things. They didn't want to write anything down – then

I lost consciousness. I remember that later I recovered consciousness briefly when they were taking me out of the ambulance, and after that I don't remember anything.

What happened afterward, I know only from what I was told. My family says that about three o'clock they got a call – all of this happened between one and two o'clock in the afternoon – and it said that a . . . a person who had been shot had given this number and we don't know anything more. That is, some one of those who were present called there.

Afterward, the people from FACh who held me prisoner later told me some things that happened in between. They told me that, in fact, I did get to the emergency post, that there I received emergency treatment from the doctor on duty who works at FACh and was in the service, and for that reason took the case. And he continued to take care of me medically at the FACh. He treated me the first time – the treatment, I understand, was only to put me on an IV and give me some blood, and then they put me back on the stretcher in the ambulance of the FACh. From what they tell me, I was not conscious at this point. They say that later, on arriving at the military hospital, they have to stop because the doctor said to and they stop at the hospital and give me a second transfusion. They say, from what these people tell me, that by this point the drop in my pressure was very, very great, so that the doctor asked them to stop to see if he could do something there before getting to FACh. Again it was something temporary, and then they continue to FACh. I have some sense of having woken up, I don't know if it was in the process of arrival, and one of the guys who was there tells me that he was happy to see me – this was Commander Ceballos – and that, unfortunately, because he wasn't there at the time the shooting occurred, but that he knew about the whole situation. This is what I remember from the conversation, and then I lose consciousness.

## Gladys Díaz

*Gladys Díaz grew up in the Central Valley city of Rancagua, where she was born in 1941 to a medical doctor and a housewife. After studying in Catholic schools, she entered the University of Chile to study journalism. She joined the MIR in 1966, the year of its founding, and became a member of its central committee. During the UP government she was a well-known radio personality for Radio Agricultura, a prominent mouthpiece of anti-Allende forces. Díaz was also president of the powerful radio journal-*

*ists' union of the province of Santiago; because of a law prohibiting the
firing of union presidents, she kept her employment at Radio Agricultura,
but was not allowed on the premises in the months leading to the coup.
Simultaneously, she worked at a small MIR-run radio station and wrote
for the leftist magazine* Punto Final.

*Because of her high profile and MIR affiliation, Gladys Díaz was a
special target after the coup; she was named in a bando on September 12.
She went underground, caring for her five-year-old son and working in
the clandestine MIR propaganda apparatus until her arrest in early 1975.
She was taken to the notorious Villa Grimaldi, a mansion on the outskirts
of Santiago converted to a torture center.\* Gladys Díaz attributes her
survival to an international campaign to publicize her case—one of the
most broadly based and vocal of many that Chilean exiles and foreign
solidarity groups mounted to save individuals and discredit the military
regime. After three months of torture at Villa Grimaldi, she was sent to
the Tres Alamos prison camp in Santiago. When the government closed the
last prison camps in 1977, under international pressure, she was one of the
prisoners considered too dangerous to be released in Chile and was expelled
to begin exile that took her to several countries. She was not permitted to
return until the end of forced exile in September 1988. Today, she is director of the school of journalism at a private university in Santiago.*

*The Pinochet government bulldozed the installations at Villa Grimaldi
before the reestablishment of civilian government in 1990. On December
10, 1994, International Human Rights Day, Villa Grimaldi was dedicated
as a peace park in memory of the victims of the dictatorship's human-rights
abuses.*

I was detained February 20, 1975, with the compañero I lived with, Juan
Carlos Perelman, who was killed—he is one of the disappeared.[†] They
tortured us together the first days—they made me witness his torture and
he had to watch mine. They took us at our house, as the result of a statement made by someone they had already arrested. It wasn't our house; it

---

\* A compelling study of torture under the military regime is Katia Reszczynski,
Paz Rojas, and Patricia Barceló, *Tortura y resistencia en Chile: estudio-médico político*
(Santiago: Editorial Emisión, 1991). The physical plant and torture procedures at
Villa Grimaldi are described in *Comisión Nacional de Verdad y Reconciliación*, 2:485–87.
Sheila Cassidy describes her detention and torture in Villa Grimaldi in *Audacity to
Believe*, 172–214.

[†] Perelman's detention and death are described in *Comisión Nacional de Verdad y
Reconciliación*, 2:546.

was a house where another of the leaders had lived and he had let us use this house for a few days while we were looking for something else. In fact, they came to look for him, and they found us. So they came up with a plan, they had a street child knock on the door, and Juan Carlos who was very friendly — if I had looked, because there was a peephole, I wouldn't have opened the door, but they would have broken it down anyway. The fact that he opened the door has something to do with why I am still alive, because if not they would have — I am willing to bet — probably they would have killed us right then.

It was the DINA. They took us to Villa Grimaldi.

We were prepared to be arrested, yes, but no one is ever prepared for the torture, because torture is just an intellectual concept until you experience it. The worst part of torture is not the physical pain that you suffer — I think that the worst part of torture is to have to realize in such a brutal way that human beings are capable of doing something so aberrant to another person as torturing them. For me, I think that was the most terrible part. It shows that human beings are capable of lowering themselves on the human scale to such a level. In order for this to happen . . . It's impossible, because I could have the greatest enemy in the world, and I couldn't do it. And I couldn't be with anyone of any ideology — or even who shared my ideology — if that man were hurting another to make that person talk, even to the point of killing him or her. I really think that civilization has made great strides, but it has not progressed enough if human beings are still capable of doing this.

I was at Villa Grimaldi for three months. They say that I am the person who suffered the most prolonged torture who is still alive. Because there are others who were tortured for a longer time, but they are all dead.

One of the things that the torturer plays with is the element of surprise. So, because of this, there is no usual rhythm; rather, they come get you at three o'clock in the morning, when you are asleep, or at five o'clock in the morning, or another day they leave you alone all day, and you can see how this ends up creating a constant state of alert in your head, such that when you hear footsteps — I was in a place that was called "the tower" that was a water tower; before you get to the tower they built some steps and they made some very small cells there. I could never lie down, because the space — I don't know exactly — but it must have been a meter by sixty to eighty centimeters, something like that. But I always had to be in a sitting position with my knees up to my chest, always like that. So then, when they would come up the steps, I became able to tell when the footsteps were coming to get you or when the footsteps were bringing you food. The rhythm of the steps is different. Since we were blindfolded, the other senses become incredibly sharpened. The steps are coming up and you know that you are going to be tortured again. And they also change the torture, sometimes it's electricity; sometimes drugs—they drugged me many times with shots—what they call the "submarine," when they stick your head in sewer water and they leave you there until you almost drown, they take you out, they stick you in again; the "telephone" that breaks your—I have a broken eardrum, I can't hear on this side.

One time I was grabbed by a karate expert who smashed me totally—I still have a broken hip today.

Torture was a daily thing, because when there wasn't physical torture there was psychological torture. For example, the days that they didn't come for me, they put on tapes of voices of children to make me think that my son had been captured. This was what I feared most, that they would find my son. I think that of all the fears, this was the greatest one.

The defense mechanisms that a person uses in certain extreme situations are infinite, the ways that one finds to defend oneself are unlimited. I sometimes dreamed about beautiful things—that gave me some consolation. I remember two wonderful dreams. I remember dreaming that I was on a beach with a warm sun, of knowing that there were many children around me who were playing and laughing. And that I went into the water and that I was feeling second by second the satisfaction of the cold water, of the sun. In fact, I have never again enjoyed the sea as I did in that dream, and the sensation lasted for several days, the sensorial effect of all that on my body. I also remember having eaten a piece of coffee cake. I remember having awakened to the sound of the warbling of a linnet, of a little bird that was outside, and how I was able to keep the sound of the bird's singing in my ears for days, enjoying it. The human being will latch onto anything.

In Villa Grimaldi, there was a paradox—beside the tower there was a path along which, out of necessity, I had to walk to get to the bathroom or each time that they took me to be tortured, and that path was surrounded by a giant rose garden. When I walked along there, there was a smell, a fragrance, and I couldn't see the roses but I could imagine them. Well, I used this moment of deep satisfaction as a source of strength. When I returned for the first time to Villa Grimaldi after I came back to Chile, and I came in with a human-rights commission from the Chamber of Deputies—you know that they leveled Villa Grimaldi, there's nothing left—but I found the place where the tower was, and I walked around trying to find the path we used. And even though they had leveled everything, there were two roses that had grown back out of the earth, and I realized how important those roses had been in my being able to survive.

Sometimes I heard other people being taken out and being tortured.

They always asked me the same things. They centered the interrogation around two things in my case: the first was to try to get information, and the second was to try to diminish the strength of my convictions, to try to show me that I was wrong, that the way to resolve the country's problems was their way. They played with me a good deal in this sense, they talked hours and hours — they would torture me all morning and then talk to me about politics. I think the Chilean soldier — I say the Chilean soldier because, I don't know, maybe a soldier anywhere in the world, but I got to know the Chilean soldier under these conditions — is so *machista* that he almost couldn't understand how a woman could be capable of thinking for herself, being strong, and even less, that a woman might look down on them. They couldn't stand that.

I think that this could be a key difference between how they treated me compared to how they treated men. I think that they also treated the men very badly, but what happened was that with me their traditional concepts broke down on them. Also because my compañeras who were arrested played a role that was very good too, which was to pretend that "I don't know anything because I am only so-and-so's woman" — beside that not being true, I couldn't do this because they wouldn't believe it, because I was a public figure. What happened is that other women did this and sometimes convinced them that it was true, so this meant that they didn't torture them as much and that they would get out sooner. For others it didn't happen that way — they killed them anyway — but I can tell you that we intended to do that, we were prepared to do that, to pretend, saying "I am just so-and-so's woman." But I was a leader, and they knew it. If I had said that, it would have been absurd.

I knew who the torturers were. All of them. I couldn't see them, but I knew who they were. I have seen them again in the courts; at least, I have seen Miguel Krasnoff Marchenko, who was the one who directed my torture — I saw him last year. Also "El Troglo" ["The Troglodyte"], Basclay Zapata. They never took off my blindfold.

One of the things that most impacted me about Villa Grimaldi was that I witnessed two murders. One I saw and the other I heard. One was that of a very young man, about twenty-two years old, a technician who was 1.90 meters tall, very strong, who they killed by hitting him with chains, and they took three of us who were in the tower — the other two are dead now — to watch his slow death. I have told this many times; I even told it on a program here on national television. It is really awful to watch how they slowly kill a person who is so strong physically that it seems like he will never die and you, in the best spirit of love, want him to die quickly. He is a young man with a Yugoslavian last name. The other is Isidro Arias, who is a cello player in the symphony orchestra of this country. They catch him, they arrest him, they throw him in Villa Grimaldi; I talk to him for about an hour and a half; they take him out and they shoot him outside the tower. I hear the shot and the next day I go to the bathroom, and in the bathroom there was a piece of newspaper where it said that he had committed suicide at the time of his arrest. I think that these were two things that I experienced that had a great impact on me. There are millions of stories.

I only talked about all this the first few days after I got out. Afterward, I didn't want to talk about it any more. First of all because mine is not a unique case, my countrymen in general experienced torture. This is a tortured country — so then, the people who believe that they didn't have anything to do with it are also tortured, because they are tortured in their values. I think that finally, today, when I see everything that is happening to my country, I think that we who were tortured were actually somewhat privileged — think about what I am telling you — we have clear consciences because we fought. This country feels a good deal of shame for not having fought. This country still has fear in its soul. And we were not afraid, neither then or now — we have our self-respect intact. Today I am not a victim; others are the victims.

## María Castro

*A native of Parral, an agricultural center 350 kilometers south of Santiago, María Castro was born, in 1947, into a large family of what she calls the "provincial petite bourgeoisie." Her father was a wholesale dealer in fruits and vegetables and a man of conservative views, while her mother, a teacher of French and philosophy in the public high school, became a Christian Democrat. Castro studied in Catholic schools in Parral and the larger city of Chillán, where she participated in consciousness-raising church youth organizations. After a year in Chicago as an exchange student, she entered the University of Chile and joined the MIR. Finishing her journalism degree in 1969, she worked on left-wing publications and, at the time of the coup, was a commentator at government-owned Televisión Nacional.*

*María Castro likens her fourteen years of underground resistance to an
"internal exile." The clandestine birth of her daughter, the assassination of
her compañero, the deprivations of everyday life, and the frequent changes
in residence and identity—sometimes at a moment's notice—did not break
her will. She survived the uncounted deaths of fellow resistance members
and experienced the life of the pobladores, whose situation went from bad to
terrible during the dictatorship. She finally went into exile in Argentina in
1987, during the heightened repression following the failed 1986 assassination attempt against Pinochet. Today, Castro is a journalist in Santiago.*

The first months after the coup were very difficult. I was pregnant, my
compañero and I had talked a good deal about whether or not to have a
child, because—actually because of the awareness of an impending coup,
and afterward, we are going to be involved in the struggle, and then what
are we going to do, and that was a very great worry. We also wanted to
have children. So I was very afraid that the coup would catch me with a
baby. So there were interminable arguments with my compañero, but the
argument that convinced me was when we talked about Vietnam and
he said to me that the Vietnamese continued to have children and life
goes on, I don't know what else, "oh, but, really, I, well . . . " Then I
purposely got pregnant and I was three months along when the coup
took place, and well, then going underground, fleeing—everything under
those conditions—also trying not to feel bad so that it wouldn't affect my
pregnancy—and there were the usual offers of asylum.

The majority of people advised us to seek asylum, to leave, and my
compañero had had heart surgery, so that he had to take care of himself.
He also had orders not to get excited, that is, there were medical instructions in this sense, so that people we didn't even know told both of us:
"but you two have to seek asylum, you have to leave." And we thought it
was really crazy for them to tell us that: "But, why should I go—it is my
country and, besides, I always knew that this was coming and I know that
here there are things that need to be done so that this will end." So we
never doubted—we had no doubt that the right thing to do was to stay
and it seemed to us very sad that the majority of the leaders of the Chilean
left did leave, because we saw clearly that the masses would have to pay the
whole cost of the repression.

With respect to the MIR, well, there were plans in effect to stay in
touch and these plans worked. We never lost contact. In general, all of the
people, also all of the journalists—we stayed in contact with each other.
We tried to organize communication networks as quickly as we could to

begin to send news out of the country about the people who were being taken prisoner, the tortures. Well, we began to work writing bulletins, sending things out of the country, all kinds of experiences with this type of journalism, but now in different conditions. We had to put things on tiny pieces of paper and use microfilm, in different situations. And besides, the repression began, my compañero was publicly named in the bandos. A short time after the coup, they detained a group of compañeros from National Television and, as a result of this process, I was involved too, so then, I was also summoned publicly.

So this forced us to go into total hiding, we couldn't live anywhere where anyone would know us. We had to establish a different kind of contact with our family, we could no longer have direct contact. We had to live totally different lives, go into what I call "internal exile." It meant a radical change in our lives. The places you frequented, you couldn't go there any longer, your family, of course not—it is a total transplant, you had to act in a totally different way than that to which you were accustomed. That was the first thing we lost.

Friendship has always been something tremendously valuable to us. We had to learn to do without friendship in the sense that we could no longer see our friends. We couldn't see any of our politically active friends, because we didn't even know what had happened to them and the others, many times, were so afraid—since they knew that our names had been published—that they didn't want to see us either, so that you have a very circumscribed lifestyle, limited to yourself, very limited as far as human contact. In other words, you have to make new friends. But since it was a period in which everyone was so afraid that no one dared talk about anything—at least at the beginning, later, it changed—once we got used to the dictatorship, we found the parameters in which we could survive.

Our family kept looking for ways to get things to us. My compañero's father had a butcher shop, and he managed to get a package of meat to us every week, especially once my daughter was born. A leftist doctor helped us and I was able to enter a clinic under another name. There, I had my daughter and then I returned to the boarding house where we were living. Some very nice things happened. Some former co-workers sent me packages with diapers, with clothes—everyone knew that we no longer had enough to live on. So I began to learn what solidarity was through what it meant to have a baby in those conditions. The people with least means were those who were most willing to help, those who showed most solidarity. A colleague who had worked at the station asked me if I wanted to go to the country to have the baby, to his parents' house—things like that, those things that comforted you and made you think that you were doing the right thing.

My compañero was a part of the leadership of the MIR and, as such, he was involved in tasks related to the diffusion of news to foreign countries, with the publication of the newspaper *El Rebelde* [*The Rebel*] which was the voice of the MIR, and communication with different groups of MIR activists. At that time, *El Mercurio* [Santiago's pro-military main daily newspaper] published the news that they had found another journalist who was called Marota. Marota had also been part of the leadership, but, at that time, there had been serious problems with his behavior—he seemed to have lost the confidence of the organization—and, for this reason, he had been punished. So Marota was caught, Marota turned over his contact, that contact was tortured and revealed where Francisco was, and then they killed him. They got there and set him up like a rat in a hole; they surrounded the place. He was out when they got there, and when he got home and was putting the keys in the lock, they fired on him—they killed him in cold blood.

Look, when my compañero died, when they killed him, we didn't have anywhere else to go, either. So another compañero from the movement, whom they also killed later, helped us. He took us to his house in the *comuna* [municipality] of Pudahuel [a working-class neighborhood], and we lived there and got to know a way of life that I had never known before. He went to get meat at the slaughterhouse in the morning and sold it and lived on that. He would get a big package of stew meat, the cheapest meat in Chile in that period, then he would sell it in the neighborhood, on credit. Those were times of extreme poverty. When he had something left over, he would come home with something for us, and if not, then he didn't bring anything. But in that kind of place the solidarity was tremendous, that is, the people didn't have anything to give, but they make something out of this nothing, and suddenly a cup of tea appears or some soup or broth. In other words, there was a very pronounced spirit of brotherhood.

I, at that time, tried to appeal to colleagues in the media, which was the social group that I came from, with very poor results. They were horrified, shocked, scared. Of course, there were always one or two exceptions, but in general, let's say, they weren't in a situation to show solidarity. On the other hand, in those other sectors which had nothing to lose, one saw different values, another way of life, that is, they shared the very little that they had. What I experienced in Santiago, I also experienced later when I was in the southern zone—the willingness to help was exactly the same. If they learned that you were in the resistance, they were ready to help, to cooperate however they could. It is a Chile that bears no relation to the one that we have today.

By 1977, there was already new MIR leadership, because the majority of the previous leadership had been caught, either taken prisoner or killed. Van Schouwen fell early, then Miguel, then El Coño; well, many compañeros fell. One loss affected the ability to lead, but it didn't make any difference as to whether the different activities kept going. I think that this was the year that they began the policy of extermination, of executing people, especially the MIRistas, of killing them, of catching them and killing them. That was a policy decision. In many cases, there were fake "confrontations." The MIR was one of the groups that had the greatest number of casualties during the dictatorship, that is, the number of compañeros killed around us—not just my compañero, the father of my daughter, but also many, many friends, compañeros, compañeras, who were on the same side you were and the next day were dead. I survived; why? I don't know why.

The year 1978 I ended up living very close to the comuna of La Granja, and that was where one of the first hunger strikes took place. It was the wives of those detained or disappeared in the churches of the southern zone, and my natural inclination, heart-felt, was to join them, but I couldn't, because my work was of a different nature. It was not in the struggle for human rights but rather in the larger struggle, that of the resistance—more global, let's say—in which we thought that the role of human rights was very important, but that it was one aspect of a whole to be attained. I remember having gone to the parish then and having talked to the women, having embraced them, having encouraged them, but, of course, in total anonymity; that is, I couldn't say to them: "Look, I am suffering the same thing you are—I also lost my compañero."

In this period, the Allana Commission [a special United Nations commission to investigate human rights in Chile, which arrived in July 1978] came to Chile, and through a priest in solidarity I was able to denounce the execution of my compañero, since by then I knew how it had happened. I talked to the Allana Commission for the report that they were preparing for the United Nations and I told them how it had happened and asked the United Nations to take an interest and support measures that would prevent crimes from continuing to occur in this country.

Already by the year 1982, there was some hope. In 1977 only a few held out hope, but when the surge came in the 1980s, in the years of the large mobilizations—in 1981, in 1982, the years of the demonstrations—already the acceptance of the resistance was much more generalized. You had even more reason to believe then, let's say, that things were pointing in another direction, that it was worth it to make all the effort necessary. But at that time — those first years, that is — the solidarity and the desire to struggle came from the poorest sectors of the people who didn't have work, from the unemployed, from the pobladores. Those were the sectors in which we kept up the struggle. Religious groups were also very important. I always found a warm reception in the Christian communities, which, without asking any questions, many times without sharing your belief in what you were doing, nevertheless, they were part of the solidarity effort.

What kept us going during those years was a very deep conviction that dictatorship was an evil too great for our people and that we had to struggle and that we had to resist, that each one had his or her work to do, and that — we thought — this post could not be deserted. It didn't seem to me to be moral, it didn't seem to me to be right, for me to take refuge in a life elsewhere that would resolve my personal problem of survival, while that of all the people who had believed in us — in our political project, in what we wrote as journalists, in what I myself said as a Christian — should be betrayed with only a "save yourselves." That is, it seemed to us that this didn't work and that you accepted your individual risks as part of this way of seeing things. Besides, we had an appreciation for the enemy that was based in what was happening in other parts of the world; that is, there was the example of Vietnam, there was the struggle of other peoples.

I didn't have a regular paid job, obviously I couldn't work as a journalist. I had some help from the resistance movement to carry out the tasks that I had. Once you knew who you were to communicate with that day, then, based on that, you had to come up with a whole plan of how you were going to see that person, without jeopardizing their safety or your own and taking certain precautions so that you would not get caught like a rat in a trap. We used the telephone to see if the other person was all right before going to see them, that kind of thing.

It was easier because I was a woman, because a women can work informally out of her home and hold sporadic jobs. I also did translations while I was underground; I didn't say that I was a journalist, but I also lived from that. I also gave English classes, private lessons; that is, I looked for different ways to make ends meet. Of course, I was also a housewife, so I had my domestic activity — I had to go shopping and do domestic tasks — and in between, I did the other things that I had to do.

My daughter was always with me, which was a joy for me. It was something that I had to decide at a given moment, because some compañeros suggested that I could probably get her out and that she could be with other compañeros in Cuba. I thought about it for a while: "Of course, it would be the safest for her." But later, I talked with other people about how it would be better for us to be together anyway, because even though there she would have material security, the presence of other compañeros would not be the same as being with her mother. So I decided that it was better for her to be with me.

Children have a great ability to adapt. What I, of course, couldn't know at that time, are the psychological consequences of this later. She, let's say, adapted well, was very cooperative, and, of course, things were explained to her on a child's level; for example: "these are the good guys, these are the bad guys," and "if you repeat what I am telling you outside this house, then we will have problems, so that you have to be sure not to say anything." And well, she never made a mistake, she behaved well beyond what could be expected at her age. So clearly, there are stages in life that she skipped, and that has a psychological toll later that we could not have imagined or known about before; that is, she had to behave like an adult. For example, several times we had to leave home urgently, leave the house and everything in it in order to save our lives—this because we had gotten word that we had been discovered and that they were going to mount an operation. So the only way to avoid the blow was to flee, and then she went with me and began to live a new life in new conditions. Well, the pressure builds up, and well, like I told you, at this time it was the most natural thing in the world for me and she didn't protest either. When we left Chile, she was about fourteen years old.

*FIVE*

# The Diaspora

## *Exile on Four Continents*

One of the hallmarks of the Chilean exile experience is the worldwide dissemination of its protagonists. The geography of Chilean exile was such that no single continent, country, or area within a country could be identified as the primary exile destination — in contrast with the case of Cubans and Miami. It is commonly estimated that Chileans settled in a minimum of 110 countries and possibly in as many as 140.[*] Exiled Socialist leader Clodomiro Almeyda claimed that Chileans had taken residence in Kenya, Bangladesh, the Cape Verde Islands, and even Greenland.[†] As a result of the diaspora, noted another exile, "There is no important city in the world where you will not find a Chilean, nor a city that is not familiar with empanadas [meat pies] and peñas [informal cafés with folk and protest music]."[‡]

---

[*] Interview, Mario Toro, Oficina Nacional de Retorno (ONR), Nov. 2, 1993. As with the number of political exiles, the exact number of host countries is impossible to establish. By the end of 1992, the ONR reported having processed nearly 8,700 heads of family from 63 host countries, including Burundi, Cyprus, Indonesia, Kuwait, and Iceland (*Memoria Anual 1992*, appendix, table 19). Rodríguez Villouta, *Ya nunca me verás como me vieras*, 14, cites 119 host countries, but her book's publication preceded the proliferation of countries following the breakup of the Soviet Union and Yugoslavia.

[†] Clodomiro Almeyda, *Reencuentro con mi vida* (Santiago: Ediciones del Ornitorrinco, 1987), 274.

[‡] Juan Pablo Letelier, quoted in Rodríguez Villouta, *Ya nunca me verás como me vieras*, 106.

One of the reasons for the global dispersal of Chilean exiles was that most Latin American countries proved to be unwilling or unsuitable hosts. The exiles' desire to remain near home was evident in the large-scale early exodus to Argentina and Peru; but, as noted earlier, neither of these countries worked out as a long-term refuge for many. Owing to their low or moderate levels of economic development, most countries in the hemisphere offered little prospect of remunerative work, except to small numbers of professionals who, given the excellent reputation of Chilean higher education and professional training, found employment in universities, private companies, and even bureaucracies. A few Latin American countries, notably Brazil, Venezuela, and Mexico, were experiencing economic booms during the middle and late 1970s and thus were able to accommodate larger numbers of professional and academic exiles. Only in Argentina were working-class exiles able to find employment on a large scale, and there they faced difficult political conditions.

Exacerbating the economic obstacles to settling in Latin America was the decidedly reactionary political climate that had begun to envelop the region in the 1960s, culminating with the installation of the Argentine military dictatorship in 1976. The generalized rightward political swing was in large measure a reaction by the elites, sectors of the middle classes, and the military establishments against the fallout of the Cuban Revolution in Latin America. Encouraged by developments in Cuba and the call of Fidel Castro for revolution, youth, workers, the urban poor, and even peasants in many countries had mobilized for change. The resulting agitation, the leftward movement of the electorate, and outbreaks of guerrilla war fostered destabilization of civilian governments, which increasingly were replaced by military regimes dedicated to eliminating the perceived threat of revolution. None was more influential in fostering the climate of reaction than the government of General Augusto Pinochet in Chile. Thus with the eclipse of elected governments in Latin America, by 1976 only Colombia, Venezuela, Costa Rica, and Mexico offered any semblance of democracy while most other countries were ruled by right-wing militaries. These regimes actively discouraged Chileans from settling or, if they tolerated exiles, closely watched them and restricted their political activities.

The United States government did not extend a warm welcome to Chilean exiles driven out by a regime it had helped to establish and which it initially supported enthusiastically. The Cold War policy of denying entry to Communists, of course, meant that for a substantial number of the displaced, the United States was not an option. Moreover, despite the economic opportunities available there, its complicity in the destruction of the Allende government and support of the dictatorship made the United States an undesirable destination for many exiles. Nonetheless, perhaps encouraged by the small but persistent anti-Pinochet lobby whose most visible spokesperson was Senator Ted Kennedy, and welcomed particularly in universities as both faculty and students, several thousand Chileans eventually settled in the United States.

Although most countries did not appear to discriminate on the basis of one's party affiliation, there were some natural political affinities that influenced exiles' destinations. The USSR and its Eastern European allies felt a special obligation toward members of the Communist Party, as did the government of Cuba. The same countries tended to welcome Socialists and MIRistas. Berlin, then capital of East Germany, became the headquarters of both the reconstituted Socialist Party and the Unidad Popular in exile, while the Communist Party settled in Moscow and the MIR in Paris and Havana. The late 1970s and early 1980s witnessed the emergence of several new socialist or social democratic regimes, such as those in Nicaragua, Angola, and Mozambique, which welcomed or sought out Chilean Marxists as advisors and technicians. While relatively few in number, Christian Democratic exiles had an affinity for countries where their coreligionists were powerful, such as Italy, West Germany, and Venezuela. The Socialist International, centered in Western Europe, took a special interest in its affiliate, the Radical Party.

Several other factors contributed to the global dissemination of Chilean exiles. Sweden, Canada, and Australia in the 1970s encouraged immigration to augment their labor force, and Sweden and Canada in particular welcomed large exile contingents. Ancestry sometimes influenced exiles' preferences, as did Chileans' perceptions of countries in positive or negative terms. The existence in Santiago of several United Nations agencies as well as other international organizations provided a job-placement network for some of their Chilean employees who had to leave.

While all the foregoing considerations shaped the geography of exile, chance was also a prime determinant, particularly for those forced to leave hurriedly. The thousands who fled to embassies, or arrived in neighboring countries without documentation, or were forced underground by the ever-widening net of repression, placed their futures in the hands of the international agencies whose mission was to match individuals and families with countries willing to accept them. Given the massive numbers of exiles, some of the host countries turned out to be exotic lands about which most Chileans knew little or nothing prior to their departure into exile.

Despite enormous differences among exiles' host countries, the testimonies in this and the following chapter reveal that the culture and the effects of exile were fundamentally similar whether one was in Costa Rica or Sweden, Mozambique or Canada, the USSR or the United States.


## Eduardo Saavedra

*At the time of the coup Eduardo Saavedra was a forty-six-year-old professor of journalism at the University of Concepción and a longtime member of the Socialist Party. He had been born in the northern city of Iquique, the historic center of Chile's nitrate-producing zone and cradle of Chile's labor movement and political left. His father was a railroad worker, and both sides of his family had deep roots in the nitrate working class. Saavedra attended public schools in Iquique and Santiago, working to pay his way, and finished his university education as an adult at the University of Concepción.*

*Home of the MIR, the University of Concepción was a special target for repression. In addition to experiencing harassment and threats, Saavedra was fired and the entire school of journalism was closed. He soon found himself blacklisted: denied employment by government and private firms. Forced to emigrate, he left in late 1974 for Brazil, a country ruled by a repressive military dictatorship since 1964 but experiencing an economic boom referred to as the "Brazilian miracle." Saavedra managed well*

*enough in a variety of jobs to send for his family. He spent a short time in*
*Algeria before returning to Chile in 1988.*

Well, I couldn't stay in the country any longer, because I couldn't work. I
went to Brazil because I had a compañero, a friend who had been the director at the School of Civil Construction, who told me that it was an industrial country, that it was a country with possibilities, that it was a
country that would allow us to make the jump later to another country.
Besides, the ticket was cheaper and it was worth a try, and that's how I
came to sell my vehicle, and with that money we went to Brazil. I went by
myself and I lived for two years alone in Brazil, and then my family came
little by little to be with me. I left the normal way, because I felt—I am not
going to say corralled—but I thought that sooner or later I was going to
have problems here.

Although Brazil also had a military dictatorship, they were pretty civi-
lized; they didn't come after me, but they never granted me residency in
the almost fourteen years that I was there, and this meant that I always
worked in bad conditions, for a salary that was too low for the kind of
work that I was doing. But they were very honest with me about it, that is,
that it was for political reasons, and they never gave me any other reason
than that.

It wasn't easy to find work being a Chilean. Brazil was still enjoying the
last of its economic "boom" and industrial development. So, then, for one
hundred dollars you bought a work permit and with this you were able to
work anywhere. There is a lot of corruption in Brazil, so much so that
even the government officials of the Labor Ministry sold the booklets,
and since the Chileans knew almost all the tricks, they took me to the
officials and they gave me the work permit, and with that I could work
every year without any problems.

For professional curiosity, I had taken a course in risk prevention at the
Technical University in Concepción, because I wanted to know more
about the work I was doing and that was very important in Brazil. For a
time, I wrote articles on risk prevention for some specialized magazines
. . . I became known from those articles, and because of that a multina-
tional corporation, NCA, called me to go work in a Brazilian equipment
industry, and I worked there for many years—it was a national industry in
the sense that it operated throughout the entire country, so they put me
in the department of industrial marketing. Then I began to do what they

called training in the use of safety equipment. So then, I became a specialist in respiratory and auditory equipment and measuring equipment and things like that—a field in which I wasn't totally unprepared—so I liked this area a good deal. I specialized in it, and after I left this company I went to work at another one doing the same thing.

I would say that there some seven to ten thousand Chileans in São Paulo. There were a lot of us. In all of Brazil, we must have numbered between eighteen and twenty-five thousand. It wasn't difficult to get work in Brazil in that period, and almost all of the Chileans were professionals, and the majority were students who hadn't finished their studies, they had two or three years toward a major in civil engineering or architecture. So that they were professionals, but hadn't finished their degrees yet, students from industrial schools, anyway. Besides, they were very well regarded professionally. I don't know of anyone that had problems in terms of their ability or things like that. Why didn't they reach a higher level— they didn't because the standard of living, at that time in Brazil, was reasonable. Life wasn't real expensive; as a result, food was cheap, so that it was perfectly possible to live. The *cruzeiro* (the Brazilian currency) at that time was worth more than the Chilean *peso*.

It was easy to integrate with the Brazilians, but there was a cultural problem on our side. We had an attitude of cultural superiority toward them. They were knowledgeable about soccer, the samba, but the truth is that our attitude was pretty disagreeable. Look, one of the good things that you should know is that exile allows you to see your nationality and to know yourself a little better. I realized that we are a pretty rotten group as a nation, we have a lot of myths about ourselves, prejudices, and when you discover that in Europe they call you *"sudaca"* [a derogatory name for South Americans], that puts you in your place. But in Brazil we were Chileans, the most cultured, the most able, the best prepared, the greatest thing since sliced bread, and we didn't realize that we were in a country, a country that was full of traditions of different cultures, with this marvelous symbiosis of the African culture, with the Portuguese, the Dutch. We didn't see any of that. Why not? Because we were superior, and unfortunately we tried to demonstrate that in many situations.

The Chileans were very active politically, but there were barriers to this. There was a lot of partisanship in Brazil; there were groups from the Socialist Party, the Communist Party, the MIR, . . . so that the same arguments that had caused problems in Chile were continued in Brazil. Also, the Brazilian military has a very strong repressive apparatus, and they didn't allow us to have any kind of street demonstrations. All of our meetings and events had to be in enclosed spaces, many times in churches. They had us pretty well controlled, they even controlled our correspondence. In terms of a movement, our compañeros in Porto Alegre, in the southern part of the country, were more active, much more effective, because they formed a resistance group that involved practically the whole Southern Cone—it was made up of Uruguayans, Argentines, and Chileans.

## Silvia Quiroga

*Silvia Quiroga was nearly thirty years of age when the military overthrew the UP government. Born into an upper middle-class family in the capital, she was the daughter of artists: her father was a music critic, her mother a painter and engraver. She attended both private and public schools and studied psychology at the University of Chile. In 1973 she was a professor of psychology in the same university and a member of the Communist Party.*

*Quiroga lost her job immediately after the coup, as did her husband, a geographer at the University of Chile. In 1974 they left legally, with their two children, for Argentina, where they expected to stay a few months until conditions improved at home. They were in Argentina when the 1976 coup occurred, and their next two years under the extremely repressive government were difficult. When the opportunity came to work in Mozambique, they gladly took it. Their six years of living in an exotic land and working to build a new, progressive society on the ruins of the colony that Portugal had given up only in 1975 were rewarding, and Silvia Quiroga still recalls her days there as among the happiest of her life. Today, she combines a counseling practice with teaching in a private university.*

When we went to Mozambique in 1978; except for "Tarzan" and "Daktari," which were TV series, we didn't know anything about Africa. So, I asked myself, will there be bookstores, will there be movie theaters, will there be cement paved streets? We knew that there was a university, but what would it be like? Would the streets be paved, would there be elevators? We got to South Africa and that was a shock because we were already on the African continent and it was the South Africa of that time with apartheid. And it made a strong impression on us to see the buses with signs saying "white" and "non-white," entrances for some and entrances for others and to realize that in the airport everyone who was working was black and those they were waiting on were white, and the attitude of the blacks themselves, always looking down — all of these things caught our attention. So arriving at the airport of Maputo and finding yourself with black people, all black to begin with, but people who look you in the eye and who talk to you and who laugh, all happy, everybody always happy — it was really special. And all of them knew about Pinochet — anyone you told, "I come from Chile," "Ah, Allende, Pinochet," they said to you. The majority of people of the city seemed to have a pretty deep knowledge. Well, and there were paved streets, and there were traffic lights and there were airports with restrooms and all these things.

We came to number some six hundred Chileans in Mozambique. When they hired people, after the Portuguese left, they brought people from all over Latin America, from Europe, many from Holland, Danes, North Americans, Belgians, Swiss, Germans — from both Germanys at that time — and there were a large number of volunteers from the socialist countries of Europe and from Cuba. See what a hodgepodge it was, it was great, there was a richness of sharing of customs. Among the Latin Americans, we were very close to the Argentines, to the Brazilians, and to the Uruguayans; we did things together. We also had things in common with the Cubans, with the Swedish, and of the socialist countries, with the Bulgarians, so then we had social activities. In general, there were thousands of foreigners, they arrived and left and arrived and left, and there was a lot of movement.

Now we had problems with the food, especially the first four years, because there was a situation of shortage even worse than what we had here. Because of the kind of agreement that we had, we didn't have access to dollars or hard currency. At the beginning, then, we ate the same thing as the people of Mozambique, rice with fish every day, a kind of a sardinelike fish, with many bones and very little meat. We had a cooperative that was like our JAP [Juntas de Abastecimiento y Precios, or Supply and Price Committees that functioned during Allende's last year to distribute basic foods and necessities at official prices], where they would give you half a dozen eggs for fifteen days for the entire family and everything rationed, with cards and with lines. Well, later our working conditions changed and we had access to a percentage of our salary in hard currency, in dollars, so then we had the right to buy in the Interfranca stores, for the diplomats and all the people who could pay in dollars, and that resolved the problem.

We were fascinated, we didn't want anything more, it was absolutely paradise for us. It didn't matter that we ate fish everyday, we were really

happy. Besides, the country was exciting because of the climate, the natural beauty that it had; it was almost impossible to get depressed there.
You went walking down the street and the flowers said hello to you; we
had the sea next door—really it is very beautiful, it is a really pretty city.
Of course, there were Chileans that didn't stay because they couldn't
adapt. Being there, you were either fascinated and happy or simply, you
were dying.

I was happy because, first, I was doing something. I was contributing to
building a society which at that moment seemed to me to be the most legitimate, that shared the same values I had. I was happy because I was
working at something that I really liked a lot and that made a lot of sense,
and which was a permanent challenge to my creativity, because one came
to work there and there was nothing preestablished, nothing, absolutely
nothing preestablished. I got to work at the Ministry of Health, always in
two areas: in the training of personnel and in training in the area of psychology for the areas of medicine, obstetrics, nursing, preschool education, and social work. I had to teach psychology, but I also had to create
the programs, and I also had to look at what their tasks were and to define,
starting with the tasks, what objectives we had to formulate, write the
texts—because there weren't any texts or because in the library we had
there was nothing about psychology. There were three or four psycholo-
gists in all of Mozambique, there were no more than that.

So I worked closely with the OMM, the organization of the Mozambican women, and that program was developed through the mass communication media—through the newspapers, radio, and TV. Through the
kindergartens—the few there were—I also worked with the parents and
through the organization of Mozambican women in the community as
such. So this was very nice because they chose the topics, we discussed
them; for example, is it good or not to hit children? So we talked about the
topic with them and then they went to their communities on a Saturday
afternoon and they transformed it into dance, into music, in poetry, or in
theater, using whatever cultural element was indigenous to them in their
language—puppets, for example. They are very gifted for dance, music,
and dramatization. It is part of their culture. Now I have no idea what it is
they said, because they said it in their language. So this was a very beautiful task and, while it lasted, was a very passionate effort.

For the children, school was very interesting. The government of
Samora Machel [1975–1986] gave great priority to education. So in order
to provide education to the greatest number of children, they had to train
teachers very quickly, and for that reason the teachers had an education

that was only a little better than that of the students. There was only one school that wasn't a Mozambican state school, which was the international school where the children of the diplomats could go and the children of the foreign workers, if they wished. We put our two children there, but my younger son, Antonio, couldn't get used to it. He was in kindergarten, and he didn't like the school because it was in English and he didn't understand anything and he didn't want to understand. So we changed him to a school that was near the house, which was called "A Luta Continua" ["The Struggle Continues"], and Antonio was happy there. Then he went very early, because he had to get there very early to get a seat, because there were sixty students and anyone who arrived late didn't get a seat and had to sit on the floor. He always did very well, he didn't have any problems. They liked him, he had many Mozambican friends.

Among the Chileans it was intense, very, very intense. Well, the Chileans were organized among themselves, there were several political parties, but we had a common organization that worked as long as we changed the names as they changed in Chile, like the MIDA [Movimiento de Izquierda Democrática Allendista, or Movement of the Allendista Democratic Left, was an electoral coalition dominated by the Communist Party in the 1993 elections; the speaker refers to this as an example of shifting coalitions and changing names among Chilean opposition groups in the 1980s]; it has several names, but we were characterized by harmony and working as a team — this was one of the few countries where this happened, and it is something that we valued a lot. Also, we had a school for the children. Every Saturday there was a Chilean school where we ourselves gave classes in Spanish and about the history and geography of Chile, and we had a choir and a folkloric dance group . . . well, one way and another, we were trying to transmit our culture to them.

We organized for our festivals — what can I tell you — for the patriotic festivals, to make empanadas. We bought them or we made them, because sometimes it was possible to get things — meat — and each of us made fifty empanadas at home and afterward we put them together. We organized a peña there, which was a very nice experience, and they appreciated it a lot too. We called it the *Peña Payota*. The *payotas* are those little houses, the straw houses that they have. So there were some houses that were abandoned there near the sea, in Maputo itself, in the city, and we fixed them up as a cultural center. On Saturdays, we held cultural activities there and we sold empanadas, and if we could we sold wine too and if not, then juice or whatever there was. Well, then we had a folkloric group, a nonfolkloric group, a singing group, like Inti Illimani [one of the two best-known exile musical groups], or that kind of a group that was called Araucaria [name refers to the Araucanos, the original indigenous inhabitants of Chile, or to the native Chilean tree; one of the major journals of Chileans in exile was also called *Araucaria*]. I was a member of Araucaria. Araucaria organized the peñas and hired or, rather, invited Mozambican groups to perform there and also groups from other countries, those who were there. So, then, it was a very nice experience of cultural exchange. And well, the Mozambicans have a very rich culture in the sense that you are never going to manage to know all their richness. So then they always participated with dance, with orchestras, with groups, and many people went.

We became integrated into Mozambican life up to a certain point. We lived in a "cement city," as they called it, because there is the Maputo of cement and the Maputo of *caniso*—caniso is the straw houses. We lived in the cement part, we lived in good houses—we lived in a house that the Portuguese left when they went, but we weren't assigned to any particular neighborhood. Now I would say that the integration at work—I felt very free to converse with my Mozambican co-workers, both male and female. I had a female boss who was much younger than I was, because she had been able to study in Portugal. She was mulatto, she had a good preparation in social work, and the place was full of young people who had had to take on positions of responsibility, without being trained for them. So they shared their fears with us, and all the work situations were pretty much shared.

The truth is that there wasn't any discrimination against us, and I never felt any. Now this has its explanation, because the Mozambique Liberation Front, the FRELIMO, was the government in power. During the period of the war of liberation, which lasted ten years, they were very careful to teach that the enemy is not the white man but rather that the enemy is colonialism, and that the proponents of colonialism may be black or white, and that friends can be black or white. In this area, they progressed a good deal in the earlier period, and well, the experience of the cooperation that they received also served in some way to confirm that. Now where there were problems was because we were, yes, in a privileged economic situation with respect to the Mozambicans and that did create tension, but it was because of economic factors, not because of pure racial discrimination.

We left Mozambique in 1984. Well, I think that the idea that we had to go back was always there. I think that one suffers from historic guilt, with respect to the coup. In some way, we felt like our generation was responsible for what had happened, so we lived our absence from our country with great guilt, like we were betraying it—now that the thing has failed, let's leave. So we, at least, always had the idea that we had to go back, besides after the year eighty-something, the political groups began to encourage people to return. It was like a moral question, that is, it was seen as a good thing and it was expected that we would begin to return then. I would say that the majority of people returned also as a result of this moral pressure, because if I had been congruent with my experience, I would have been delighted to have stayed there. I came to the conclusion that one's national identity is very fragile, and that you are from the place where you have a place to work and where you have a job to carry out. So it wasn't that we came back for the beans and the Andes and the *congrío* soup [a succulent soup of conger eel], although that is also important—it meant going back to the cold.

## Guillermo Meza

*Guillermo Meza, born in 1933, grew up in the northern town of Chuquicamata, the site of the largest U.S.-owned copper mines in Chile. His Communist father was a white-collar employee of Chile Exploration Company and, for a period, mayor of neighboring Calama; his mother worked for the same American company as a nurse. Meza studied in local public schools and the University of Chile. In 1973 he was a nonpartisan supporter of the UP and professor of education at the Universidad Técnica del Estado, a university noted for its radicalism.*

*Along with the majority of that university's faculty, Meza was fired and unable to find work; his apartment was searched and he felt a noose tightening around him. With friends, he left Chile legally in February 1974 and went to Venezuela, the country that took in the greatest number of Chilean exiles. As Meza notes, Venezuela was attractive to exiles because its economy was booming in the wake of the 1973 OPEC oil price hike and because its government, one of the few committed democracies in the hemisphere, extended solidarity not only to Chileans, but to refugees from other Latin American dictatorships. After returning to Chile in 1986, Meza went to the United States two years later to take a teaching position at the University of Nevada, Reno, where he remains today.*

I was in Arica the day of the coup. I had been sent by the university to a branch that was located there. I was arrested there because I was at the home of some friends that the police came looking for. After a few days, they let me go, since I wasn't on the list of the people they were looking for in that area. When I managed to get back to Santiago — it took several days since traveling by land was very difficult — I found that my apartment had been searched and sacked by the police, and besides, that I had been thrown out of the university. For safety reasons, I couldn't live in my apartment any longer, so I was forced to stay with friends for many months. I couldn't find work and I had to begin to sell the few personal things that I had been able to salvage from my apartment. The situation was desperate. The police circle seemed to be closing in, and the resources that I had to live on were scarce.

Some of my friends and I were leftists but weren't active members of any party, and that made it more complicated when we tried to see about possibilities for leaving the country. The Pro Paz Committee asked for party contacts; to get asylum it was the same thing: you had to have the support of some organization. I could have gotten that, but it was hard now that everybody was underground.

Faced with this critical situation, two friends and I decided to leave the country by land, in February of 1974. After gathering a little money, two hundred U.S. dollars, we started our odyssey toward Colombia by way of Peru. We had managed to get visas for Colombia. The trip was really long, some three months. Our car broke down in Ecuador, where we had to abandon it. Then we continued traveling on country buses, along with pigs, hens, till we got to Bogotá.

The Colombians showed us great solidarity. We didn't have anything, not work, not money, not clothes. They were extraordinarily nice to us and to all the Chileans. I remember a curious fact that demonstrates the solidarity of the Colombian people. One day I went out for a walk, and when I was passing by a huge building in demolition I heard some other Chileans talking. These compatriots were living in that building. The demolition crew had left an apartment for them. The entire building showed the effects of demolition, except that apartment in the middle of the building. It was a very nice gesture.

From Bogotá, I made some inquiries about going to Venezuela. This country was enjoying a very good moment economically, and there was a great demand for professionals in the areas of health, education, and in oil. The government of Venezuela created an educational institute some 500 kilometers from Caracas, in Maturín, and nobody wanted to go there because it has a very harsh climate — it is very hot and very humid. They hired me and I arrived in Maturín with three other Chileans. Then the institute grew and they needed more professors, and they asked us if there were more qualified Chileans who would be willing to go there. There got to be more than forty Chileans among two hundred professors.

The solidarity of the Venezuelans was impressive. *Acción Democrática* [Democratic Action, or AD], which was the party in power, gave a good deal of help to all Chileans. But, of course, to some more than others and, especially, to those linked with political parties. We who were from the independent left were obliged to fend for ourselves. There were many organizations that helped. But the most important thing in Venezuela was that there was plenty of work. And the most important way they could help was to find you work or you could find it yourself, because there was plenty; besides, salaries were good. I left Chile with two hundred U.S. dollars, and I survived several months with that. I get to Venezuela and my first salary was fifteen hundred U.S. dollars. That was extraordinary, that was a fortune. In that period, that was a very significant amount and enabled me to help many Chileans—friends who were very badly off, and who needed money to be able to eat or to get out of Chile.

My arrival in Venezuela really had an impact on me. The country is very different from Chile, beginning with the landscape, a lot of color, very green. The climate is tropical—it is very hot; there is a lot of rain and the humidity is high. The people are extraordinarily communicative, extroverted, and happy. The food is also very different with a lot of rice, meat, and beans. But, in general, I would say that we adapted well.

In Maturín, they welcomed us well, in spite of the fact that with the arrival of the Chileans, Uruguayans, Brazilians, Argentines, we were a real invasion. Sometimes there were some problems with some Chileans who wanted to take advantage in inappropriate ways or to get things to which they were not entitled, like, for example, to try to get a job for which they were not qualified. That generated some resentment, but it wasn't much of a problem.

My experience shows me that the Venezuelans were extraordinarily generous. We, on our part, came with the ideas and values of our country and we were not able to find a place for ourselves in the new context. Sometimes we wanted them to recognize things that were valid in Chile, but not in another country. As far as my work, it was an excellent experience. I was respected, I had an excellent relationship with my colleagues and with my students. I had many opportunities to do other things, and if I had problems, they were no greater than those that I could have had in Chile. After a time, I got a job in Caracas and moved to the capital.

As far as the personal side, I can say that life was very nice in Venezuela—the people very warm, very nice—a life that was incredibly

happier than that in Chile. The unfortunate thing is that when you remember that time, many faces come to mind of people that you care
about and appreciate a great deal. In general, I would say that Venezuela
as a country was very open to receive us. Now I am speaking of a middle-
class sector, professors and professionals. There was another group of
people who were nonskilled workers who did have problems finding jobs,
problems of adaptation, of alcoholism, family conflicts, separations,
depressions.

Within this, there were some strange things in exile, like those meetings that a group of friends started at a billiard parlor in Caracas. It was
called the Golden Billiard, the owner was an Argentine. By the end, more
than a hundred of us got together every Friday to converse, to discuss and
exchange news of Chile. It was an escape for the exiles to go to this bar on
Fridays. Some sang, there was music. We took up a collection to buy a
guitar for those who had musical ability. The majority of the people who
went were middle class, workers, and some professionals.

Another thing to point out about Caracas is that an elite of exile leaders developed—an elite that received aid from international organizations, who had honorary positions in the Venezuelan government but who
didn't work in the government, but rather concentrated on political work.
Very linked to the AD Party and who sometimes lived in very luxuriant
conditions. They received special treatment that was sometimes pretty
shocking.

There were others who did not receive this kind of protection, like
Mario Palestro, a ex-Socialist deputy. He had some very hard times, did
unpleasant work, especially for someone of his age. Also Carmen Lazo,
another Socialist deputy who also had to work hard to survive. José Car-
rasco, a journalist, who worked very hard in solidarity with Chile and who
had a very hard time, subsisted with the bare minimum. Mario Díaz, another journalist, was in the same situation and finally died due to a long
illness. He had to go to Cuba where they took him for medical care that
he could not afford in Venezuela because of his precarious economic situation. People who were very honest and very committed. And among
these people, there were extraordinary foreigners who were more Chilean
than many of our countrymen. This was the case of the Argentines Tomás
Vasconi, Irene Decar, and Luis Vitale—people who have dedicated their
lives to writing and researching our country and who have an incredible
amount of affection for our country. Well, they returned to Chile and live
there now. Three intellectuals of very high caliber.

I returned to Chile in 1985 because they asked me to come back again as the director of a high school where I had worked at the end of the 1960s.

## Enrique Ramírez

*Enrique Ramírez was the owner of a small print shop in the capital. His father, a Spanish immigrant who worked as an agricultural administrator, died in 1936, when Enrique was five years old. His mother took him to Santiago, where he grew up in the working-class neighborhood of Estación Central. He worked to put himself through school, finishing at the public school of graphic arts, and eventually establishing his own modest business.*

*A man of leftist ideas but no party affiliation, Ramírez was arrested after the coup and released, but his oldest son was imprisoned at the Chacabuco concentration camp in northern Chile. Fearing that their other two sons might be arrested or drafted into the military, he and his wife began making plans to immigrate to Canada. Rámirez took a remarkably practical approach to exile: He prepared by taking a course in welding that he hoped would get him a good job in Canada, and while in exile worked at accumulating capital to facilitate the family's return to Chile. He again owns a printing shop in the capital.*

When I arrived, I was the last one in the family to get there. A year before, our two youngest sons had gone; we sent them as tourists to Canada in April of 1974, when our oldest son was already a prisoner. Friends met them there and they began to do the paperwork and they went right away to study at the university. Later my wife went, and after he was freed, my other son went. I went last because I was concerned about arranging things here, not selling anything and leaving my shop running.

It was an abrupt change for me, because I was a man forty-five years old, and from one day to the next, after having a kind of position of authority here — being the boss — I arrive there and I look out the window and see a white, strange landscape, children of all colors who are playing in the snow. It was the month of February — it was a very strange sensation. So I said, "Well, the only thing to do is work quickly," so I started working on it, and on the fifth day, through a friend, I was told that a hotel in Toronto needed someone to clean the kitchens, and they said, "Look. you have to talk to such and such a person." "But I don't speak English," I said. "It doesn't matter. Tell them this: 'I'm looking for a job.'" I had to be there at eleven o'clock at night and find that man and tell him,

"I'm looking for a job." So that is what I did and he told me "O.K." and he gave me something to eat. It was a hotel with sixty floors. Since I worked at night, and I still had a certain image of a Chilean who worked at night. This was the first shock that I had in Canada, because I had an Italian following me around who was always hammering at me. I had forty meters of kitchen to clean, then move on to the meat area and clean it. The truth is that I got off at eight o'clock in the morning extremely tired. The two weeks that I worked there, I worked really hard. The only good thing about it was that since there were many juice machines, every little bit I drank juice from the machine. I had never drunk so much juice in my life.

Later I went to an English class. That was glory for me because being there six months and having a salary and studying—it couldn't have been any better! What I liked most was to meet people of so many different nationalities in the class, meet them and realize that that black girl or that Chinese man or South Vietnamese person, when all is said and done, reacted the same way I did in the same situations, and are like you, and that is a very rich experience. Well, English, in reality, you only learn it theoretically because you can't learn it in the time that the class lasts.

Before leaving Chile, when I knew that I was going to come to Canada, I took a welding course at INACAP [Instituto Nacional de Capacitación, a government technical school program] and I got a certificate. So, when I arrived there, I took the English course and went to look for work at a metallurgical plant as a welder. This was also a good experience because I realized that you don't get a job there because this or that friend recommends you, but rather because you know or don't know how to do the work. When I had recently started at the company—it made office furniture—they didn't hire us immediately, rather they gave us a trial period. We started to work at nine o'clock at night and they tested us. Then at around twelve or one the boss came around and said who would stay and who wouldn't. He told me, "You are O.K." I was on the assembly line welding; I liked that a lot because it gave me a sense of accomplishment in my work as part of the line.

I was surprised, when I went to the factory the first day, that there was no one group among the workers; rather there were groups by nationalities, from Africa, from Pakistan, from India, and we were only two Chileans. But this distance that I noticed the first day didn't exist three months later, and there was a sense of community. I realized that because, one of those first days, I had a cart full of pieces that I had made, and suddenly they all fell. And I looked around and no one made any move to help me. And that same thing happened three or four months later and there was a totally different reaction, because people came from all over and, among all of us, we stopped the thing. That was really nice, I liked that.

I spent eight months working nights there. The strange thing is that I had to shout because of being sleepy. I had never felt so sleepy, I shouted and sang. One night I was on top of a machine with an enormous key, taking it down so that I could change the molds. It was February, and suddenly I said, "What in the hell am I doing up here at four in the morning? I ought to be at the beach, in El Quisco [a beach town south of Valparaíso]." It was such a strange feeling that I couldn't convince myself to stay up there at four o'clock in the morning. This is what hit me most during the period in Toronto, the working at night. But, in reality, I didn't have to suffer or have anything serious happen to me.

In general, for me, the years went by like a show, like a strange situation. I enjoyed it many times because of the strange jobs that I had. There always was that willingness, at least, on my part to work all the time, it didn't matter in what. And what I always liked was that there wasn't, on the part of the rest of the people, a sense that if you worked in something that was not so prestigious, you would lose status. That didn't matter. I liked that; I saw that there.

I always lived with my head partly here in Chile, always thinking that the fact of being in Canada was an accident, that this would happen later, that I would return—I was always thinking that. The truth is that I knew that I had to be there for some years, but I never thought of that as being my destiny. It was just a stage—I had no choice but to be there and live as best I could. The bad thing was that I never bought a house. I should have probably bought an apartment—they were really cheap at that time. I remember that for sixteen thousand dollars, we could have bought an apartment and we didn't buy it because we didn't think that we were going to put down roots there, we thought that it wasn't going to last.

We continued to follow our customs. The food we ate was the same as we ate here in Chile. There was everything that you needed to cook. That was really no problem. Perhaps having to stay indoors because the days were so short could be bothersome, but it wasn't a serious problem. But my wife never got used to it. She felt more urgency to come back, and says now that she will never leave again, that she would not go back. This is not really the way I think. I think, more and more, that it is better there. I enjoy the life, the cleanliness, the landscape, I like it better.

We only got to know a few Canadians well, because of the language and communication problems. But we always had good relationships with many Chileans and the friendship and the affection could be felt. There was a lot of communication; there were more possibilities of contact than one has here in Santiago itself, and, naturally, always thinking about what to do to get rid of Pinochet and to go back, those were the themes. Also, each one talked about his or her life and experience at work. Naturally, there were many emotional crises. It was very frequent for marriages to break up. The worst effect of exile were the marriage crises.

Then, something like a plan took shape and I realized that everything that I was doing was aimed at returning to Chile, in reality. I took a course in offset printing, which lasted seven months, and that course gave me the ability to know about and choose machines that I could buy and take to Chile. It was very useful to me because I brought with me some machines that are in great demand here, so when I got here with the machines I sold them; I went back and did this several times, and in some five or six months I earned some thirty thousand dollars bringing in and selling machines. There wasn't any difficulty about bringing in this kind of thing— you pay the taxes that are due and they let the merchandise in. There was an immediate market for that type of machine. The first time I brought two, and I sold them immediately. Then I went back and I bought three. I did this several times, and finally, I stayed for good in the year 1981.

## Eduardo Montecinos

*Born and educated in Valparaíso, Eduardo Montecinos was twenty-eight years old at the time of the coup. The son of a printer and a technical school teacher of dressmaking, he joined a Socialist Party youth organization at the age of eleven and held a number of party posts, including membership in the central committee. He attended technical schools and eventually studied journalism and communications at the University of Chile's Valparaíso campus.*

*Awakening in Valparaíso on the morning of September 11, 1973, Montecinos found all strategic locations occupied by the navy, which had returned from maneuvers overnight to initiate the coup in the port city. Captured in a sweep a month later, after hiding out in a party colleague's house, he was held in a number of detention centers, including the naval vessel Lebu, before being sent to two separate concentration camps in Valparaíso province. He was beaten and subjected to psychological torture; he lost between forty and fifty kilos ("the food was terrible") and saw his wife only once during his eleven months of detention. Montecinos was never charged with any crime and was expelled from Chile a year after the coup.*

*He, his wife, and three daughters are Costa Rican citizens living in San*
*José, where he owns a book importing and publishing business.*

I was expelled on September 11, 1974, that is, one year after the coup. My
father paid for my airfare. CIME brought my family four months later
and paid their fares, and I will always be grateful for that. January 14 or 15,
1975, my wife and my two daughters arrived. These two daughters who
left Chile completed their elementary school, high school, and university
studies in Costa Rica. The oldest is a publicist in the Housing Ministry.
The second is a lawyer, she just graduated, and the little one was born in
Costa Rica — she is in her fourth year of humanities and she is fifteen.

I knew very little about Costa Rica, but what made me decide on it at
that time was that I had a very good friend and trusted comrade, a Socialist leader, Ernesto Tapia, who had gone into exile through the Costa
Rican embassy in Chile. You have to remember that the dictatorship had
long arms. We had serious concerns about some of our party comrades
and about other parties that might be infiltrated in exile. That is, I think
that there were a series of things that I was looking for, too: apart from
there being people from the party, that they were friends too. So, those
things made me feel more confident about coming to a country about
which I knew nothing at all.

And on the other hand, there was the attitude of the government of
José Figueres Ferrer [1970–74] before I arrived, of support for Chilean
immigration. The subsequent governments also had a very open attitude, they were very helpful to the Chilean colony. In my case, there was
a very favorable opportunity, because it is different to arrive after you
have been expelled than as an exile. The idea was that I would get political asylum because I had been expelled from my country; that is, I didn't
have a country. So President Oduber [Daniel Oduber, president 1974–78]
granted me political asylum in January of 1975, so that my irregular situation in Costa Rica didn't last more than four months. Then once I had
the political asylum, I had permanent residency, the possibility of working freely without having to get a work permit. So that, in that sense, I
was rather lucky to be able to integrate into this country.

When I arrived, there was already a functioning solidarity committee
formed by parties on the left, by the Chileans who had arrived earlier, but
I really didn't have to resort to this kind of help and organization at any
point. Rather, it was the group connected with the newspaper *Pueblo* that
took me in. *Pueblo* here has a progressive point of view with respect to religious questions. It was directed by a priest, Javier Solís, who without

even knowing me, except through Ernesto Tapia, worked to have me freed so that I could come to Costa Rica and work at the paper. I ended up working there for a year and eight months, selling as well as writing— I was the director of the publicity department.

The work at *Pueblo* did not keep me from working in a group with other Chilean friends on independent trade-union newspapers. We put out the magazine of the National Bank for a year, we did brochures, posters, everything that had to do with graphic art. We earned little, but we managed economically. We did this as a team. We worked in commercial film, writing scripts for some shorts for the Costa Rican Tourist Institute. I was a television actor; I made over fourteen commercials. I had a radio program for a year, in the radio station of a Costa Rican Socialist friend, Radio América Latina. And later I directed the San Martín press for a progressive group in this country; I was there for a year and eight months.

I did this until I went to work in the bookstore of the University of Costa Rica for four and a half years, always at someone's recommendation and always trying to work in activities that you think will give you the most ideological and spiritual satisfaction.

At the same time, we had these small "*camarones*" [shrimp], as they are called, income from always making brochures, magazines, art, everything related to graphic art. I gave independent classes at the University of Costa Rica on book publishing and graphic design. After some ten years in the country, I began to edit books for a friend's publishing company. I was there for a year, and then I began to publish my own books, *La Nueva Década*, and then I began to import books and now I think that I am one of the major book importers of Costa Rica. It has meant a great effort on the part of my family and of friends who have helped. My wife has always worked in her profession, in education. Now I am president of the Costa Rican Book Council, which makes me very proud. I have been president for almost three years now. One of my responsibilities is to represent Costa Rica in all the international events that take place.

It is difficult to know how many Chileans there were in Costa Rica at the moment of greatest influx of exiles. We had always spoken of a group of more than four thousand families. At one moment in the center of San José and the Immigration Office, one saw hundreds of Chileans every day. I think, without including the Chileans who came to Costa Rica for other reasons, you know, that the greatest influx came starting in the year 1975–1976. Later, an incredible number of my countrymen began to arrive in Costa Rica, which meant that the Chilean presence could be felt too much in Costa Rica at times, and there were always problems getting work, aid, I don't know what all. People who came here stayed for a while, who saw the possibilities. There was a good number of people who were wandering around lost in the world, who went from one country to another, and you didn't know if they wanted to work or what they wanted to do, but probably the greater part of the four thousand families became integrated into Costa Rica and we started to get to know each other and to hold activities.

Now there is a group that we never saw much of in Costa Rica — the working class. Almost all of us were people with some university study who found jobs quickly, for example, in press agencies, in newspapers — there were many journalists — some went to work in customs, and mainly in the university, and in the arts — in theater, in music, in everything related to art, painting. You have to realize that Chileans created here, before our exile, a group of organizations. They helped to form the insurance system, the University of Costa Rica, the Ministry of Education, the direct tax system, the Central Bank [this refers to Chilean experts hired to help create the educational, social, and economic institutions that Costa Rica developed beginning in the 1940s]. And in our period, people came who developed the theater a great deal in Costa Rica.

The change that exile represented is so strong that you took refuge with friends, and were constantly, let's say, thinking about how long this exile would last. According to the analysis of the group of friends I was closest to in that period, already here in Costa Rica, we always talked about five years as the maximum as opposed to two or three years as a minimum. And in that critical stage, we drank a good deal, looked for adventures — every night a change of scenery. We spent most of our income on alcohol — this was a country where with little money you could eat well, you could buy things...

We talked about how we lived in an improvised fashion. If something characterized our exile at that time, it was improvisation — let's say, for example, that the books that we got we put on planks with bricks, with blocks, which shows that we were planning to leave and that we didn't have anything linking us to the country where we were. The big leap, in my case, the definitive one, was one day, talking with my wife, and I had some money — "I am going to throw away the bricks, I am going to throw away the planks, we are going to buy some furniture." I bought a color TV, I bought a new refrigerator, I bought a piece of land. They even made fun of me because when I had more money, I went out and bought living room furniture — in Chile we say a "living" — made of leather, which is what I still have and they are still really expensive. All of this cost us a great deal of money, but it was not done out of a desire to gain status but out of a desire to feel that we belonged here. This was some two years after we got to Costa Rica. We told ourselves that if it came to that, "if the change comes tomorrow, we will leave here and . . . " And that was like saying, "Well, O.K., I am still able to live, able to have something that is mine." In Chile, I wasn't interested in money, I didn't have a car, I didn't have property, I didn't have anything. But there comes a moment in which, well, this was done for my daughters, who were growing up here, so that they wouldn't have to suffer because of exile, so that their house would be like the others and have a record player, a television, a living room, etc. After that beginning, we — joking a little, but because we had experienced it — began to laugh at the people who did not change after the years that they had been here. Many people left and the only thing that they had was a car or something, but not a house.

There are Chileans who simply cannot adapt. We went dancing, we went out with Costa Rican couples, and we tried to understand what they were like. There are even the romantic-type relationships. These weren't necessarily always between two Chileans; some were, but the rest got together with Costa Ricans. My oldest daughter has a Costa Rican compañero. It happened here, like it must have happened in many other countries, that the older adults found that even the carrots were different, the tomatoes or the lettuce, and that they couldn't get whatever. We were able to get everything, everything. But also, from a social point of view, it was always said that the Costa Rican is lazier, that he or she is irresponsible and misses work. But this is because in our situation we were somewhat in competition with them because of being foreigners. In Chile, I go and I see that they are not as hardworking, or as punctual, nor are they so sharp as one would think because of the economic boom, the model country in Latin America. This is a very personal view.

I don't think that we did anything special to keep our Chileanness or to transmit Chilean culture to our daughters. We lived a time in which we were very close as a family. You have to remember that the majority of us didn't have anybody. So my daughters' family are their aunts and uncles, but they aren't really aunts and uncles, but rather the closest friends of the family. Obviously, we would go out together, we continued to maintain strong ties among the Chileans. But what we did mostly was to have a Chilean folkloric group which was very successful in Costa Rica, but then that fell off.

Now exile cannot be good, ever — it cannot be good, but it can be less bad. You have your pride, you have your ideals, and that was cut off, totally, for our generation who are in their fifties, they cut it off for us when we were very young. And in the space that we have, we simply feel cheated, that we were not able to contribute our small part to do something for Chile. Perhaps this is the only thing that I resent, not being able now to help with the experience and the baggage I gained in this trip around the world. The Chileans have made a contribution to the culture here in Costa Rica, but the loss of talent that exile has meant for Chile can never be recuperated.

Although my family and I are Costa Ricans, the question of possibly going back to live in Chile is one that you always ask yourself, constantly. For example, if I had to decide today, with a stable economic situation, with my family here, who made their life here, who are studying, who have studied, it would be very hard for us to be able to reintegrate ourselves at this moment in Chile. But if in some moment of our lives we have the opportunity to be in Chile, temporarily at first, maybe later permanently . . . I really would like to be able to walk in a more permanent way through the streets of Valparaíso — we natives of the port of Valparaíso are very attached to our city. And for a very simple reason, because there I think I will have the opportunity to talk about the past and about what happened to me with people who I think will understand me and I will understand them. Growing old in Costa Rica would be hard for me because, really, my experiences are, let's say, so different from those of the Costa Ricans that I could not, probably, I think, enjoy those memories and sharing that life.

## Viola Carrillo

*Viola Carrillo went into exile as a young child. Born in Lota, center of Chile's coal-mining region south of Concepción and one of the country's poorest areas, Viola was seven years old in 1973. She was the daughter of union leader and Communist Party central committee member Isidro Carrillo and his wife, parents of twelve children. After the mining company was expropriated by the UP government, Carrillo was elected to a managerial position. He was arrested the day of the coup and shot after a sham court-martial, with four other miners, six weeks later.\**

* Carrillo's October 22 execution is described in *Comisión Nacional de Verdad y Reconciliación*, 1:348–49.

*Under constant threat of violence to her children and lacking the means*
*of economic survival, Viola's mother opted for exile, a possibility rarely*
*available to people in her family's social circumstances. Two of her sons had*
*already been arrested; one of them, Vasily Carrillo, would later become a*
*leader of the Communist Party's armed resistance unit, the Manuel*
*Rodríguez Patriotic Front, and participate in the August 1986 assassina-*
*tion attempt against Pinochet. The international Communist network and*
*the Red Cross arranged passage for her and the other ten children to the*
*Soviet Union in June 1974. Viola's story offers the perspectives of a child*
*and a young woman on a long exile that culminated with the collapse of*
*the Soviet Union in 1991.*

Before we left was terrible for me. We were always afraid. I remember, I
had to go to my aunt's house, and we went with her to see my father and
got back about nine o'clock at night—we came back with the sounds of
gunshots all around us. Later, when I got to Moscow and there was a
different atmosphere, I slept better. Of course, it was hard because we saw
my mother crying all day long.

The welcome that we received was very nice. The Red Cross met us
and they took us to a very nice hotel, but I don't remember which one it
was. I think that we were almost the first Chileans to arrive in the USSR.
There were others, but just a few. In the school where we studied, where
we were all children of exiles, we were the first Chileans.

Later, we went to Zaporozhíye [an industrial city on the Dnieper River,
with a 1980 population of some 800,000], in the Ukraine. I don't know if
the Russians or my mother decided that, but I remember my mother saying that she wanted to be in a smaller city than Moscow, with less noise.
We went to live in a hotel, because we were waiting for them to finish
building some apartments, that later they gave us completely furnished.
At the beginning, we didn't understand anything. We also missed the
food; we thought the food there was awful. Since we were living in the
hotel for two weeks, my mother didn't know what to do about our not
wanting to eat. Everything was totally different. She could not prepare
food because we had to go to the hotel restaurant. We all drank the tea
and ate the pastries, but we didn't like the other food.

We got there in July, and at the end of August—because the school
year begins in September [the opposite of the Southern Hemisphere
school calendar]—nine of us children went to a boarding school. It was almost like going back to Moscow, because the international boarding
school for children from countries which had political problems was lo-

cated in Ivanovo, closer to Moscow. I studied there for ten years. There were many children who came from their different countries directly to this school, without their families, their parents, with nothing. I met people from Angola, Guinea, Colombia, Honduras, Spain, Greece, Iran, Iraq, Ethiopia, Somalia. There were so many different cases. I remember some Guatemalan classmates, two brothers and two sisters. They were children of labor leaders, their parents had been shot. The children were gotten out of the country by the Red Cross, and they came to the school. The Angolans who came to this school began to arrive in 1976, when UNITA was fighting with the MPLA [The União para a Independência Total de Angola, a Western-supported group fighting the Soviet-backed Movimento Popular de Libertação de Angola in the aftermath of independence from Portugal in 1975]. So orphans came, children of the disappeared, of prisoners. Those were the children who came to the school.

The winter was really strange. I saw skates for the first time. We were children and we fell trying to learn how to walk on snow. We threw snowballs at each other. At school, this was the strangest part for all the children coming from different places.

Among the most difficult things for me was to live so far from my mother. I was a crybaby. In the school, at that time, we had many acts of solidarity and they talked about Chile and the news got there quickly. In my school, I had to talk about my father many times, so the first period was hard because everything made me think about him, it was like a trauma.

It was easy to learn the language, to study, we had access to everything, we played sports. I can't complain. When I talk about my childhood, I say that I was happy, in spite of the fact that I was always missing something, but I had many things that other children haven't had. I began to study piano, but later I gave it up. I was very devoted to sports: I skied, I skated, I participated in the student relay ski competitions.

The school was very hard; at least, harder than it is here. The level was high and the professors were good. From what I remember, the professors were the best in the Soviet Republics. And it had to be that way because it wasn't just any school. The children came from all parts of the world, and they had to begin to teach them to speak Russian and start from there. Each class had between twenty and twenty-four students maximum, and the total was some six hundred students. I think that all the teachers used psychology. They were well prepared.

For my mother, exile was terrible. She always tells us that it was very hard to make the decision to leave. She left in Chile her aged mother, her oldest son a prisoner, my father dead. And then, in the USSR, she had to be separated from her children because, even though she would have liked to, she couldn't have us all together, because in order to support us she had to work. But in spite of everything, she has always appreciated all the help that we got. She says that if we had stayed in Chile, she could never have provided us with the educations that we got. That was a great help to her.

She worked in a metallurgical factory, because Zaporozhíye is an industrial city, where there are a great number of metallurgical factories. There is an automobile plant. She learned Russian very well. She can even argue in Russian. After 1974, more Chileans began to arrive, and in Zaporozhíye there were some twenty Chilean families. During the vacations, we got together with the other people who had arrived from Chile to talk, to have peñas with empanadas and red wine from Georgia.

At my house, when we got there in the summer, we would have lunch and talk for hours and hours about Chile, our memories of Lota, my father. What I remembered most was Lota. The places that I had gone with my father, because my father took us on a lot of trips. In the summer, there was the white beach, the trips to the rivers and to Concepción. We went to the park in Lota every weekend. And I also missed being able to visit my father's grave. I think that because of that, we didn't forget anything and not the language either. Because at school they gave us Spanish classes, but not for very many hours. What we spoke most was Russian.

All my brothers and sisters went to the university. Some finished their degrees, others didn't. I have a brother who got a degree as a mining engineer; it was the idea that the majority of my brothers had because they had seen my father working in the mine. I have a sister who studied civil engineering, another who is still studying computer science. Then a sister who studied and works as a translator. Another sister got her M.D. We also have a teacher. I studied journalism in Leningrad and then in Lomonosov University in Moscow.

They gave opportunities to the foreigners there and even more to us. The Russians, to apply to the university, have to take exams, get a certain number of points, and all that. We didn't have to do that. They gave us scholarships. I, for example, said that I wanted to study journalism. They asked me, "In which city?" And I made the choice, although you didn't know for sure that you would be able to go there. At first, I didn't see any jealousy on the part of the Russians toward us; the Russians were in solidarity with the foreigners. Later, there began to be resentment and you heard people say that it was because of the foreigners that they were badly off. Because they said that Russia gave a great deal of foreign aid and didn't have anything for them, but it did for others. But this was more recently.

I witnessed the great changes in the USSR, I saw the good ones and the bad ones. Everything was changing: They would have to pay tuition in the universities, they would have to pay for medical care. Of course, I think that there needed to be changes. They couldn't continue to live that way, with the bureaucracy that existed in the USSR. But not the changes that they made. They took away all the benefits, they confused a great many things. The young people were in favor of the changes. Many times I saw young people demonstrating downtown. They supported change because they thought that this would bring the market from outside and they were enamored of McDonald's and Pizza Hut. They thought that with these things they would be on the other side. They were motivated by consumerism; it didn't occur to them that eating things from other places would bring other things with it.

All of this created lots of problems for the foreigners. I had finished one year at the university and I had to leave the student residence; I didn't have any place to live. And for everything you need legal papers, because if I wanted to go to another city, I had to have a visa to travel. And the Red Cross, which helped us, that was in charge of us, washed its hands of us. When we had any kind of problem, there was nobody to help us. In the Red Cross, they told me: "We are not concerned with the Chileans any longer, because you have a democracy now." We were left abandoned in a foreign country.

## Iván Jaksić

*Iván Jaksić was born in Punta Arenas, Chile's southernmost city, in 1954, one of two children of a retired public employee and a secretary. He grew up in Punta Arenas and in Puente Alto, an industrial suburb south of Santiago. He studied in the local trade school to be a machinist, and participated in the leftist politics common among secondary-school students. After finishing his apprenticeship in a factory, he changed course and entered the University of Chile's school of philosophy, a part of the traditionally radical Instituto Pedagógico. Despite his support for and involvement with the left, Jaksić became disillusioned by what he considered the heavy-handed efforts of faculty and student militants to transform the school of philosophy into an instrument at the service of the UP adminis-*

*tration. Although he rejected this "sectarianism," he was unwilling to join the right-wing opposition or condone the military coup.*

*Jaksić recalls a 1974 DINA raid on the Instituto Pedagógico as "a turning point in my life." Of the forty students and faculty arrested, including close friends, some eventually joined the ranks of the disappeared. Having avoided arrest, he fled to Argentina burdened with "survivor's guilt." By 1975, conditions for Chileans in Argentina had deteriorated to the point that, ironically, he returned to Chile for his safety and managed to re-enroll in the university. Nevertheless, he was soon after expelled from the university and drafted into the army. His second exile, this one in the United States, began when he refused to comply with the draft and was consequently declared "in rebellion." His testimony clearly portrays the senses of loss and displacement that accompany permanent separation from the homeland. Like the majority of exiles, he has not returned to live in Chile and today is professor of history at the University of Notre Dame.*

I started my life in the United States with the knowledge that my return would be uncertain. I had a vague hope that the regime would soon fall and that I would be cleared of the charges. During the first few months of my stay in Buffalo, I was primarily thinking of what I had left behind. I focused on reestablishing contact with friends both in Chile and in other places around the world where many had been exiled. Obviously I could not neglect two pressing necessities: making a living, for I had no means of support other than the help of friends, and learning English, which was imperative if I was to perform well enough to maintain a student visa. The learning of English was less of a problem than I thought, for the need to communicate was something of a personal demand in a place that had few people with whom I could communicate in Spanish. Still, some Chilean exiles arrived, and with some of them I tried to address the first problem. I worked in a variety of jobs, from unloading trains to house painting to carpentry and typing. Eventually, I received a graduate assistantship and I was able to concentrate on my academic work.

My impressions of the United States were filtered by my primary personal concern, which was Chile. The United States was a curious country to me, but I did not devote much time to thinking about the new surroundings. What I found most striking was the treatment I received as a graduate student at the university, the respect with which my opinions were considered in a seminar context, the general civility which I encountered in that university environment, especially in contrast to the persecution and vindictiveness I had known in Chile. But though I had

lived in some very poor areas in Puente Alto and Santiago, I was not prepared for the neglect and squalor of urban Buffalo. I shared a room in a
neighborhood adjacent to the city's red-light district, a desperately poor
and violent part of the town. Every night, I would zigzag my way home to
avoid the solicitations, fights, and general pandemonium of this crime-
ridden area. The way I lived and was treated in that neighborhood, if you
can call it that, in contrast to the life at the university, was a sobering in-
troduction to life in the United States. I did not have great expectations
coming to the United States, but even if I did, I was quickly disabused of
any expectations of great comfort and wealth.

My hopes of a quick demise of the military regime gradually faded as
the months and years went by. I started to despair. My approach to life in
the United States was very similar to that in Argentina: I was waiting, literally ready to leave at a moment's notice. But the late seventies were the
glorious days of the military regime in Chile. Despite President Carter's
emphasis on human rights, Chile was beginning to receive the accolades
of the business world for its economic policies. Return looked almost impossible, and were it not for Juan Rivano, my philosophy teacher and
friend who counseled me to concentrate on my studies from his home in
Sweden where he lived in exile, I would have grown extremely alienated
and morose. Still, I jumped at the opportunity to claim the amnesty that
was offered in 1978 to violators of military law.

I did not hesitate to claim this amnesty in person in Chile in the hope
that I would be able to return to my country. I can now say that this was
complete madness, but at the time this was my strongest personal desire.
What I found upon my return to Chile were the realities of a secure military establishment. As soon as I reported to military headquarters to
claim the amnesty, I was summoned to military court, tried within an
hour, found guilty as charged, and sentenced to four years of military service. Although in the end I was dismissed because of my poor physical
condition, and I could leave Chile to return to the United States, I faced
the moments I had dreaded for years when I was led under military escort
to the basement of the Ministry of Defense to be interrogated, humiliated, and eventually released to start a more permanent, if unplanned, life
away from my homeland.

In the years since 1978, I fought against, but gradually came to accept,
the facts of my exile. After graduation from SUNY [State University of
New York at Buffalo] in 1981, and the attendant expiration of my student
visa, I moved to Sweden. I lived there for half a year working as a janitor
before I managed to return to the United States, where I thought I would

have better chances of finding an academic job. I decided for myself that I would maintain a linkage to Chile, but that I would also try to find a job and secure a place I could call my own. I did not have the support networks in Chile, either social or political, that would have allowed me to return to some form of professional activity. Basically, I confronted the fact that I had to move from a situation of exile into an experience of immigration.

The positive side of this transition is that I became, in the early 1980s, much more conscious of my life in the United States. I started to view it as, maybe, a more permanent situation. I had friendships going back to the early days of my arrival, but I was now more open to cultivating relationships with more people, of more and different backgrounds. I did find some reluctance and distance, perhaps even a trace of distrust in some, but mostly I encountered a warm and interested people. They did not seem prepared to develop the depth of friendship I had known — I now recognize — in trying circumstances in Chile, but I did learn to challenge the pervasive Latin American stereotype that Americans are aloof, cold, and reluctant to engage. Although the stereotype had some measure of truth, I found that once the barrier of language was removed, communication with Americans could be fluid, sincere, and fulfilling.

Despite the rewards of involvement in the life of the United States, I also encountered the realities of the job market in academia during the bleak early 1980s. Besides the agony of securing a job, jumping from one place to another on temporary teaching and research assignments, I also discovered the difficulties of establishing legal status as a permanent resident, and on a more personal level, understanding that the energies I devoted to life in the United States inexorably dashed any hopes of returning to Chile. I married, I formed a family of my own, I started to appreciate life in a community — first in Oakland, then in Milwaukee, and now in South Bend — and became a citizen. I did maintain a linkage to my country by becoming active in human rights, mostly through professional organizations like LASA [Latin American Studies Association], and consultation with other human-rights organizations. I did not pursue any involvement with Chilean exile groups partly because they were almost nonexistent in the U.S., but mostly because those that I knew were dominated by the sectarianism I had learned to dislike in Chile.

I returned to Chile again in 1985, when my father was gravely ill and in fact died shortly after my arrival. By that time, it was clear to me that I was a visitor in my own country, that though I could now enter and exit without problems, there was really no place for me there. I was now a professional historian, a Latin Americanist, with neither prospects nor contacts that could provide me with some basic security, or even a role in what was basically a new social and political environment. Clearly, my life was now in the United States. Besides, I understood early in my professional life that teaching and scholarship have been activities I was fortunate to pursue in the United States, but could never have done in post–1973 Chile.

However, the price I paid for this option — or rather, the lack of an alternative option — was what I truly consider to be exile. It is not the temporary situation of banishment, the months and years of waiting, the expectations of a quick return that are constantly disappointed, but rather the longing for the certainties of life in one's homeland, the mundane comforts of a shared understanding based on language and culture, the sense of roots in an environment that has a certain texture of air, and light, and tones of voice and fragances of sea, mountains, and food, from which you are, perhaps permanently, removed. There is also the longing for the life that could have been in the absence of the nightmare of military rule with its attendant violence and disruption, the desire to have lived a life without catastrophic breaks, a life in the place it was meant to be. I search in vain for a literature of resolution on the matter of exile. No one who has confronted it has truly found a solution other than a sense of sad resignation. But, in the end, this is the choice I made when, exactly twenty years ago, I decided I would not go to the barracks.

[Note: this interview was conducted in English.]

*SIX*

# The Diaspora

## *Exile in Western Europe*

While exile dispersed Chileans around the globe, between a third and a half of all Chileans forced out of their country spent most or all of their exile in Western Europe. Some of the Western European countries had been very supportive of the defeated side from the moment of the coup; the Italian, Swedish, and French governments opened their embassies for asylum and with others, including Belgium, Germany, and Holland, were especially generous in accepting refugees and providing moral and material aid. These countries commonly offered a range of programs and facilities to equip the exile for subsistence and employment: language courses, free or subsidized apartments, job training and placement, and sometimes counseling. These incentives, combined with Chileans' admiration of European culture and institutions and the clear advantages of settling in developed countries, made Western Europe a major exile destination.

Despite marked differences in language, religion, climate, customs, and diet among the non-Communist countries of Europe, those countries had important traits in common that provided Chileans residing there with comparable experiences. At the beginning of the Chilean diaspora, only Spain and Portugal were dictatorships, but the 1974 military coup in Portugal and Franco's death in 1975 launched short and effective democratic transitions in those countries. The remaining Western European countries were stable political democracies featuring well-protected individual liberties and a range of social democratic policies. Although suffering the initial consequences of the 1973 OPEC oil boycott, even the poorer countries offered comparatively high standards of living. Except for Spain, Portugal, and Italy, the Western European countries still faced labor shortages and welcomed not only Chileans, but other South Americans fleeing dictatorships, and by the 1980s, refugees from the Central American civil wars to complement their usual sources of guest labor.

Western Europe clearly offered advantages over most of the other common exile destinations. Although many professionals were forced to take unskilled service jobs, at least initially, even some of them could achieve a material level that was comfortable by Chilean middle-class standards. Members of the working class who went to Western Europe, if successful in finding employment, normally exceeded their accustomed standard of living by far. With adequate language proficiency, many obtained access to higher education and professional positions; as exile author Jorge Arrate put it, exile was "an immense scholarship program" to some of the world's best universities.* For exiles' political purposes, Western Europe was ideal: With well-informed, politically conscious, and affluent populations, open political systems, and strong socialist and social democratic parties and labor movements, Europe offered fertile ground for building vigorous solidarity movements and raising funds to sustain the resistance and relieve poverty in Chile.

Despite the advantages, exile in Western Europe was harder in important ways than relocation to Latin America. Arriving in Sweden or Holland, one encountered unknown languages, cold climates, strange foods, and people who, despite their official policies of welcome and solidarity, seemed as individuals to be cold and aloof. Faced with these challenges to integration, Chileans always felt a separateness, often a greater affinity with other non-Europeans than with their hosts. In Europe one had to work hard to keep Chilean culture alive and transmit it to children exiled in infancy or born abroad; thus the ubiquitousness of empanadas and the peña and the immense popularity of the folk protest groups Inti Illimani,

* Jorge Arrate, *Exilio: textos de denuncia y esperanza* (Santiago: Documentas, 1987), 106.

headquartered in Rome, and Quilapayún, located in Paris, which constantly traveled to sustain Chileans' culture and spirit of resistance.

In Europe, too, the full psychological weight of exile was commonly felt: feelings of defeat, of guilt, memories of torture, of leaving dead, jailed, or disappeared comrades behind — these and a myriad of other legacies of a sudden, sometimes violent, forced uprooting profoundly affected the exiles, compounding the challenges of adaptation. There was also the contraction of personal space: Many of the men and some women lost the public roles that political involvement had given them in Chile, forced by new circumstances into the private realm; and the typical Chilean extended family was replaced by the nuclear family unit. These changes choked off customary outlets and sources of solidarity, magnifying problems of adjustment. Among the symptoms of these traumas were chronic depression and exaggerated incidences of divorce and suicide. And caught in limbo between the inclination to put down roots in the host country and the hopefulness of an early return to the homeland, almost all exiles experienced the syndrome of "living with the suitcases packed."*

## Luis Caro

*Father Luis Caro was born in Santiago in 1947, the son of a merchant and a housewife. Growing up in a very Catholic family, he attended Catholic schools and seminary in Santiago and joined the Redemptorist Order. After a novitiate in Argentina, he returned to Santiago for theological studies in the Catholic University. In the late 1970s his order sent him for further study to the University of Louvain in Belgium, where he became involved with Chilean and other Latin American exiles.*

*His contacts with the exile communities throughout Western Europe led him to redirect his efforts. With the support of the Chilean Bishops' Conference, Caro established a one-man Pastoral del Exilio [Pastorate of Exile] in the early 1980s to provide spiritual support for exiles. The next few years found him traveling constantly throughout Western Europe, to*

---

* Two fine studies of these problems facing exiles in Western Europe are: Ana Vásquez and Ana María Araujo, *La maldición de Ulises: repercusiones psicológicas del exilio* (Santiago: Sudamericana, 1990); and Diana Kay, *Chileans in Exile: Private Struggles, Public Lives* (Wolfeboro, N.H.: Longwood Academic, 1987).

*large cities and small villages, wherever his flock was located. As spiritual
and personal counselor to the exiles, he came to know their lives and
problems intimately. These experiences give Father Caro a unique perspective on exile in Western Europe.*

I ministered to Chileans all over Europe. There were communities in the
principal cities of the different countries, in London, Amsterdam, Frank-
furt, Rome, Lyon, Malmö, Stockholm, countries that I visited periodically. Also, we were even starting groups in the Eastern Bloc countries, in
Berlin. This pastoral work included not just a pastoral ministry that was
strictly religious, but also that was at heart a kind of social action for the
groups representing the different Chilean organizations.

One part was religious and the other was intended to maintain the
spirit of nationalism in people who were away from their own country,
also to keep alive the conviction that they would return. We worked with
the *Comité Pro Retorno a Chile.* We kept informed of the activities of
the different political parties in order to be able to coordinate the actions
that were carried out outside the country. There was work with the local
churches, with area pastors, with the Protestants as much as with the
Catholics. This was so that we could provide services for the Chileans, according to the needs that came up involving their family, their children.

As far as our pastoral work, we had international camps in the summer
in different countries, and people gathered there from all over Europe.
We had periodic days of reflection, weekends together. This was partly to
keep spirits up, combat the defeatism that sometimes threatened to over-
whelm those who were far from their own country. These days created a
space different from that of political confrontation. Exile was hard in the
1980s—you have to remember that the Socialist Party had eighteen divisions, tendencies. One of the tasks was related to that, to try to achieve a
more united effort, coordination, of making people see that we should be
working for a common task.

As far as the women, they were totally transplanted from one world to
another. The men continued their political work and the women were
supposed to take charge of the household, the children and, often, work as
well. There was a high percentage of couples that broke up because of
their exile. There was a good deal of maladjustment: people, for example,
who had been mistreated in Chile—the tortured, all those who suffered
oppression, those who were fugitives—arrived psychologically damaged.

Add to this being uprooted—culturally, socially, politically. The people
who had a played an important role politically, many times were nobodies

in exile, had nothing. They wanted to continue being leaders there and be important. But they were just one more refugee among all those who were there. So, all this had its effect in the sense that inside the family the man lost authority. He was no longer the provider, because they were all in the same situation. It was the state that supported many of them. On the other hand, cultural differences, the Latino mentality that "I am going to Europe and I am a Latin American macho, and, as such, I will have many opportunities," led to the destruction of many homes. In exile, they continued leading a fictional life, a totally unreal political life. Every afternoon they had their hearts in their mouths, saying "we are going to overthrow Pinochet," that "we will return soon," but all of this said at a distance of some twenty thousand kilometers from Chile. This idea continued to be fed there with "I have learned that in Chile they are doing such and such," and then a series of imagined things. I took part in meetings in which I even said to the leaders: "Why invent things, why tell the people that they are taking Santiago block by block when it is not true?" So people were living with the idea that "yes, tomorrow we will return to Chile."

I knew the reality — I knew that it was absolutely nothing like that. So that when the bishops came through, we would get a large number of Chileans together so that they could hear a different version from what they normally heard or discussed in exile. We had the power to get many people to come.

In Belgium, there were many Chileans. We estimated that there must have been some seven to eight thousand Chileans. The greatest concentration of Chileans was in Sweden. In the years that I was in Sweden, they numbered some forty thousand. I spent nine years living in Belgium, from where I covered all of Central Europe especially, and later, I spent three years in Scandinavia. The farther north the greater the material well-being for the exiles in Europe, but there was less spiritual peace. They felt, one could say, internally more uprooted, more anguished. On the other hand, more toward the south, they were more comfortable. They felt like they were in their own ambiance, but the material living conditions were worse. In one case, in Italy, they were never given official status as refugees. There is a general law that they do not accept refugees there. Through other mechanisms they were permitted to live there, but they were on their own; all of them had to work or they had no future. In Sweden, it was different. There, everything had been provided for, everything was ready, they were assured of everything.

In the south, there was more integration. If one compares, for example, the situation in Belgium—in Belgium you could walk down the street without your presence being so obvious. In Sweden, however, you are instantly identified by your dark hair. All of them are blonds there, and you have dark hair. I visited, for example, small towns in the extreme north of the country. That's where the camps were for those waiting to be granted refugee status. There, in this little town, it was a very great contrast to see these dark heads among so many blonds. It was a scene that seemed strange to them. The sensation was so strong, I myself felt very different.

Besides, the landscape was totally foreign to us: everything well made, so pretty, everything so orderly. And the *chileno*, with his "Listen, here, you son of a bitch, come on over here," shouting from one place to another—they aren't used to that kind of atmosphere. So, then, you can say that these are two different worlds. The world of order in which everyone goes out in their cars, the mass is over, they get their cars, they go home, and that's it. And these others going around town swearing up one side and down the other, the joking, the laughter, all that. You realized that this is totally different from what their world is like.

There came a time, around the 1980s, when a certain Arab or Lebanese group realized that there was a potential market and began to import things from Chile. Practically wherever you would go in Europe, there were Chileans, and in all these Arab establishments there would be jars of abalone, the mussels from the Chilean fishing boats, salmon, hard brown sugar, and they had *El Condorito* [comic book that includes political satire], Chilean newspapers and magazines.

The greatest problems for Chileans were those of adaptation—many times because of the language and the work. It was difficult for them to find work if they didn't know the language. The younger you are, the more quickly you learn it. Something very interesting: the women learned the language faster than the men—those who had contacts outside the home. Those who were shut in, no, but, normally, it was the woman who had to be the one to go to the children's school, who had to learn a whole series of things. She was the one who had to go shopping and had to begin to get oriented. On the other hand, the men continued with the mind-set from here: they went to political meetings. They went because a leader had announced that he would make a visit to the city. So, three days before, they were making preparations, they had to discuss it until all hours of the night.

The Chileans continued to have the same problems as in Chile, political differences that continued in exile. One example is when Ambassador [Harald] Edelstam died. He had been the ambassador of Sweden in Chile during the coup; he was someone who put himself at risk for the Chileans. While he was ambassador in Chile, the police shot and wounded people who were inside the embassy, and he handcuffed himself to the stretchers and accompanied them to the hospital and brought them back. When this gentleman died, we had a program in the town where I lived, and we organized it in cooperation with the Lutheran Church. Well, getting the Chileans organized meant that I had to write to each one of the groups. At that time, there were – in this little town – thirty different organizations of Chileans, thirty I had to make contact with. First, there were the individual conversations, one by one, and then with all of them together in different groups to organize the mass, a religious service in honor of this gentleman. All of us were in agreement that this was something that we had to do, but each of them wanted to say how it was to be done. So finally, I said to them: "But I am the priest. I know how I am going to do it." The problem is that all of them – each of them – wanted to use the occasion the meeting gave them to say something against the others present there or to talk about their group.

There were some eight hundred Chileans in that city. But what happened? In Sweden, the municipality gave the aid to the cultural organizations. Each Chilean party had three or four organizations. So, then, if a group has the Víctor Jara organization, the Pablo Neruda organization, or another organization, which group is it? In this case, you knew that it was the Communist Party. The Club Deportivo Barrabases, or Colo Colo, you knew who was behind them. Many times, it was the same people who were in all of them. That is, the twenty active members of the Socialist Party were the same ones who were in this cultural group, in that cultural group, in such and such a study group – so that each one of them was in competition to beat out the others, to have more events in order to get more money from the municipality.

We also found in Europe, and it was widely recognized, that the well-known people were in certain institutes: people who were important in Chile continued to be so outside. You only have to think of *Nuevo Chile* [a think tank for exiled intellectuals, which was very influential in reshaping the left's approach to politics in the post–Pinochet era] in Amsterdam. We see that, later, when they return to Chile, there they are again. They have a group of institutes, the same ones that they had in Nuevo Chile. For example, who was in the *Chile América* [see chapter 7] in Rome? They were the members of Congress, political leaders, ex-ministers, chamber presidents. There were certain groups that had a position of privilege in Chile and then again in other countries. On the contrary, the majority of

Chileans—we could say the anonymous ones—had a very different experience in exile. An exile of sacrifice, of privations, of hard times, with difficulties learning the language, in getting oriented, finding work, and living decently.

In Belgium, a friend from the air force told me, "Lucho, I don't know what to do. It is so hard for me to learn French and the worst part is that I am forgetting Spanish." He said it in a humorous way, but it was the truth. It was true for many Chileans, especially for all the people who were older when they left. For people over thirty going into exile, it is very difficult to learn the language. On the other hand, the children after three days are playing with the children who live there and they are already beginning to answer them. They are communicating; they have a facility, so that in twenty days a young person is integrated into the world of the young without any great difficulties.

Also, there were many problems of delinquency and drug addiction. That was another of the things that affected the family. If we were to analyze the things that affected families, we would find a series of factors. There is the case of drug addiction, alcoholism—even among women, which was not usual in Chile. In exile, the women felt they had rights. And this didn't just mean being liberated in the sense of changing partners, but even of fomenting lesbianism and things like that. Certain groups, in meetings of Chileans, make a big thing now out of being part of a group of lesbians. In this sense, exile affected the family a great deal.

When one starts to look around and tries to understand where all this started, you see that there is no father, mother, brother, relative, there is no one to make you ashamed. So, many things were permissible because, bad as they might be in Chile, for example if a couple is going to separate, there is always someone close to them who will say, "Think it over again, reconsider." In exile, on the other hand, it was the opposite, because there were organizations that gave them psychological support, support for women in their decisions. Then: "The best thing that you can do is to separate, go away and leave your husband." So this reinforced already difficult situations.

## Luis Peebles

*Luis Peebles was born in 1947 to a very wealthy family in Antofagasta, the largest city in Chile's northern Atacama desert and a major port for copper*

*exports. His father was the Coca Cola bottler for northern Chile, from La
Serena to Arica, and his mother a housewife. He studied in private schools
in Antofagasta and New York City, and in 1966 enrolled in the medical
school at the University of Concepción, where, like so many of his contempo-
raries, he was swept up in the ferment surrounding the founding of the
MIR. He finished a degree in psychiatric medicine and, still in Concepción
and active in the MIR, was arrested after the coup. After extensive torture
and imprisonment, Peebles was released and left for Belgium.*

*With other Latin American exiles and some Belgian colleagues, Peebles
established the Colectivo Latinoamericano de Trabajo (Latin American
Work Collective, COLAT), a self-help group of a communitarian nature
for the study and treatment of the psychological and general medical
problems of exiles and refugees. He thus not only lived the normal problems
of exiles, but observed the impact of exile on thousands of others. His views
offer valuable insights into the challenges that exile placed on the mental
and physical health of the tens of thousands of Chileans and other Latin
Americans who settled in Western Europe. Today, Dr. Peebles practices in a
psychiatric hospital in the Santiago suburbs.*

Our intervention was intended to make things easier. With our medical
tools, we tried to help people recover their health, to prevent disasters, to
prevent consequences, for example, that originate in the family, in the
woman, in the man, in the child, products of the experience of repression.

So we began to study, and we saw it in ourselves, how we lost our roles
as active members of political parties, as heads of households, of feeling
we had dignity, and became dependent on our wives, on our parents, on
our lawyers, on our torturers, on the Pro Paz Committee, on the Vicaría
de la Solidaridad. How we became children, how we went through an
inverse process of socialization and how we were transformed from
macho men to dependent beings—the complete opposite of what theoretically we think of as the strong male who knows everything and does
everything.

We had observed that women in general went though a different
process in the repression in the sense that she helped put food on the
table, she went to work for her household, to get her husband out of jail,
and she joined and organized with other women. Women had a communitarian experience, they had a political experience—an area from which,
many times, they had been marginalized until the coup. They began to
live solidly with their feet on the ground, to look around and understand

what this coup meant, what the dictatorship in Chile meant, but from another point of view—not from the point of view of having to make changes and transform the structure of the world.

Upon arriving in exile, this had repercussions. The children had been left in different places. Many times they had seen their parents arrested or had lost them, they had left their school, left their neighborhood, they had lost their dog, they had lost their toys because they had to flee, they were traumatized because their father was an "enemy of the nation." Their father had changed, he had gone from being a person of dignity to someone with no dignity, and eventually they didn't talk about their fathers; they began to be educated and socialized in a different way. This had repercussions in people's sense of self, in the role that they play in society, and in how they think about themselves. Along with another doctor, Jorge Barudi, I tried to make a contribution in this situation.

Besides the people who came to us tortured, physically or psychologically, who were very damaged and needed psychotherapy—something which we began while we were prisoners in Chile—we had a specific program for our children. At three o'clock in the afternoon, they got out of school and then they didn't have anything else to do and until six or seven, the time we got home. They ran loose, and since there were no servants in Belgium, you couldn't leave them with the maid. So we created a child-care center, a special kind of kindergarten, where we used the Montessori method, how can I explain it—our interpretation of the idea of education in an atmosphere of freedom and permissiveness that was nondirectional.

We created a school for doing homework, a kindergarten after school, which was held every day with all our children, children who were from three to four years old, up to five, six, seven, eight, ten; and then we began to have it on Wednesdays and then Saturday afternoons. We began to have workshops for the children, for our children and our friends' children, and we took turns at the beginning supervising, taking care of the children, but we took care of them by playing with them, soccer or in the sandbox, whatever, and then we began to meet with the parents. We began to talk about these things, we began to have true therapy groups for people to express themselves about the problematic situation that we were living.

We found that the Belgians, the natives, the people from there, stank— they didn't bathe during the week, just on Saturdays—they were racists; we began to impute a series of defects to them. We "blamed the dead man," as they say in Chile. In other words, we had to blame someone and so we put the blame on the people of the country. It was a defense mechanism, a way to protect ourselves, which allowed us to defend ourselves a little and keep a feeling of superiority. And besides, they contributed to it, because when one arrived as a Chilean they opened the door for you, they gave you everything — you were a hero of the resistance against the dictatorship, against fascism in Europe — and there were a series of things we experienced that were very dramatic. Because, in general, all the heroes of the jails had not been heroes at all, but rather had been atrocious traitors who had succumbed under torture, who felt enormous guilt because they had a disappeared friend that they had turned in, or because they had not been able to act as they had always thought that they were going to. Or others had fled into exile, even though the MIR had said that the MIR does not seek exile.

So this was the situation and that was how COLAT was formed, a collective where we worked as professionals, not so much as staff but rather as alter egos for our own patients who came to work, as parents of children in the workshops. They worked on a magazine, for which they wrote poetry if they wanted to, where there was freedom of expression for whatever the refugees wanted to say, open to the refugees from whatever country. In practice, we limited ourselves to Europe and, more practically, to Belgium, but we were constantly going to neighboring countries and we formed other self-help action groups in Denmark, in France, in Holland, in England, among others.

We gave COLAT, in the year 1977, the character of a health institution, where we treated and prevented health problems, especially mental health. We wanted to achieve a critical integration of refugees and European society, in which the refugee would not have to refute anything — to refuse to be integrated into society, which is the phenomenon that normally occurs.

According to the anthropologists and sociologists who have studied the phenomenon of transculturation, in order to be integrated you have to lose some of your culture of origin. So we tried to maintain a set of characteristics of the culture of origin for people, this many times by teaching elements of the culture to the children. We taught them Latin American songs, a little history, and we talked to them about a faraway country that had snow-capped mountains and about aunts and uncles and grandparents and about a set of concepts that were totally abstract to them because the children didn't know anything about them. In this way, we tried to prevent in the children the effects of transculturation, the effects of victimization as refugees, or of marginalization. Because clearly, without a doubt, we were experiencing a process of marginalization. The majority of the exiles were marginalized, certainly, so that in a certain sense we dealt with this with the children. The children had a good time, the greatest benefit was to the community itself—those who carried it out—because for them it was much more therapeutic to channel their energy into this kind of thing.

Our group was financed, at the beginning, by the Catholic University of Louvain. Amnesty International, the university parish of Louvain, and soon our principal source of funding was the organization Bread for the World, part of the World Council of Churches. Bread for the World is an NGO [nongovernmental organization] with German funding, and the World Council of Churches has its headquarters in Geneva.

In COLAT, at one point we numbered some thirty-five to forty people, half of whom were university-trained professionals; the others were not professionals, but they had received training. The majority were Latin Americans and Belgians, and then maybe someone from Holland, and then perhaps a German, and suddenly they began to come from all over.

I have the impression that women when they go into exile—in contrast to men—have been able to acquire some tools that men haven't been able to. For example, a certain greater independence, a certain greater ability to confront the problem, and when they got here and didn't know how to speak the language, it didn't seem to bother them and they went out and swept floors and cleaned houses. The man who, generally, has come out of jail and has been received as a hero can't, usually, go out and clean floors, so the women went out to clean floors and began to learn to speak the language and the men stayed at home taking care of the children. This is a job that they had never learned in Argentina, Chile, Uruguay, and Brazil that there they had to take care of. So then, they felt that exile was, in some sense, a continued punishment, a consequence of the repression. This continuing moral stance as a political prisoner or as a fugitive in Latin America became there something that attacked their very identity as a person and also imperiled the identity of the nuclear family. This, because looking at the man and the woman as two distinct people—they had been separated in 1973 and reunited in 1978 or 1980 or whenever, and they took a new look at each other and they were different, they were two people who had evolved inside in different directions.

The children adapted immediately. They learned the language quickly and they began to be crutches for their parents, for a childlike father that used his children to ask where such and such a street was, to be a mediator with their surroundings. And when there was no father present, the child still played this role for the mother, who replaced the absent father with one of the children as a substitute. These phenomena created dysfunctional families and created a number of problems. This was a common characteristic in all the places of exile.

Another of the consequences of exile was the great number of separations that occurred. In a tally that we made one time using patients' registration cards — which, of course, is not a systematic count made over a long period of time — there were some 43 percent of the couples separated. My impression is that it was even higher and that, in general, it could be even twice as high, that is to say, 80 percent — this in Belgium. In exile, I separated from my wife. I found a new relationship there, my wife found a new relationship — each of us had children with our new spouse. I think that this is a very typical case — it is a typical case of destruction of the family. And it doesn't end there, because when I got back to Chile my mother was dead and I had left my two older children in exile.

## Miriam Casanova

*Miriam Casanova (introduced in chapter 2) settled initially in Poland with her family, before moving in 1975 to Ferrara, Italy, a city of some 150,000 in the northern Emilia-Romagna region, where her Italian-descended husband had relatives and contacts. While Italy was a relatively congenial host country, from Casanova's perspective, she was forced to make important adjustments in domestic and cultural life. Her experience in exile illustrates some of those changes as well as the development of new perspectives on Chile and Latin America.*

In spite of the fact that my husband had relatives, we stayed at the home of some friends while we looked for someplace to live. We didn't have any money, my parents had sent some from Chile so that we could survive. With that, we covered the basic necessities. The Poles gave us some bedclothes, which were the bedclothes that we had. In Ferrara, we bought some mattresses and we slept on the floor at first. We didn't have a table, we didn't have chairs, we began little by little — I who had been comfortably off in Chile and had never lacked for anything. We had always had a maid who did the heavy things; besides, I was rather spoiled and never did anything in my house. I think that I have never worked so hard in my life as I did during that period in Italy. In Warsaw we worked, but everything

was easier. In Italy, we experienced poverty at the beginning, lack of resources, great consumerism, and little money. I even washed the household linens and, besides, worked in the music field.

I did a good deal of solidarity work for Chile—my husband supported
us because he earned a large enough salary for us to live on. I made trips
all through Italy for several years. I also taught some classes, I worked with
children with mental handicaps and worked with preschool teachers—I
was in charge of the games, music. I learned all the folkloric music for
children and I taught them to Italian girls who didn't know how to sing—
they didn't know their own songs. I taught Italian folklore to people from
Ferrara.

People in Europe don't have household help, except for the rich; the
most that the middle class can have is someone who comes once a week to
do housecleaning, and that's it. I had to go along with this, but I also think
that we kept the same roles; we are lucky in that we have always been a
couple, in this sense, with a good deal of freedom.

My husband changed for the better as far as housework, because he
didn't know how to boil water, and there, many times when I wasn't there,
he had to take care of things and he learned to help out at home—I would
say that this was one of the few positive things about our exile. More cooperation from a husband like mine who had been comfortably off. And
that because the situation in Chile was different, one was able to pay
someone to do things. I had never done anything before either, because in
my house when I was little we had a servant, my mother was at home; I
spent my time on other things outside the house and didn't do anything at
home, but that was something very common among the middle class in
Chile. I don't know if this is true in all the countries of Latin America. In
contrast, in Europe one learns about the double shift that women work.
In Europe you learn that women have jobs and also work at home and
take care of the children, and so forth. It is a very self-sacrificing life for
women. I think that with the young couples, we were seeing for the first
time a kind of couple with more participation from the man. In general,
at our age, also having had a rather machista education, the roles were
very much the man, the master of the house, and the woman, the one who
has to do the household tasks.

I think that Ferrara was a very difficult city, very small, very provincial,
and very closed. A city that had been isolated for centuries. It is true that
more toward the south life was more pleasant for Chileans, even for the
Chileans who lived in Rome—and the majority went to Rome, they felt
very comfortable in the Roman life of that period. There, the people were

much more open. The Roman was more like us, more communicative, more accustomed to dealing with the outside world, with foreigners.

My husband managed to get Italian citizenship, so that we also got Italian citizenship, but not because we asked for it, but rather because it was automatic. But the truth is that we always lived like Chileans. It may have made things a little easier for my husband, besides my husband already spoke Italian perfectly when he arrived; since he was a child he had gone to Italian schools, they spoke Italian at home, so this helped him to integrate better than we did, who lived in a world of foreigners, of Latin Americans.

Another interesting thing: I never learned so much about Latin America as I did in Italy. Everything I learned about Latin America had never even entered my head when I was in Chile. Learning about the Latin American world allowed me to learn about the culture of other countries, it allowed me to think of myself as Latin American—because in Chile you think of yourself as Chilean—and they said the same about us, they said— the Central Americans who were there, the Nicaraguans, the Venezuelans, the Colombians, and so forth—said that they had also learned about Chile through this contact. Because after the coup, many Chileans went to Venezuela, too. A whole world opened, but the truth is that the condition of being Latin American, you feel it there, and when you realize the number of things that we have in common with other countries, that is impressive too, isn't it?

## Astrid Stoehrel

*Astrid Stoehrel was twenty-two years of age in 1973. Her father, a wealthy industrialist living in Concepción, owned one of Chile's largest textile plants, the Fábrica de Paños Bío-Bío, and her mother managed the household. After a divorce her mother finished an interrupted education and moved to Arica, Chile's northernmost city, taking the teenaged Astrid along. Astrid took a degree in early childhood education at the University of Chile, Arica, where she subsequently obtained a teaching position. An independent leftist, she was married to a MIRista who was arrested after the coup. Upon the husband's release from prison in 1975, they left with their young daughter for Ireland, and after nine months moved on to Sweden to join other members of Stoehrel's family in exile.*

*Home to the largest Chilean exile community in Europe—at least thirty thousand in the 1980s—as well as to refugees from all corners of the globe,*

*Sweden offered policies and programs that gave Chileans an enviable level of economic comfort and educational opportunity.\* Moreover, Sweden had formally declared itself a "multicultural nation" in recognition of the results of its generous immigration policy. Yet while making life comfortable, Swedes did little to assimilate their guests, who commonly associated more with other refugees than with their hosts. Returning to Chile in 1993, Stoehrel experienced the family fragmentation so common among exiles and returnees: she had divorced, and her daughter stayed behind in Sweden. She now works part-time at the Organización Internacional para las Migraciones (OIM) in Santiago.*

We got to Sweden in 1976. At this time, the state provided 240 hours of language study. While you studied Swedish, you were paid for this. It was enough to live on; in Sweden, there is always enough to live on. After these 240 hours were finished, both of us applied immediately to continue studying Swedish in the university and for this there are study loans, and you can also live on those. The study of Swedish is not that difficult; it doesn't take a long time to learn, but you never learn it correctly. What makes the most difference is practice and we were all lacking in that. Swedish society is rather difficult, it is rather closed; so then there were few opportunities to practice.

It is very difficult to make close friendships with Swedes. At the beginning one is most friendly with the professor of the course, but after that, it's a long time. When I was studying Swedish in the university, all my classmates were also refugees or immigrants — Latin Americans from Argentina, Uruguay, but there were also Kurds, Turks, Arabs from different countries. So you have more contact with these people and not with the Swedes.

Then I began to study education, and then I realized that the Swedish that I had learned was really pretty rudimentary. So I decided to try to work for a time to be able to better solidify my command of it. I worked for seven years as a preschool teacher in a kindergarten. In 1984, I decided that I didn't want to work with children any longer and I began to study a totally different field in the University of Stockholm, a degree in social sciences with a specialization in research in intercultural relations and migration problems. I finished that in early 1988 and then went to work at the Office of Refugees and Immigrants of the city of Stockholm.

---

\* Patricio Orellana, "Exilio y desexilio" (unpublished, 1991), Vicaría de la Solidaridad, 220.

My husband did a thousand things, all the jobs that were typical for the refugees there; for example, cleaning, taking care of old people in a home at night, working in a mental hospital, driving trucks, delivering newspapers, doing auto repair, painting. He is also a musician and he spent a lot of time forming bands, first of Chilean folkloric music, but later salsa and merengue.

I think that in Sweden the salaries are more or less equal; there is little difference between skilled and nonskilled jobs. Besides, there are subsidies, so you never drop in level, because there is a minimum that the state sets each year. We had a lifestyle similar to that of the majority of the Swedes. The apartments are all very well equipped there; we lived like the Swedes — there was no great difference as far as material conditions. We managed to get a car, we took vacations in southern Europe like the Swedes; in Spain, principally because of the language.

There were different forms of discrimination. My physical appearance is not so clearly Chilean as that of the majority of those who were there, and for this reason, that discrimination — in fact, because of being physically different from the rest — I didn't experience it. There were many who were asked for their papers just because of the way that they looked, and because of that, they had to always have their identity cards with them. Many people wouldn't sit next to them in the subway, for example, or on the buses; the Swedes wouldn't sit next to a foreigner — this kind of thing. Where I felt the discrimination most was in the working situation — if you apply and a Swedish person is also applying, it is very unusual for you to get the job; you will be in second or third place. In this aspect, I did note quite a bit of discrimination.

We did not live with the famous syndrome of packed suitcases. I think that really that is a defense mechanism that one has, denying the wish to go back. So it is better to say, "Well, for as long as this lasts . . . " And, anyway, that's the way that it was: we didn't go back even for vacations. We criticized harshly the people who had left because of Pinochet and, nevertheless, went back to Pinochet on vacation. I remember when we had just arrived, a Swedish friend shows me a school near where we live and says to me, "This is where your daughter will go." My daughter was three years old and they begin there at seven. I said, "In four more years, I won't be here, I will have already left." That is, we never thought that it would last so long.

The majority of women who were married in Chile and depended economically on their husbands had the opportunity there to become independent economically, and with that, then, a world of other doors opened.

There was also a kind of change of roles in which the women became stronger, when you suppose that culturally and historically it is the man who has been strongest here. This made many question their relationships and finally decide that they could also live alone, that they could also have another life and be better off. I think that, fundamentally, this was, at least in part, the reason for separations.

Later there is something else. Swedish women like the Latin type, and the men were very successful because of this. But Chilean men are quite possessive, exclusive, and Swedish women aren't. So, at the beginning, many men left their Chilean wives — they went off with Swedish women, thinking that they were going to form the same kind of relationship, and finally, after a few months, realized that they weren't. The Swedish women threw them out and when they wanted to come back to the Chilean women, the *chilenas* didn't want them to. On the other hand, Swedish men were a little afraid of Latin women because behind the chilenas there was a whole family; it wasn't just the Chilean woman alone.

As far as keeping up the Chilean culture in my daughter, I tried when she was small, because later it is harder to put her in a folkloric song and dance group, so that she would share that experience, and for the language. At the same time, the government tried to create classes in the native language in the state schools. So my daughter always had, besides her other classes, two to four hours weekly of Spanish. The family got together for Christmas, New Year's, birthdays, and we prepared Chilean food, although later on we incorporated Swedish things, because it was more practical, much easier, much quicker.

Since there are so many groups of immigrants in Sweden, you stopped seeing the problem of Chile as the only one. At that time, you saw the whole process that Nicaragua was going through, then El Salvador. I also got involved in that more than just in the Chilean situation.

The truth is that it was hard to get used to the winter. Not so much the cold, because, after all, I think that here in Santiago it is colder than it was there, because there all the houses are heated, the buses are heated, everything is heated. That is, you get cold the moment you set foot outside the house to catch the bus and go to work, but the buses there operate on a schedule, so that you know that the bus will come by at five to eight and it comes at five to eight, so that you don't have to be standing there. But it is the darkness, the darkness is awful. There is very little light: the sun comes up at 8:00, at 8:30 the light begins to appear, and by 3:00 it is already totally dark and that is long. I had a friend who said to me, "I love

Sweden but I don't like the cold, nor the winter, nor the dark, nor the Swedish people."

There are things about exile that change you for the rest of your life. For example, my daughter stayed there. I do not know if she will have the desire to return and try it here. This is something that is very objective and concrete that will affect me forever, even wondering whether she will come. Anyway, I have to acknowledge that what drew me back here, the twenty-four years that I lived here, are the smells, the landscape, the colors—in short, all of that which for me is so strong here; for her it is there.

Eighteen years there was practically my whole adult life. I got used to many things that Swedish society provides: work itself, job security, punctuality, schedules, work relationships, respect for the individual. This is something that impressed me from the very first moment: the lack of hierarchy that exists when compared especially with this country and, I suppose, also with the rest of Latin America. These are the kinds of things that are hard to accept again, that, even so, you would still like to try to change.

## Luis Ortega

*Luis Ortega was born in Valparaíso in 1950. His mother was a housewife and his father a career customs officer and member of the Radical Party. Ortega studied in private schools in Viña del Mar and finished public high school in 1967, two years after joining the Socialist Party's youth organization. At the University of Chile in Valparaíso he became active in student politics, serving for a term as president of the Chilean Student Federation (FECh) in Valparaíso. This prominence as a student leader made him a target, and he was arrested two days after the coup and sentenced by a military court to five years and one day for possession of arms and other alleged crimes. Ortega remembers vividly the response of the admiral who presided at his trial to the defense's argument that the alleged crimes had occurred prior to the declaration of the state of internal war on September 11, 1973, and thus were not covered by junta decrees: "Mister Attorney, you must understand that the war began on September 4, 1970"—the day of Allende's election.*

*Paroled after a few months, Ortega did underground work for his party, but feared additional persecution. Advised by friends to leave, he obtained a World University Service (WUS) scholarship to complete his university studies in England and left for exile in March 1975. Owing to his own decisions and determination, his exile was markedly different from the common patterns among Chileans in Western Europe. He returned to Chile in 1985 with a doctorate in history, and today is a professor at the Universidad de Santiago de Chile.*

I think that the feeling of guilt that I had began the day that I decided to leave Chile because, at this time, the motto of the compañeros of MIR was "The MIR does not seek asylum," and because some of my Socialist compañeros said that the first act of resistance is to stay. I remember that many times my British friends who ran the center for the reception of refugees and those from the solidarity campaign would invite us in the evening to have a beer at a pub, and I remember having said many nights, "No, thank you," because it was very hard for me to enjoy myself knowing that in Chile there were compañeros who were prisoners, compañeros who were in the hands of the DINA, that there were compañeros without work and that many people — because I had experienced it — were living in fear. I also believed very strongly that I had to take advantage of the opportunity that I had been given, and because of that I committed myself to studying English very hard.

In June or July of 1975, there was a meeting of the party. It was the first time that I saw Carlos Altamirano [head of the Socialist Party during the UP government and leader of its left wing] after the coup. We thought that the economic crisis, the split within the armed forces, the international pressure, and the resistance would put an end to the regime very soon. I remember that Altamirano said in that meeting that, besides our being defeated, we had to get used to the idea that this was going to be a very long process, ten to fifteen years. This really depressed me, but it was at that moment that I said, "I have to live like the English, because if I am going to be here for so long I have to do what they do — if not, then I am going to fail." And that was very important because in September I went to the university and made the very important decision to separate myself socially from the Chilean community. I kept up a very intense political work until the year 1979, when the party split, but except for a friend, the son of my compañero Armando Barrientos, I decided not to socialize with the Chilean community, except for the events on September 11 and 18 [September 11 is the anniversary of the coup and September 18 is Chilean Independence Day] or a party or two, but not to have Chilean friends but rather English ones. I was very criticized, but I think that it was the right decision because I adapted very well. There are people, some of my British friends, who say that I am as English as the best of the Englishmen. I broke with my Chilean identity, I decided to be British, and that was hard for me.

The British are a very complicated people, very closed, but I discovered that once they accept you they include you in the group, and they consider you a friend. They are great friends. I went to live in the southeast part of London, in a working-class neighborhood. There, I made very good friends at a social club that was run by the Labour Party and the Communists. Later, I started to play soccer; I integrated socially in an area where there were no other Chileans, and I made good friends. Then my life began to revolve around English things, like going on Saturday afternoons to the stadium to watch soccer. I decided to end this thing of living in Chile and in exile at the same time; I ended much of my correspondence with Chile, except with my parents and one or two friends, and I centered my life there.

I had a scholarship that allowed me to live very well. I always wanted to do things, I wanted to go places that I had studied about when I was a student in the first and second years of history—to Egypt, to Greece. So, with other classmates in King's College, I entered into what is the work circuit on Friday, Saturday, and sometimes on Sunday, and there were many opportunities. One was to go count boxes in some factory, but there were other better ones because, besides the money they paid, you could eat free, and one of these was to be a waiter at a restaurant. Near the university, there was a kind of employment bureau and I got my first job there as a waiter in an Italian restaurant, a huge restaurant with four or five floors where there were very good tips; you could eat a lot and it was enjoyable. In this restaurant and others in which I worked later, I ended up working as an assistant in the kitchen. Later, I worked in a Spanish restaurant in my neighborhood, afterward in a Greek restaurant downtown, and in a series of restaurants—which allowed me to learn a good deal about international cuisine and allowed me to save the money with which to finance my trips to Greece, to Italy, and after, in 1978, I discovered Spain—although I am not Catholic, after seeing the Holy Week processions in the year 1978, I always went to Spain in Holy Week.

With Leonardo León, beginning in 1980, I edited the journal *Nueva Historia*, which was a project that allowed us to attract and concentrate on what was being done historiographically in foreign countries about Chile. In England, at one point, there were around fifteen of us historians, doing our doctoral or Master's theses. We went to the World University Service and they told us that they were willing to help us as much as they could. Later, at the Institute of Latin American Studies at the University of London, we talked with John Lynch and Harold Blakemore and they were very enthusiastic and supported us. We thought that this was the weapon, the means that we had, that would allow us to go back to Chile, at some moment to reintegrate ourselves in Chile. What's more, we named it *Nueva Historia* thinking of the journal *Historia* of the Catholic University of Chile, where the historiographic right was gathered, and a little, I would say, to bother them. *Nueva Historia* became a historiographic phenomenon of exile that was very interesting because it represented, in some way, my identity as a Chilean that was reborn in me through the journal. We stopped publication in 1989; it ended with the end of the dictatorship.

## Mónica Pilquil

*Mónica Pilquil's parents were Mapuche Indians who had migrated from the heavily indigenous zone around Temuco to the capital, where her father ran a shoe-repair business. Born in 1953, she grew up in the working-class district of Quinta Normal, studied in public schools, and became a political activist in leftist student organizations. After the coup she worked on the fringes of the resistance; one of her sisters was arrested and her compañero, by whom she was pregnant, disappeared after being arrested in July 1974. For the next three years she underwent the depressing but common routine of looking everywhere—police stations, military bases, prisons, hospitals, morgues—for her compañero, and joined with other women in the* Agrupación de Familiares de Detenidos Desaparecidos (*Organization of Relatives of the Detained, Disappeared), sponsored by the Vicaría de la Solidaridad of the Archbishopric of Santiago. She also did volunteer work for CIME in getting people out of Chile.*

*Mónica Pilquil's situation grew dangerous when her association with an anti-regime group was discovered, and with the aid of CIME she left for Holland with her young son in October 1977, to join her sister in exile. She approached exile without illusions. She broke away from her compatriots, mingled with other Latin American exiles, married a Dutch man, and returned to Chile in the agitated year of 1985, only to return to Holland. Never abandoning her ethnicity, she became a founder of a pan-European Mapuche exile organization formed in the 1980s. A widow with two children, Mónica Pilquil runs a bakery in Cerro Navia, one of Santiago's poorest districts.*

I went to France first. It was so terrible to arrive there. Everything was so strange—it was like going from one landscape to another, a different world, people who talked differently. My sister and my brother-in-law had come to meet us, and then I remember that we slept in the home of some Chileans who lived in a big group there together in one house, because it was really expensive, I think. They rented the house for one family, then several got together, and there we were and I remember that my brother-in-law told jokes about Chile and people were really listening, like they were nostalgic to hear things about Chile. My son was three and a half years old then, and from there we left for Holland, which was even stranger. I began to look at faces and I said, "Some dark, some blond." And then, when we went up to the apartment, people were looking at us. There in the apartment, my sister and my brother-in-law begin to tell me, they say to me: "We are glad that you've come." I told them that I was sad that I had come, but that, even so, I believe that it is important for me to come, because what else am I going to do? I went with a great desire to do things.

The people of Holland welcomed us. There were never problems having to do with the people. I got to know Holland from one end to the other.

I began to get in touch with the compañeros from the MIR. I was denouncing the situation of the disappeared. The MIR invited me since they knew I was a MIRista. They took me to different cities in Holland so that I could tell and relate what it meant to have someone disappeared and what you did, how you struggled. In this period, you couldn't do much, but anyway, I told them about it. From that, I began to get to know all the compañeros who were in exile. I saw them all the same, it didn't matter to me if they were Socialists, Communists, and that is what I have always said to my son, "Don't worry about such things, be very open."

Later, the compañeros of the MIR wanted me to give the same speeches and also to sing and, on top of that, to make empanadas and *pan amasado* [kneaded bread]. "No," I said, "that's enough." I remember that one day I was going to sing, and fortunately I had a sore throat, and I spent that day thinking. I said, "These guys really think they are hot stuff, well, and who do they think I am?" So, after that, I began to think, and I said to myself, "I am not going to do what they want." I kind of began to rebel: "I am not going to involve myself much with the Chileans, I am going to be more open than that." And I began to meet the Peruvians, the Bolivians. They told me their problems, how they had left. I met the Montoneros [members of the largest Argentine urban guerrilla group, defeated by 1979; survivors went into exile], the whole range of exiles, because we took classes together and the Latins got together. I worked at a Bolivian restaurant. I learned to make Bolivian food, to serve it. I liked it. Chileans came there, Latinos.

They gave us classes in the Dutch language, but learning Dutch is a psychological matter. When I was feeling good, it seemed like I understood everything and I talked — I talked a lot — and then somehow it got harder. So there were years in which I understood more than other years, and it depended on my mental state. I took a long time to learn it really well, some five years to learn Dutch well. I also studied to be a social worker. I studied in an academy with contacts in Latin America. That's why I liked it, that's why I wanted to learn.

I always asked myself, "Why am I not in Chile? Why am I here?" Economically I was fine. I missed my compañero, of course, and I always wondered what I was doing in exile when I could have been looking for my compañero in Chile. I was really very much in love with him — imagine, we had been married for five months and they took him away. I can't say that I haven't gotten offers of marriage, or to live with other compañeros, a whole bunch of things, but I was totally closed to that and I didn't want to be used, I didn't want anything. I felt very committed to the Chilean cause and, like I tell you, I got involved with the situation in El Salvador. In the year 1981, I met my compañero who was my second husband. He was Dutch. His name was Vicente.

In the year 1985 I came back to Chile for an internship in social work. I was the social worker for the Agrupación de Familiares de Detenidos Desaparecidos. It was a terrible period, because there were lots of deaths, lots of protests. Well, Paul was born in Chile in 1985 and we returned to Holland with him three weeks later. That's why he says, "I was born here, but I am from there."

It is interesting that when I came to Chile for the internship, I arrived with a new compañero here. Then all those in the Agrupación begin to talk about me: "She has another one, she's already forgotten about her compañero." I remember that one day I had to sit all my compañeras down and say to them: "Look, you bitches, it's true that I have a compañero, but this compañero knows what happened to me, I am young, I am living a different moment. It's true that my compañero is disappeared, and if he appears then we will deal with it ourselves. I don't know if my disappeared compañero will want to live with me later, or if I will want to live with him—I don't know what is going to happen, but, meanwhile, I am living, I am alive, it's another period of my life, and he accompanies me and is with me, and, in fact, he came with me here to work with you"—because he was a foreign press correspondent.

And he began to take photos and we went to all the protests. I was arrested some three times that year. I was in the protests of the year 1985, that is, at the time of the *"degollados"* [the case of the "degollados" refers to members of the underground central committee of the Communist Party who were kidnapped and killed by security forces, who cut their throats]. There was also the case of a disappeared person that I had to deal with when I was doing the internship, and due to this I was taken prisoner too, so many things. And being pregnant with Paul. The bunch of women started to notice. "Damn, if this girl isn't something," and one of them said, "This compañera, all the times that she has been arrested and, really, she has shown that she is with us, and that's good. Her compañero has always shown that he is very committed." And then they began to accept me.

They also became fond of Vicente, they called him Jesus because he was so beautiful. But they said to me: "You all in exile have it easy, you have a good economic situation." Then I felt bad, because I told them that I didn't have it that easy, that for me it had been torture to go into exile, to get used to a new world, torture knowing that they were there fighting and I couldn't be with them. But I also realized that in exile we are also fighting, we do other things and the world isn't so small; that is, it isn't only the Chileans but also the Salvadorans, the Nicaraguans, the Bolivians, the Argentines, and the whole world has the same problem that we have. I feel Latin American now, I don't feel Chilean. I told them a little bit about the experience that we had with the guerrillas from El Salvador. When I studied to be a social worker, I did an internship with the Committee for El Salvador and my compañero and I organized a peña. I sang with him and we didn't hire artists, because that way we could get more money to send to the guerrillas since the Dutch government didn't want to send money to the guerrillas; it didn't agree with that. So we put ourselves at risk for them. I told them that experience and that I don't feel quite so Chilean any longer but rather Latin American.

I thought on the way back to Holland: "It was like a new exile to be back in Chile in the year 1985. I feel bad, I want to go back again." And I began to feel anguished and I was constantly thinking about it. And my compañero was so good to me, I remember, that he made me a brazier, he lit coal on the balcony and bought a bottle of wine, and we felt like we were in Chile. We began to say, "Listen, do you remember when the Flaco [nickname, which means "thin"] was taking pictures and a cop hit him on the rear end," Vicente said to me. We started to remember everything that had happened during that year. I felt really bad then.

Back in Holland in 1986, we formed what we called the Foreign Mapuche Committee. I was the treasurer of this Foreign Committee. We would meet, we had a headquarters in Holland, we met two or three times a year. Sometimes we met in Sweden or in Germany, but usually it was in Amsterdam. There were some five hundred or six hundred Mapuches in Europe, all over. We formed this committee because the Mapuches felt different, they felt that in exile people treated them better than in Chile. In fact, there were plenty of festivals. We had a musical group in Holland that I sang in—there were four of us. I was the only woman and we dressed like Mapuches and I appeared in a tape on television. I always sang Mapuche music.

We had a publication, it was called *ADMAPU*. This was because we agreed with the political ideas of ADMAPU, which was the political organization that existed in Chile during the dictatorship [from the Mapuche meaning "essence of the earth"; founded in the mid-1980s]. They had their struggle against the dictatorship too. They were demanding autonomy, the return of their lands, respect for their religion. The Chilean exiles were happy that the committee was formed. They felt proud, they supported it, they always welcomed us.

# SEVEN

# Political Life in Exile

## Fighting the Dictatorship from Afar

Mass exile was key to the armed forces' objectives of gaining and holding absolute, uncontested control over Chile. Yet exile turned out to be a double-edged sword, for while it removed the bulk of the active left from the country it also gave regime opponents the means to disseminate their message throughout the world and mount a vigorous campaign to deny the military regime the legitimacy it sought. Upon arriving at their destinations, militants of the Socialist and Communist parties, the MIR, and even the smaller MAPU established local party units wherever a handful of coreligionists were found, and regional, national, and international entities soon followed. The national labor organization, the Central Unica de Trabajadores (CUT), and the UP also recreated their institutional structures, and in a matter of months the Chilean left had been replicated in dozens of countries around the world. Along with the institutions were transplanted the fissures that had divided the left along party and factional lines, exacerbated by the post–coup blame-laying. While these divisions gave rise to rivalry and occasional acrimony, they were not so deep as to undermine the exiles' common political mission.

At the local level the political groups carried out organizational activities, disseminated information on Chile, organized marches and demonstrations, held peñas, or political gatherings with typical food, wine, and protest music, and made and sold empanadas to raise money and consciousness. As a result of the latter activity, the traditional empanada, a meat and onion pie of humble origins, became the universal symbol of Chilean exile and the struggle against Pinochet. One exile claims that there was a serious discussion of erecting a monument to the empanada.* And Ana Laura Cataldo recalls of her Canadian exile, "I worked in the solidarity movement for Chile. We made 500 empanadas every Saturday to collect money and be able to send it to the women in Chile. We sold empanadas to our friends by telephone, and we delivered them to their houses. I must confess that since I came back to Chile, I have not made another empanada and I don't plan to ever make another in my life."†

One of the most important tasks was to mobilize support among the citizens of the host countries for the campaign against Pinochet. The worldwide prominence of the UP experiment, the respected figure of Salvador Allende, and the brutality of the coup and subsequent repression had created receptive audiences in many countries whom the exiles sought to organize in mixed committees of Chileans and sympathetic nationals. Some of these committees were general, while others were built around existing organizations of students, labor, left parties, and human-rights advocates. These groups were quite often effective in lobbying their governments to condemn Chile in international forums and to support high-profile campaigns for the release of selected political prisoners in Chile.

Exiled leaders of the UP parties operated at a different level from the rank and file. In addition to overseeing their organizations, they were active in soliciting support among world political and government leaders. Some were active in existing international political organizations, and others in *sui generis* organizations focused on Chile — in both cases working to secure diplomatic and large-scale financial support for the exiled opposition and ultimately for the restoration of democracy in Chile.

The exiles' mission of creating an effective international opposition to the military government was a difficult one, despite the widespread sympathy for Allende and his government. The Chilean economic "miracle,"

---

* Almeyda, *Reencuentro con mi vida*, 279.
† Interview, June 26, 1994.

which began in 1977, made Pinochet the darling of the powerful business sectors of the countries whose loans and investments fueled the economic growth, and for whom a few human-rights violations were a small price to pay for the new opportunities opened to them by the military regime. Thus, in the developed capitalist countries there were countervailing views of Chile and competing interests at work to influence governments' policies toward the Pinochet dictatorship.

The exiles' success in keeping the regime's dark side in the news and the public consciousness and in achieving repeated condemnations of the regime in international forums is testimony to the dedication, persever-ance, and skill of the uprooted left. The survival of a small opposition movement inside Chile, the limited but significant opening of the regime in the mid-1980s, and ultimately the victory of democratic forces in the 1988 plebiscite on Chile's political future can be attributed, in no small measure, to the efforts of the exiles, including those who returned to con-tinue at home the political work begun abroad.

## Julio Pérez

*Julio Pérez (introduced in chapter 3), a former member of the MIR who went to Canada in 1974, experienced exile politics at the grass roots. In Montreal, home to thousands of exiles, the parties and spinoff organizations mounted activities of all types to raise funds and consciousness among their hosts. The intensity and variety of political life in exile are reflected in Pérez's testimony.*

Upon my arrival in Montreal, in May of 1974, there were already the be-ginnings of a movement to reorganize the political parties. Until that mo-ment, the solidarity with Chile was directed by a group of Canadian and American priests and nuns who had been expelled from Chile and who had gone to Quebec. They knew the medium well and were the first to mobilize along with religious organizations, unions, political parties, and community groups of that province.

The Chileans formed different organizations, reproducing in a small way the outline of the political structure that existed in Chile. Unidad Popular organized around the Chilean Association in Montreal, the peo-ple who supported the MIR around the Bureau of Political Prisoners, which was affiliated with similar organizations that existed in the rest of the world and whose principal task was to get political prisoners released. Independently of these groups, there were the traditional Chilean parties of the left, now with the aggravating factor of the great splintering that took place in exile.

The tasks were many: to sensitize the representatives of different organizations so that they would sponsor specific political prisoners and put pressure on the Chilean embassy in Ottawa, so that there would be lawyers to defend them, to verify their status as prisoners and to try to get them visas to get into Canada.

There were constant street demonstrations that ended up at the Chilean consulate in Montreal or at the Chilean embassy in Ottawa. Support of leading Canadian figures was obtained, so that they would send letters to the Chilean ambassador in Ottawa, to the United Nations, to judges in Chile and important members of the military regime, demanding that the prisoners be released. The same thing was done with thousands and thousands of signatures that were sent to the Secretary General of the United Nations and of the OAS.

Also, there was the uphill battle to keep the Chileans in the country informed. We used as a source of information the telephone books from different cities in Chile. Pages were distributed around the world and envelopes sent constantly with information as to what was really happening in the country. In that period, the censorship that the dictatorship exercised on the media was strict. In each form of media, there was a censor who censored any information that could harm the image of the dictatorship.

Solidarity committees were created in universities, high schools, and industries, and in this work we traveled to different towns and cities in Quebec. We organized informational programs and debates about the situation in Chile. Also, there was an intense effort to work closely with Amnesty International and the Red Cross of Canada and with the Canadian political parties — like the New Democratic Party and the Québécois Party in the province of Quebec. These parties sent representatives on numerous occasions to Chile to get more in-depth information on the situation or to try to get some prisoners released.

On several occasions, along with the Canadian unions, we carried out extensive campaigns to boycott the distribution of wine and other Chilean products that were on the market. Also, we tried to prevent the defense industry in that country from sending parts or machinery to Chile.

Pratt and Whitney was one of these aerospace companies that did business with the Chilean air force, sending spare parts and aircraft and helicopter engines.

Collecting money was a very important task and the results were impressive. The solidarity of the people of Quebec toward the Chilean resistance was very great. The union central committees often gave instructions to their members to contribute an hour's salary for the struggle in Chile; this fact alone meant a great deal of money. They also offered material support and facilities for copying newsletters and magazines, for holding meetings or peñas.

Nevertheless, and in a seeming paradox, I think that the solidarity of the Chileans in Canada was limited to a small group — I would say, a tiny group. Those who were really concerned about what was happening in the country and did the thousands of tasks were always a very small number. Many of the exiles even refused to buy magazines, newspapers, or newsletters that were put together with great effort to try to keep the Chileans outside the country informed. This seemed to me to show a lack of solidarity on their part, when the majority of them worked and lived in even better material conditions than they had in Chile. Nevertheless, in the peñas and the fiestas, where there was good music, many empanadas and wine, there was always a large crowd.

Another task of the groups organized in exile was to collect tons of clothes, shoes, and supplies needed for work that were sent to the churches in the lower-class neighborhoods in Chile, to be distributed to those most in need.

## Eduardo Montecinos

*The political activity of Eduardo Montecinos (introduced in chapter 6) in Costa Rica shows a different and unusual approach to fighting the dictatorship from abroad. Despite a lengthy affiliation with and leadership roles in the Socialist Party, he was disturbed by the replication in exile of the Chilean left, with all its inter- and intra-party fissures. He and a group of like-minded exiles opted to take advantage of Costa Rica's political system — open, democratic, but with a weak labor movement and left — by creating a nonpartisan organization to lobby the government and public opinion against Pinochet, focusing on human rights and democracy, and eschewing many of the usual forms of exile political activity.*

In my case and that of many of my friends, we never believed in party activity by remote control. We could be sympathetic to the Chilean parties, but we couldn't be active party members in Costa Rica; rather, we needed to integrate into that country—this is the activity that we wanted. So then, that created a great separation from the other, more orthodox groups that met as Socialists, as Communists, and so forth.

Different organizations were formed. There were activities to collect money, for whatever purpose, with many problems because of the internal conflicts within each political party and the big differences that could come up between them, but at the same time, it was natural that people would organize around the parties. In each flight that came to Costa Rica, it made sense to determine which group was closest to them so that they would help them or help them find a place to live. Then, it was a natural thing that if they came with some link to the MIR that they would hook up with the people from the MIR and that if they came with some connection to one of the groups of the Socialist Party that they would hook up with that group. As a result, there was not a homogeneous group, but rather there were groups that helped or provided connections.

This form of organization was important because of the lack of confidence that grew up around a person if that person could not show in some way what connections they had, or where they had been active, because imagine the number of people who came here for adventure, for economic reasons. There was, for example, someone who came from the Gran Avenida of Santiago [a major north–south artery in Santiago, known for cheap shops and constant hustle], who first brought a friend from the left, and later, the friends from the left brought their mother, sister, cousin. So that it was very hard to determine which were political problems and which weren't. That is one of the problems that even made you act very cautiously, even rather egotistically at times, in not opening yourself up immediately to people you didn't know very much about.

We were a group that did not believe in this division of labor based on political parties, rather that what united us were concrete solidarity efforts. So we created an organization that was called *Por Chile* [For Chile]—very large—that included Costa Ricans in our solidarity work. We had cultural events, even in the National Theater several times, which resulted not only in a presence but something deeper in the Costa Rican reality, going beyond a "marriage" with the leftist groups of Costa Rica and including the entire Costa Rican society. This was the great difference, I would say, in our solidarity work. Later, the few funds of the Por

Chile group were assigned without any political interest. At one point, we helped the poblaciones in Chile; at another, we helped the groups that asked the most for help, like at another point, we helped Almeyda's [Clodomiro Almeyda, leader of one of the two major rival factions of the Socialist Party] party, with which I had no ties nor any desire to have a relationship. But we were able in some way to provide this small help. I don't think that the amount mattered that much. At one point, those internal differences in the Chilean colony, especially because of the funds, meant that almost every group or faction of the parties had its own link or tried to have this link with Chile with respect to solidarity. But not us.

The truth is that the presence of masses, the demonstrations, and so forth, were very poor; that is, no one was able to mobilize the Chilean colony. We are a disaster. And these people believed that we could do everything using the Chilean organizations as a base, eating empanadas, dancing the *cueca* [traditional Chilean dance], or – I don't know – talking about politics. Those of us who formed Por Chile always gave opinions in the press and had stronger links with the Costa Ricans – we wanted the Chilean problem to also be part of the Costa Rican one, regardless of whether they were on the left or not, but that they also feel committed. To the point that this quiet work for so many years has produced results because we have managed to get the most conservative newspapers, like *La Nación*, for example, to do articles on us. They end up attacking the military junta; that is, they came down on the side of democracy, and members of congress from all the parties always condemned it.

So the work of our group was to link the situation of Chile with the people who had pressure groups in Costa Rica. Obviously the unions are very weak, the left kept getting weaker so that now, practically, as an organization it no longer exists.

So I think that the vision, in a certain sense, was right, to draw in the larger population of the country, not to draw in unions and leftist groups that were weak and that could be conflictive at some point. It was easier to get the chancellery involved in the rescue of some important compañero who was detained or had been expelled. Pascal Allende [successor to Miguel Enríquez as head of the MIR] was there, many more people, with the aid of the government of Costa Rica; and most of the time Costa Rica voted to condemn the situation of human rights in Chile. In some cases, we had some problems, but this work, I believe, with the authorities, members of congress and ministers, with the majority parties, which are *La Unidad* and *Liberación* [Social Christian Unity Party and National

Liberation Party], with the judges and the university authorities, has always generated a great deal of sympathy in defense of the Chilean people
and democracy.

## Gabriel Sanhueza

*Gabriel Sanhueza (introduced in chapter 3), a journalist and militant of
the MIR, spent his transitory exile in Argentina. Despite having violated
the MIR's policy of staying in Chile to resist, he was recruited to organize
support for the MIR's activities in West Germany, arriving in November
1974. After a successful stint of organizing groups and raising money, he
became disillusioned with the MIR's operations and broke with the party.
His testimony illustrates the degree of support that exiles found in Europe
as well as the frictions within the exile community.*

The MIR realized but didn't want to acknowledge that it needed resources and people outside the country to help them with the policy of
not seeking asylum and staying in Chile. They had not been able to set up
the work outside that would help them stay in Chile, something which the
Communists, the Socialists, all the parties on the left, had. Then a compañero from the MIR who was in Argentina made me a very concrete
proposal: "You have to go to Europe, you have the ability to put something together, to get something. Get money. We have a great number of
prisoners, of people disappeared, so you go to Germany and wait there for
orders. And the MIR will thank you for it." I saw it at that time as my
moral obligation, as an ethical question that I had to help them in this situation, and they got me the ticket and the travel documents.

The Germans established a quota system for the Chileans; since they
have a federal system, the states that were under the Social Democratic
Party created more openings. I was assigned to Bochum [an industrial city
in the Ruhr Valley, of approximately 400,000 in 1980], a working-class
city with a very large university. Some three months after my arrival, I
was visited by people from the MIR Exterior from Paris, saying that we
had to begin to organize things. In fact, we had already done it, because
the concern in Germany about the situation in Chile was very great.
Three days after arriving, I was already talking at least to students, telling
them what had happened in Chile, what the coup was like, and we formed
an aid committee.

I was very impressed at how the different sectors of German society converged in their concern for Chile. There was the evangelical German church, the students, the unions, the minority groups like lesbians and gays, journalists, even people from the Red Army terrorist group. And this was because Chile represented many dreams, dreams of a free socialism, a critical church, a labor movement creating a different kind of labor relations. This and many other dreams were present in the Chilean process, and, as a result, the great interest in being in solidarity with Chile.

Well, we became a money-generating machine, and if there is anything that the MIR owes those of us who did this work it was our having gotten them millions of marks. We wrote proposals, held campaigns, we opened bank accounts to receive the aid. We even thought up totally false projects; for example, the project of a farm for the wives of the political prisoners so that they could have something to do. At this time, Germany had a great deal of money, and if we were to make a count we would come to the conclusion that we turned over a lot of money to the resistance, a lot of money.

The Germans have an incredible organizing ability, so that at one point there were 140 *Chile Komitees* all over Germany that met once a week to find out what was happening in Chile. These were controlled by the MIR, MAPU, and the Socialist Party. On their part, other parties also had their organizations and their networks, like, for example, the German Communist Party and its groups supported their Chilean counterpart.

At one point, it was asked whether part of this money shouldn't be invested in Argentina because the situation was more conflictive than in Chile and that more could be done, and that it was important for us to have a platform nearer Chile. And on their part, the Uruguayans, Argentines, and Bolivians had a hard time raising money. This was because the solidarity with the situation in Argentina, Uruguay, was much less than with that of Chile because of the characteristics of the Chilean process and the sympathy it generated.

In 1977, there was a formal break with the MIR. The truth is that there wasn't any reason for me to be there, that is, I felt totally distanced from the MIR as far as what we wanted: from the utopia of the MIR, from the mission of the MIR. But what motivated me to leave it was that, as an instrument, it was antidemocratic in the sense that they didn't discuss the mission or the objective of the party, nor why this or that. You had to serve and respect and accept. So, then, the most important problem for me, more important than strengthening the MIR, was to try to achieve what the MIR, in its best moments, wanted: a revolution, social justice, getting back rights for people that didn't have them, these sorts of goals. This was the purpose, and for that you pick a party — you can choose something else, like the church, if you wish — but in the MIR it was twisted so that everything was directed to strengthening the instrument, but the objective had been largely forgotten. This was a criticism, and, on top of that, the instrument wouldn't even allow you to discuss it.

I remember that the breaking point came when we wrote a letter criticizing many of the positions that the MIR took and I insisted that this letter be distributed by the party to all the MIR people in Europe; that if not, I was leaving — if my letter wasn't distributed and discussed, I was leaving. They wanted the letter to be given to specific leaders who would answer me; they said that the letter couldn't be circulated because there weren't resources for that, that it wasn't the time, that this wasn't right. So this went on for some two months, and finally they expelled me, with the allegation that "you have become a petit bourgeois, you have become addicted to whiskey," whatever they could find to say. When they threw you out of the MIR, it was because you had made mistakes, not because there was some problem in the party. Several left, several.

## María Elena Carrera

*María Elena Carrera (introduced in chapter 2) was a Socialist leader and senator at the time of the coup. After passing through Peru and Cuba, she settled in Berlin to help lead the Socialist Party and restructure the Unidad Popular as head of its women's organization. Her experience in East Germany and connections to the party and the worldwide UP apparatus provide insights into the lives and work of UP leadership in exile.*

I settled in Berlin in June of 1974, after having spent four months in Cuba. The welcome I received in the German Democratic Republic was incredibly good. There was a tremendous solidarity in all the countries that I visited, and from the stories that I heard, I think that the solidarity with Chile worldwide was more even than that given to Vietnam in the period of the war. The solidarity with Chile was very extensive in Europe and the United States.

The German Communist Party or the German government tried to organize our exile — which was never massive in scale. We were never more than twenty-five hundred people, but yes, these were all people supported by their parties, people from parties, but from all of the parties —

not just Communist and Socialist but also from the other parties. Among the German Communists there were several who were children of people exiled at the time of Hitler. One of them was the son of a member of the central committee of the party who had been exiled in Mexico. He had gotten there as a child, and so he had experienced what it is like to be in exile. I think that this also helped in our being treated with care, with a dignity that I really can't thank them for enough.

It was a big job to organize the exiles, to help what was left of the party in Chile, to organize the party outside. In all the countries where there were Socialists there was an organization of the party, and in all the countries where there were Chileans there was a Unidad Popular organization. I don't know exactly how many countries, but I do know about the women. We had organizations in thirty-five countries, women of the UP. When I left here, I was the leader of the women's organization of the UP, and along with another senator, the Communist senator doña Julieta Campusano, a great woman, we began to organize the women again—and, in fact, they are easy to organize. Chilean women are tremendous; you have to tie them down to keep them from organizing. So we began just with letters with our signatures giving the necessary authorization for the organization—letters that were passed around, photocopied, and sent to places where we knew that there were women—and very soon thereafter, there was an organization like Unidad Popular had had of Women in Exile and I was the head of it.

Our political line—not just of the women, but rather of the UP in general—was that we had to wage in Chile a battle on all fronts to get rid of the dictatorship: a political battle, an organizational battle, battles of all types, and, if possible, even military, but I never had much hope that we would achieve that. One of the fronts was the diplomatic front, the front of world public opinion, and that front was the one most accessible for those of us who were in exile. We would have to develop it with very simple and clear political lines—that we would accept, appreciate, and be thankful for solidarity wherever it came from—from the socialist camp, from the capitalist camp, from the developed countries, from the developing countries, from all continents, from all races, from all political persuasions, from all religions, and that's what we did.

Of course, the solidarity with our prisoners and our disappeared—that was an area of work that was very strong. We had to get them visas, work, or at least be able to say that they had work so that they would let them leave, so that they would give them the 504 [1975 decree law that allowed political prisoners to petition for commutation of their sentence for exile]. All of this was a very systematic task, and eventually we really got to be specialists at it. All the people that were prisoners, including Gladys Díaz, received our solidarity and our efforts. I personally had an enormous list, a huge card file that got smaller as we were successful, and with the disappeared, well, we fought for them to appear, and some of them did reappear.

Our vision of what was happening in Chile was very clear. We had reports that we received from people who traveled clandestinely or sent news by secret mail. Then, with this kind of report we would inform the United Nations and we had, in this respect, a good organization, an office in Rome and an office in New York, and we had people who were very well-connected in Geneva. We had a good organization, so good that it allowed us to do a little solidarity work, too. We opened our doors to other people who were suffering from dictatorships in other parts of America. We had contacts with Argentines, Uruguayans, Brazilians, Salvadorans.

## Patricio Rivas

*Patricio Rivas (introduced in chapter 4), a member of the MIR's central committee, went underground to resist the dictatorship. He was expelled from Chile in March 1976, after a long period of detention and torture, and immediately picked up the anti-regime struggle in exile. His political life in exile exemplified that of the MIR leadership: He spent his full time working for the party. Anything but party work was discouraged as the MIR first regrouped and then launched its policy of sending members clandestinely to Chile to organize for the armed struggle. The words of fellow MIRista Patricio Jorquera describe this life in exile: "My exile was constant party activity. You had to commit yourself 100 percent to the party."\* Patricio Rivas currently teaches political science at a private university in Santiago.*

In Europe, there were more than a thousand MIRistas scattered in different countries. This created difficulties for our party work. On the other hand, there was a psychological political problem due to the fact that the majority of the MIRistas who were in Europe had received asylum, and, as you know, the MIR took active status away from all of those

---

\* Interview, June 12, 1994.

who exiled themselves rather than being expelled. So that they had a great guilt complex. So, if you feel guilty, you are a coward, you sought asylum. This was Peyton Place and it was hard to work with those people because they were carrying around a very heavy psychological weight.

I decided that, to facilitate the work, each area would become a Regional Committee, reproducing more or less the structures of the Chilean MIR before the coup. That year I was reorganizing the groups in solidarity with the MIR around the world. The international work of the MIR was very good at one point, as good as the international work of the Vietnamese. It was a very efficient effort in spite of the lack of resources; besides, the motto was to work with the minimum to give priority to the internal work of the organization in Chile.

We had annual meetings in Mexico of all the exterior committees to coordinate and plan the work. Our tasks consisted of the development of our international relations, and these were political—with political parties, unions, youth organizations, with women. On the other hand, there was the financial responsibility which consisted of collecting funds for the resistance in Chile. We sent the money by zones. For example, Italy sent money to the Regional in Concepción and another country to Santiago. In this way, we created a very strong group spirit. The other part was the underground work. This consisted of getting false passports so that active members could get into Chile. On other occasions, French friends traveled to Chile with large sums of money for those working actively inside the country. There's the case of a French psychiatrist who went there some ten times without arousing any suspicions.

In 1978, the MIR decided on the policy of returning to Chile. I went with the first group that returned, but later they pulled me out of the group and sent me to take charge of the clandestine relations in Central America, with the *Frente Sandinista* [the Sandinistas in Nicaragua], with the *Frente Farabundo Martí de Liberación Nacional* of El Salvador [the FMLN], with the Guatemalan guerrillas, with the movements in Colombia. These organizations demonstrated extraordinary solidarity with us, especially the Salvadorans. This help was due to the fact that none of these groups followed the line of the pro-Soviet Communist parties and decided to support us. This was the logic, more or less. The second thing was that we were the only ones who were fighting in the Southern Cone of Latin America, so then, if they were planning to open a guerrilla front, it had to be us. This was more or less the geopolitical perspective.

Also, they helped us to prepare our active members for their return to Chile. Our people went to training schools in Cuba and Germany or the

USSR, and those didn't give the kind of instruction that we needed. I told the Cubans and the Germans, "With what you know, you wouldn't last a day in Chile—your techniques are very out of date." They were thinking about the resistance against the Nazis in Europe, with a contact in the street and a briefcase. So what we did was to move our people to Central America, so that they would get real training in urban and rural guerrilla warfare. We had people in Guatemala, El Salvador, Nicaragua, and Colombia. In that period—1978 to 1983—we didn't lose a single person.

There were some political and ideological differences with the Central Americans. They were very militaristic—for them, it was a matter of firing more shots, more bombs; for us, it was a matter of masses, of greater participation. We were seen to be too "intellectual."

In the year 1980, they sent me to talk to the Colombian M–19 [one of the major Colombian guerrilla organizations of several operating in the 1970s and 1980s]. In that period, the leader was Jaime Bateman. I go to this meeting and make contact with this person. He was a mulatto; he comes half an hour late, dying laughing. An incredible lack of rigor in security measures—I was very scared. In Chile, I would never have waited for half an hour for him. Then he says to me, "You know, the meeting between the MIR and the M–19 can't take place here—we have to go into the jungle. Come with me tomorrow to the jungle, we'll meet in the Bogotá airport. Get vaccinated against everything in the jungle and buy yourself clothes for the jungle." I went to get vaccinated and bought clothing that looked like that of an English colonial in Africa.

These were flights that left once the plane was filled. Meanwhile, we ate chicken; then, once we had taken off, Bateman takes out a huge pistol and gives it to the stewardess. I was rather perplexed, but when the plane is going to arrive in Bucaramanga—a town hidden in the jungle—the stewardess goes by with her cart full of weapons. "Mr. Pérez, your gun." The whole plane was armed; all of them wore pistols. It is a country of crazy people—a country from García Márquez [Colombia's Nobel laureate, best known for the magical realist novel, *One Hundred Years of Solitude*].

## Benjamin Teplizky Lijavetzky

*Born in 1932, Teplizky was brought up in an upper middle-class Jewish household in Santiago. He studied in public schools, took a law degree at the University of Chile, and practiced and taught law from 1961 to the coup. A member of the Radical Party, he served as director of National Television and in other high-profile roles during the UP government. In 1994 he was named Minister of Mining in the Eduardo Frei administration.*

*Teplizky was arrested on the day of the coup and released in January 1975. After nearly two years in Israel, he went to Rome to assume the directorship of Chile Democrático, the original and most influential of several multiparty organizations fighting for the restoration of democracy in Chile. Established in December 1973, primarily by Chileans who had been outside the country at the time of the coup, Chile Democrático played a leading role in garnering international support for the anti-Pinochet campaign and for political and human-rights organizations in Chile. Benjamin Teplizky died in August 1997.*

In 1976, the central solidarity organization in Rome that was called Chile Democrático had a small crisis. There were two ideas as to what this organization ought to be. One part of the left thought that it ought to be an organization with a political direction – for political struggle, doing battle – and the other tried to convert it into an organization of international solidarity, an NGO [nongovernmental organization] for human-rights matters and for the diplomatic isolation of the military government. This tendency was in the majority in the year 1976. Then the groups representing UP, MIR, asked the Radical Party to send me, because I had been president of the UP coalition of parties and had very good relationships with the political forces of the government and outside the Congress.

The structure of Chile Democrático was rather unique. It was a federation of parties, of party leaders, that provided their people to Chile Democrático – because we didn't have resources to pay salaries – lawyers, engineers, professors, union leaders, directors of social organizations, etc., who could give some of their time to Chile Democrático. This organization had a council where all the parties of the Chilean left were represented, from the parties more at the center-left all the way to the ultra-left – like the MIR – and from this base we tried to form a relationship with the rest of the Chilean democratic parties that were in favor of a democratic project. The Christian Democrats were not directly represented, but we had a very good relationship with the part of the Christian Democrats that was in exile – with Bernardo Leighton, with Claudio Huepe, Renán Fuentealba, with the Tomich family, with Belisario Velasco.

The form that I asked it to take was a good one—it wasn't a political direction, but rather to work in this triple dimension of human rights, the creation of a network of institutions of human rights in Chile, and an NGO of an international diplomatic nature.

We divided the activity of Chile Democrático into sections. We had a section dedicated to direct contact with the international organizations, with the whole system of the United Nations. We had another section that worked directly with the so-called national committees, that is, the committee that existed in Algeria or in Sweden or in Mexico, in Havana, in Buenos Aires, etc. There were committees in some eighty countries of the world. Now those committees that we called "national" were the committees of the people of that area, of the people of those countries. Along with each national committee, there was a Chilean committee that had a variety of names: in Australia, there were a number of Unidad Popular committees like in the old days; in Mexico, they were called *Casa de Chile* or *Secretaría para América Latina de la Solidaridad Internacional*; in Algeria, they called it the Chilean Antifascist Committee; in Sweden, the Chileans organized around committees that were financed by the cities, small clubs with three or four people, of a specific nature like cultural, sporting, or social. We had specialists in the topic of human-rights organizations—that was the United Nations Human Rights Commission, with headquarters in Geneva, or the United Nations Subcommission on the Prevention of Discrimination and the Protection of Minorities. We had people who worked with the union organizations, people who worked with artists, with intellectuals. We coordinated all of this from Italy.

All of this was financed with the aid of many international organizations, including aid from development funds that governments sent to the NGOs. The country that gave the most money in solidarity with Chile was Holland, because it has a culture of real political solidarity; also the Scandinavian countries, the Chilean Committee of the Socialist International.

Chile Democrático had its own instruments of communication, but we gave a great deal of support to one publication—in my opinion, one of the best among those published by the exiled Chilean intelligentsia—which was *Chile América*. It was published by a center next to our building that wasn't directed by Chile Democrático, but those of us who were executive secretaries or presidents of Chile Democrático formed part of the board, with Viera Gallo, Julio Silva Solar, Bernardo Leighton, Fernando Bachelet, and Fernando Murillo. So we had I don't know how many books, pamphlets, magazines, films—helped by several of the countries of the Socialist bloc—among other things, which were done on the subject of Chile. So then we were true worldwide preachers with all this quantity of "know how," of knowledge of the topics. In Mexico, the exiles worked on a publication that touched on a topic that was almost taboo for the old Chilean left, a true and objective analysis of the relationship of Chile and Latin America with the United States. The United States contributed a good deal to human rights through underground diplomacy in key moments. Jimmy Carter was one who did this, Ted Kennedy, Tom Harkin—I think that he is still a congressman [currently senator from Iowa]; [journalist] Jack Anderson with his report on the destabilization carried out by the CIA in Chile—all of this was organized by those in exile.

After 1976, Chile Democrático became a rearguard organization for defense of human rights, for the promotion of development, and for denouncing abuses, and it wasn't a political organization, with a battle or combat line like some of the compañeros of the ultra-left wanted—"so that the whole war of liberation would come out of it." But we managed to convince those compañeros that the only thing possible here was to help to make the history of the internal struggle less painful and to help in the development of strong values, from the international level toward the national. We were sure that this work of an international diplomatic nature that we were doing, by itself was not going to overthrow the military junta, that this would be determined inside the country—as, in fact, it was—but the force of this solidarity movement was such that we realized that it had become a force in favor of Chilean democracy.

The African and Arab countries and liberation movements offered us material aid, but we said what it was that we would do and how it was that we wanted to do it. These people offered resources for waging war—something which is not part of the history or the tradition of Chile and that would have been rather difficult given the failure of those who chose the path of armed struggle in our country. Because there were people of good or bad faith—history will say which—who believed that we could wage a war of liberation here in Chile, and that is crazy because of the very nature of Chileans. So we found it amusing when these commanders of revolutions in their own countries said to us: "What you need are battalions, squadrons."

We gave aid—in the material sense—through the international organizations to all the organizations working in Chile for human rights in a sometimes heroic and dangerous way. We supported the Vicaría de la Solidaridad and the Chilean Human Rights Commission without having direct contact with them because our location in the spectrum of the

Chilean left would have been the kiss of death. We helped the Chilean Human Rights Commission by denouncing abuses before the Human Rights Commission of the United Nations, before the General Assembly, and to other international organizations. Some of the funds for the development of the Agrupación de Familiares de Detenidos, Desaparecidos — families of the executed, of the political prisoners, etc. — now it can be said — came from Chile Democrático. There, the relationship was a direct one because these were organizations of the left.

After the years 1984–1985, when the struggle inside the country became a political one, we realized that our time had come — in the sense that the different orientations that the forces had in Chile were going to produce a split in Chile Democrático — because the force of Chile Democrático had always been its unity. But, in fact, beginning in the 1980s the forces which in Chile had already begun to develop their own structures — which was what we had expected — began to go off in different directions. There is no doubt that the option that the Communist Party took for armed resistance to the dictatorship divided Chile Democrático because the objectives were now different. So then in 1986, when I had been at the helm of Chile Democrático for ten years, we decided to dissolve it.

## Anselmo Sule

*Anselmo Sule was born into a middle-class family in the agricultural town of Los Andes, north of Santiago in the Aconcagua Valley, in 1934. His housewife mother died three years after his birth; his father, a wholesale dealer in agricultural products, died during Sule's adolescence, making it necessary for the youth to work his way through school. He attended public schools in his hometown and law school at the University of Chile, finishing his law degree at the young age of twenty-two. A member of the Radical Party from age fourteen, Sule quickly rose through the ranks of party leadership and was elected senator in 1969. At the time of the coup he was a lawyer, professor, senator, president of his party, and also president of the Unidad Popular coalition. After returning from exile in 1988, he was again elected to the Senate in 1989, but lost his seat in the 1997 election.*

*As a very high-profile member of the UP, Sule was imprisoned from November 1973 to August 1974, with other prominent leaders of the Allende government and its supporting parties, on Dawson Island in the*

*Strait of Magellan. Following his release from Dawson Island he was
rearrested and became the subject of an intense campaign of international
pressure led by the Socialist International. The personal involvement of
leaders such as Sweden's Olaf Palme, Italy's Bettino Craxi, Spain's Felipe
González, Portugal's Mario Soares, and presidents Daniel Oduber of Costa
Rica and Carlos Andrés Pérez of Venezuela resulted in Sule's expulsion
from Chile in February 1975. Later, as a vice-president of the Socialist
International during his exile, Sule organized similar campaigns of
publicity and pressure against the dictatorship and worked to establish
and finance numerous NGOs within Chile. Forced to operate within the
regime's rules, these academic, human-rights, and social-service organizations nonetheless were subtly subversive and played a crucial role in
preparing the populace for the return of civilian government.*

They expelled me in February of 1975, sending me to Venezuela, a country that gave a really incredible welcome to exiled Chileans. There was
great help from the political parties, from the government – Carlos Andrés Pérez was president. All the exiles had a place to work, especially
they opened the universities to us. I worked in a state agency similar to
our CORFO [Corporación de Fomento, the Chilean state development
agency]; it was rather light work that allowed me to put in intense effort at
the international level. In the first stage of the dictatorship, the work was
basically done on the outside. Because of the extreme conditions of repression, the work that could be done in Chile was rather limited. It was
underground work and was very dangerous. The work stirring up interest,
of educating, of collecting money, of defending those sentenced to death,
defending the prisoners – all that was done from the outside and that was
my work.

After two years we moved to Mexico, strictly for economic reasons. In
that period, Venezuela was one of the most expensive countries in the
world, and with what one family needed to live in Venezuela, the five top
leaders of the party lived in Mexico with our families. Besides, we were invited by President López Portillo. We all had work; many refugees were
even given furnished apartments; they offered us dual citizenship. In
Mexico, the truth is that we were really overwhelmed by the support that
they gave us. So we centered the external leadership of the party principally in Mexico.

A very important aspect of my work was through the Socialist International. I was the president of the Radical Party, which is a member of the
Socialist International, and then they elected me vice president of the In-

ternational in 1976, in the congress in Switzerland. At that time, the Socialist International was in its heyday with a great world-class leader like
Willy Brandt was and with an exceptional team of other leaders.

You have to recognize that, without a doubt, the most unrestricted,
unconditional, massive, automatic, obvious support for Chile was on the
part of the socialist countries and the Communist International. But what
was decisive and really very important was that of the Socialist International, and this for obvious reasons. The Socialist International had a
significant presence that countered that of the United States; we had easy
access to the international decision-making organizations and to the
United Nations, and in this aspect there was a total commitment to the
cause of Chilean democracy on the part of the Socialist International. At
the same time, it agreed to coordinate this work worldwide, a natural role
for it.

The attitude of the Socialist International was, for all those years, to
put the Chilean case as the first item on its international action agenda at
the United Nations, in the organizations in Geneva, in the Latin American Commission on Human Rights, in the OAS – in any place where they
were able to take action. There was an effort by the government leaders
in Europe and America who belonged to the Socialist International to
counter the American president and Congress. There was extraordinary
work done to finance the different underground, semi-underground, or
legal organizations in the country; this established a system of integration
of the NGOs that still exists today.

I think that Chile was considered a priority for all the democratic solidarity movements in the world because Chile was like the Switzerland of
America, in the sense of being a peaceful country, a democratic country,
with significant development in culture and in health, education, and retirement benefits. Chile had two Nobel prize winners. Also a stability that
was almost unique in Latin America, and the coup – because of its bloody
nature – had a very great impact worldwide. There was a reaction from
the democratic forces within the different conservative, social democratic,
liberal, and Christian Democratic sectors. The coup took people by surprise – no one had thought there would be revolution with empanadas and
red wine – Chilean style – and besides, Allende's prestige. Allende's gesture, his suicide, Allende's final words – all those things reached all parts
of the world. They caused an impact in the strangest, most exotic countries; in the smallest towns, people knew about the Chilean experience
and the dictatorship. I made a trip through Turkey, both the Asian as well

as the European part, and everyone knew who Pinochet was and who Allende was.

Outside Chile, in the majority of the countries, there were not any serious difficulties in carrying out actions against the dictatorship. But it was very common, in whatever place that you were in, that you would get information about possible attacks on the leaders in exile by the DINA. I remember that once I went to West Germany for a meeting of the German Social Democratic Party with Willy Brandt. It was a very strange trip because in the morning I had been with the leader of the German Democratic Republic and in the afternoon I met with Brandt; I lunched with Honecker [Erich Honecker, head of the East German Communist Party and government] and dined with Brandt. Only Chileans could do such things. Well, but when I got to the airport, a Mercedes Benz was waiting for me with incredible security measures—a Mercedes Benz that even tanks could run over and I don't know if that would have any effect. It was even halogen bomb–proof. There was a group of police and party leaders because they had received information that there would be an attempt on the lives of the leaders of the Unidad Popular parties. This created problems for the host countries; because of this, we met more in Havana or in the GDR [German Democratic Republic] than in other countries.

Toward the beginnings of the 1980s there was a moment when, without previous agreement, we said: "Okay, conditions are now different within the country. Those inside the country have to take over—as is obvious and natural—the complete leadership of the process. We have to become a support group." Thus we began to move the decision making, and it was a crucial thing that the majority of the leaders on the outside didn't want to maintain control and decide for the people inside and impose judgments. Obviously, there were isolated cases, but these were neither massive nor decisive. So that even, in general, the meetings that occurred before between the leaders in-country with those outside took place outside; after the early 1980s they began to take place in the country itself, and the meetings of these leaders outside Chile practically disappeared.

As far as the resistance movement in the country, we as the Radical Party had until the year 1979 a totally underground leadership, and after 1980, when leaders began to achieve public notoriety, so to speak—they began to act in a de facto semi-legal fashion. It was not public knowledge that the party was led by such and such a person—there were no declarations made. We began to form a national alliance; there began to be much more intense action on the part of the group of twenty-four [one of several configurations of anti-regime political leaders in the early and mid-1980s leading up to the formation of the broad alliance that won the 1988 plebiscite, the Concertación por el "NO"] in which we had a representative. They began to form the bases for a return to democracy at the beginning of the 1980s.

The NGOs were essential in the process of transition. Many organizations began to receive aid starting right away in 1973, and there was incredible help, which allowed for the protection, the defense of the political prisoners, and this aid was able to help many families that were left totally orphaned economically. It allowed us to transport many people, sometimes clandestinely, and allowed us to maintain an information network through educational institutions.

The support that the Socialist International gave the NGOs was constant, incredible. I don't have numbers for the quantity of aid, but it was significant. It's true that in exile the leaders — who were numerous — never paid for their travel, their lodging, and all that organization was costly. I found myself in hotels in Holland, in Norway, or in Sweden that cost from two hundred to three hundred dollars — and in this period three hundred dollars was equivalent to one thousand dollars today. These were extraordinary amounts that were invested, for a ticket there was another thousand dollars, and you saw that there was always an army of Chileans in all the meetings. The presence at the United Nations was not just in New York, but in all the places where there were meetings of the FAO, the ILO [The United Nations' Food and Agricultural Organization and International Labor Organization], etc. However, I should clarify that the greatest sums of money, especially after 1979 or 1980, was earmarked for Chile. I think that after 1980, 90 percent of what we took in was sent to Chile and the rest used outside to pay for support activities.

# EIGHT

# Exiles' Return, 1978–1988

## *Struggle on Many Fronts*

Although both the departed and their families longed for the day when exiles could come home, after the illusion of a brief military regime faded, so did the idea that exiles would be able to return in a reasonable period of time. The military government's initial policy on return was defined in Decree 81 of November 1973, which required exiles to obtain permission from the Minister of the Interior to enter Chile. This meant, in practice, that legal return was impossible for most exiles. Many of those who maintained Chilean passports had them stamped with a letter "L," signifying that the bearers were on a list of those prohibited from returning. Having had some success in portraying exile as a humane alternative to prison, or a worse fate, for "enemies of the nation," and relying on massive exile of the left to keep his power secure, Pinochet felt no inclination and little pressure to change policy through the 1970s. When foreign correspondents covering the 1980 plebiscite asked the general whether exiles would be allowed to return, he responded: "I have only one answer: No."* Only the MIR and the Communist Party systematically defied the regime's policies on return, beginning in 1978 and 1980, respectively, by introducing members clandestinely for political work and armed resistance.

Despite Pinochet's opposition, by 1984 most exiles had obtained the

---

*Comité Pro Retorno de los Exiliados Chilenos, "Documento presentado a la Organización de las Naciones Unidas" (1980), 10.

right to go home. This far-reaching policy change occurred within the context of the popular protest movement that shook the tranquillity of military rule between 1982 and 1986 and led to a slight, grudging opening achieved, in the words of a close observer, at the cost of "dozens of innocent deaths, thousands of arrests, and serious abuses of fundamental rights."* Among the concessions that the regime unwillingly made were a loosening of press controls, granting permission for student and professional organizations to elect officers, and allowing the opposition to hold occasional rallies. None of these concessions had such far-reaching consequences as the liberalization of policy on exiles' return.

The issue of exiles' return had been formally raised in 1978 with the founding of the Comité Pro Retorno de los Exiliados Chilenos under the auspices of the nascent human-rights movement, but no results were obtained until 1982. In that year, sparked by the 1981 economic crash that greatly exacerbated unemployment and poverty, unauthorized protests began that would lead in 1983 to a broad antigovernment mobilization, the "national days of protest." In September 1982, street demonstrations protested the Supreme Court's refusal to permit the return of the expelled president of the Chilean Commission on Human Rights, Jaime Castillo Velasco. Since Castillo Velasco, a Christian Democrat, could not be portrayed as a dangerous radical, his case served to broaden support for the return movement beyond the families of UP exiles. Against this backdrop, and in a clear attempt at preemption, the government convened a commission to study the return policy in October 1982, and on Christmas day of that year issued the first of ten lists of persons authorized to return.

This cosmetic concession quickly proved to be a cruel hoax. Issued periodically through October 1983, the lists contained a total of only 3,562 names—a miniscule proportion of the exiles—and when duplications,

---

* Genaro Arriagada, *Pinochet: The Politics of Power*, trans. Nancy Morris (Boston: Unwin Hyman, 1988), 66. See also Cathy Lisa Schneider, *Shantytown Protest in Pinochet's Chile* (Philadelphia: Temple University Press, 1995); and Gonzalo de la Maza and Mario Garcés, *La explosión de las mayorías: protesta nacional, 1983–1984* (Santiago: Editorial ECO, 1985).

dead persons, and persons who had previously returned were subtracted, fewer than 2,000 individuals were authorized to return.* Nonetheless in October 1983, as part of its response to the rise of the protest movement, the regime scuttled the lists and reverted to its previous hard line on exiles' return.

The regime's policy reversal did not settle the issue, however, because the outbreak of the unexpectedly potent protest movement—after nearly a decade of absolute military control—made clear to the exiled opposition leadership the importance of reestablishing itself inside Chile. On one hand, the protest movement gave hope of forcing the dictatorship to grant major concessions or even to step aside. If such ambitious goals could not be achieved, the opposition still would need to be back in Chile to organize and proselytize for the plebiscite on the continuation of military rule to be held, according to the 1980 constitution, in 1988. Thus in 1983 and 1984, aided by the formation of numerous pro-return groups abroad and the beginnings of international pressure to allow exiles to return, an energetic campaign emerged for the total abolition of restrictions on exiles' return.

This campaign focused on redefining exile. Rather than the humane alternative, the "golden exile" that the dictatorship had projected, the movement presented exile and the prohibition of return as grave violations of human rights, specifically of the Universal Declaration of Human Rights' section 11 which established "the right to live in one's homeland." The legal department of the Vicaría de la Solidaridad flooded the courts with thousands of petitions for return, while FASIC began publishing its periodical *Chile Retorno* in December 1983. Meanwhile, the influential news magazine *Hoy* boldly carried large supplements on exile in seven consecutive weekly editions between January and March 1984. Titled "Vivir sin Chile," these supplements featured staff reports from Europe, interviews, photographs, thoroughly researched accounts of exile life, bibliographies of exile writings and artistic accomplishments—in short,

---

* Vicaría de la Solidaridad, internal memorandum, Oct. 31, 1983, caja 53; "Vivir sin Chile," *Hoy*, January 25–31, 1984, 47.

taken together these amounted to a book that offered Chileans the first mainstream, nongovernmental view of the entire exile phenomenon. These developments, and the united voice of the UP and Christian Democratic opposition on the issue, inserted the question of return into the narrow but growing space the regime grudgingly allotted for public discourse.

Beginning in mid-1984, return policy came under more direct fire as prominent opposition figures began flying into Santiago without authorization to enter the country. In July, two members of the popular exile musical group Inti Illimani flew into Santiago's international airport and were denied entry. On September 1, six UP leaders arrived on an Air France flight from Buenos Aires; Chilean agents entered the airplane, roughed up the six, handcuffed them, and after the French ambassador visited them on the airplane and publicly denounced Pinochet's policy on return, re-embarked them to Buenos Aires. The six leaders returned the following day on an Avianca (the Colombian airline) flight; denied entry again, they were flown to Bogotá, where they conducted a hunger strike and were received by Colombian President Belisario Betancur. These events, covered extensively by the international press, created a public-relations embarrassment and a serious enforcement problem, as the international airlines had begun openly defying the regime's long-standing threat to cancel the landing rights of any airline that did not deny passage to Chileans lacking documentation authorizing their return.*

Yielding to these mounting domestic and international pressures, the Pinochet government adopted a new policy of lists, this time naming those persons prohibited from entering the country. The first list, issued September 5, 1984, contained 4,942 names; the twelfth, dated March 15, 1987, named 1,471 individuals. In an attempt to cast the October 1988

---

* These events are described in *Cauce*, June 15–21, 1987, 22–29. The six made a third unsuccessful attempt to enter Chile on October 11, after the new lists had begun to appear, in an attempt to force the lifting of all prohibitions against exiles' return. See *Chile Retorno*, FASIC's periodical publication, for general reporting on matters related to exiles' return.

plebiscite on Pinochet's continuance in power as legitimate and fair, the government decreed the end of forced exile on September 1, 1988. Nonetheless, a substantial number of exiles who had taken foreign citizenship and had been declared "undesirable aliens" were still forbidden to return. And for those exiles facing charges of anti-regime activity (see Sergio Buschmann, below), returning to Chile meant surrendering to the military government.

The regime's concession on return policy was apparently based on a serious miscalculation of the opposition's determination and ability to send its cadres home. Indeed, there was plenty to discourage exiles from returning: Recovery from the economic crisis had not begun; blacklists would prevent the employment of leftists; and the regime's repressive apparatus was still fully intact, as demonstrated by the brutality with which the continuing protests were put down. Yet the dedication of many exiles to ending the dictatorship propelled them home to take advantage of the slight, tenuous opening that had been achieved for political work. Some returned without jobs, others in the employ of their still illegal parties or of the private academic, human-rights, communications, and social-service organizations that had been established with international financial support, often through the exiles' efforts, and which were hated but grudgingly tolerated by the regime so long as they did not overtly violate the "political recess" that the regime still tried to enforce. Meanwhile, the MIR, since 1978, and the Communist Party, since 1980, had been sending cadres back to Chile clandestinely to organize and mount an armed struggle against the regime—a policy that placed those parties at loggerheads with the rest of the left and with the Christian Democrats.

Returning home for political work in any form was dangerous, for the level of repression employed to counter the protest movement between 1983 and 1986 rivaled that of the regime's first four years and generated a large wave of new exiles. But with continued international financial support, the opposition reestablished itself in Chile as a result of the 1984 opening and worked rebuilding their parties, pushing the limits of tolerated political activity, and mounting a drive to defeat Pinochet in the 1988 plebiscite.

# José Muñoz

*During their sixteen and a half years in power, Chile's armed forces and carabineros became synonymous with dictatorship and extreme human-rights violations. Yet the decision to carry out the 1973 coup was far from unanimous among both officers and troops, and the minority that opposed it, or whose loyalty to the new order was suspect, paid a price. The assassination of General Carlos Prats in Buenos Aires is well known, as is the case of General Alberto Bachelet who died in prison in March 1974 as the result of being denied medical attention. José Muñoz (introduced in chapter 2) estimates that some four hundred members of the uniformed services were cashiered and stripped of their pensions and benefits; many of these went into exile, and an unknown number were detained, tortured, and a few killed.*

*Muñoz returned from East Germany in 1978 with the political mission of publicizing the roles of constitutionalist soldiers and police. In conjunction with progressive military men from other Latin American countries, he has worked to develop pressure groups within the ranks to steer the military establishments away from their common conservative or reactionary political orientations and to instill respect for civilian governance. In contrast to the majority of those who returned to Chile to fight the dictatorship, José Muñoz continues to pursue his quixotic mission that has no terminal date. He owns a security company in Santiago.*

Well, one of my first concerns, when I returned to Chile, was to try to reconstitute, from my point of view, what the military coup had been like; that is, what happened to my colleagues? How many of them were affected? This was a lengthy task because of the difficulties that this involved, that is, beginning to dig into this topic which was very unique and complex, especially during a dictatorship. The thing that I did most often when I arrived was to show myself publicly everywhere.

They were watching me and it became obvious; someone was there, but it never went beyond that. I managed to make contact with some ex-colleagues in Investigations who had been outside the country, another who was an ex-major of the carabineros, and we had the level of trust necessary to talk to each other because, in Chile, people were afraid to talk to other people. So then, one who was an ex-military man did not have many civilian friends; we were friends just because of the common formation that we had received—they put us into a very special bubble.

Then, in the year 1985, I was a member of Police Studies for Democracy, which functioned under the auspices of the Jesuits, thanks to the understanding and support of Father [Mario] Zañartu. I would say that this was the first time there was a study of this kind. Only carabineros and Investigations took part, so for this reason it was called the Center of Police Studies. The number grew to six at this stage in the formation, and these were the first attempts to change public opinion with respect to police-related topics. We even asked ourselves: "How can we present an alternative to the police process that is occurring in Chile?"—we thought that police work was still something important. To promote this idea, we had seminars, talks, and put out some bulletins.

Also in the year 1985, in Buenos Aires, there was a conference announced with the purpose of forming an organization. It was called OMIDELAC, the Organization of Military for Democracy, Integration and Unity in Latin America and the Caribbean. After this conference, in this interval, I had made contact with some members of the military who, in some way, were carrying out some form of opposition work in a very slow, but constructive, way, as was the case of General Pickering. General Pickering and General Sepúlveda [Mario Pickering and Mario Sepúlveda Squella] had been the closest colleagues of General Prats, and resigned when he resigned. They appeared from time to time criticizing the military dictatorship.

I talked with General Pickering and told him about this meeting that was going to be held in Buenos Aires, that had been organized on the initiative and through the efforts of many progressive military men—there were as many Uruguayans as Chileans and also some from El Salvador. We must remember that Latin America had suffered dictatorships in Argentina, Brazil, and elsewhere. This convention was born out of the concern for how this sector of society could begin to participate in a public way and in a political way, based on its experience, and make a contribution to the democracy, integration, and unity of Latin America and the Caribbean as an alternative, and to put pressure on the armed forces so that they would stop for a time being the rearguard of history and become progressive forces in their countries. Very few people know about the progressive military men that were imprisoned for many years. The political prisoner held the longest in Latin America is an army captain, Captain Napoleón Ortigoza, who was imprisoned twenty-five years by the government of General Stroessner [Alfredo Stroessner, dictator of Paraguay, 1954–1989]; finally, thanks to international solidarity and the efforts of OMIDELAC, he was freed and I think that he is living in Spain. Many progressive officials were leaders in national liberation movements.

In 1985, there was great international pressure and great solidarity with Chile. This led to the creation of OMIDECHI, the Organization of Military for Democracy in Chile. I was the executive secretary. It sent a message that the subject of the armed forces should be a topic for public debate — a topic that before was totally taboo. The organization wanted to point out that not all the members of the armed forces should be put into the same bag — that is, that they were not all fascists — but rather that each has a personal responsibility in accord with his rank and category, and to let the public know that there had also been military people who were constitutionalists and who had made contributions and who had sacrificed themselves, who had been assassinated like in the case of General Prats, like the case of General Bachelet, like numerous enlisted men who were tortured, others exiled, because our case is also a case of violation of human rights.

We talked to the organizations of the detained and disappeared and the executed, and the only thing they wanted was to hang anyone in a uniform from a lightpost. Then they understood and recognized that you had to make distinctions and that we had to work together — that in the union offices, in the workers' areas where there were portraits of Neruda, of Recabarren [Luis Emilio Recabarren, an early labor leader and founder of the Chilean Communist Party], or of so many heroes that have contributed to the process of the country, there should also be the pictures of uniformed personnel like Prats, Schneider [General René Schneider, assassinated by rightists after Allende's election for opposing a coup], because they had also been social leaders.

We presented an appeal to the Supreme Court for the uniformed personnel because it was the opposite situation from what people were saying about the right of civilians to return — but not those in uniform — because the uniformed personnel had a double charge against them: an administrative one and a criminal one. We created a great public controversy about this topic. Every year we had cultural events — we ended the year with a cultural artistic event in memory of General Bachelet, as the person who symbolized this group. We had seminars, forums, talks, and we especially made sure to have public actions.

For the elections, we formed an organization called the National Organization of the Armed Forces, Carabineros, Investigations and Police for Aylwin and Democracy, which lasted about a year, with the intent of mustering all the ex-uniformed personnel to vote for Aylwin. This effort was recognized and we worked in conjunction with the Concertación [the broad center-left antigovernment coalition initially formed to contest the 1988 plebiscite]. In 1988 or 1989, we created another organization that was called the Workshop for the Armed Forces and Democracy with the participation of four generals, a naval officer and officers from the air force and the carabineros. It had become a rather important bloc which had as a goal thinking and talking about subjects related to military policy, and perhaps the most innovative part was to have conversations with the representatives of the political parties on these topics, to generate some ideas and plans for a future democratic government.

There are still many things to do.

## Julio Soto

*Julio Soto was born in the capital in 1944. His father was a construction worker who became a small contractor, and his mother was of peasant background. He studied in public schools in the working-class neighborhoods of Central Santiago, but was able to finish secondary in the private Liceo Francés. Despite his humble origins, he entered the Catholic University, where he studied philosophy, and continued his education at the University of Louvain in Belgium, the fount of modern Catholic social philosophy. He spent his exile in Mexico and today is a consultant to the Ministry of Education and a leader of the Christian Democratic Party (PDC).*

*The PDC, a moderate reformist party based on social Christian principles, was founded in 1957 and has been Chile's largest party since 1964, when its candidate, Eduardo Frei, was elected president. While the party and most of its leaders did not suffer the degree of persecution that the UP parties and their members did, the PDC was declared in recess immediately after the coup and formally dissolved by the regime in 1977. Upon his return from Mexico in 1982, Julio Soto turned to the task of rebuilding the party. Since the Christian Democrats did not attain legality until 1988, Soto's work was illegal, clandestine, and occasionally dangerous. At the same time, his brushes with police and the relative ease with which he was able to carry out his mission reveal that the military viewed illegal PDC activity as far less subversive and dangerous than that of the left, and tolerated it within limits.*

After 1982, when I saw clearly that the Pinochet government had to go, I came back to fight against it. I came especially to work with young people – this is my vocation – and I worked for seven years with young people until 1988, training young people from my political party. I worked in an institution that financed activities for political formation. I traveled all over the country; I know many people that today are thirty or thirty-five years old.

The year 1982 was very dangerous here. They picked me up in Puerto Montt, but it was carabineros that stopped me. We got together in a residential hotel to work with some twenty young people and they arrested us there, but they let us go after two days. In Valdivia they also picked me up in the retreat house of the archdiocese, and then they took me to the police station and they had me there for four or five hours, because the archbishop intervened, saying that this was pastoral work – but we were doing political training. In the community of Angol, we were having a class for young activists, and we had to take off running into the countryside, because a truck with the military was coming – in fact, it came and . . . This happened to me several times, this happened to me in 1984.

I received threats because of my participation in the teachers' organization. They threatened the political leaders who were for the democratization of the Colegio de Profesores [Chilean teachers' union]. In the year 1983 we created the Comando por la Democratizacíon del Colegio de Profesores [Group for the Democratization of the Teachers' Union], and we worked out of an apartment in Amunátegui Street [downtown], where there were Communists, MIRistas, Christian Democrats, Socialists, etc., and they threatened us there twice and we had to leave that apartment. They put a bomb in the door of the apartment one time while we were meeting, a noise bomb, and so we left there. They had me pretty well identified – absolutely – it even appeared in the papers. I wasn't unaware how crazy it was – of course, I was very conscious of that and even more afraid. From 1982 on, my actions are the result of greater fear, of a greater sense of reality.

I was in charge of training for the Christian Democrats for six years. We were training people for the future. My idea was to prepare young people who would replace the older generation. Now there is something really dramatic here, and I realize now that these young people lived in a system with no rules and the only thing that I could do was to teach them some democratic norms. They came to the classes and then went back to their población, where the norm was the survival of the fittest. So then there are generations of young people in all the political parties who are, in effect, children of the dictatorship, that is, the offspring of those who don't have rules or whose norm is violence. So then, pragmatism –

political action with no ethical base—is a very important characteristic of the political work in this country—politics without ethics. The younger politicians were formed in a period when there were no norms for living together in a healthy way, and they learned that—they learned to survive. I am more afraid of the young people than of the older ones.

Almost all the young Christian Democratic deputies in Congress, all the cabinet heads, the leaders of the services who are young today—almost all of them know me. They are almost all people who were exposed to my classes one way or another—the workshops, I mean—and for this reason everyone knows me.

## Julieta Campusano*

*Julieta Campusano was born into a working-class family in the north of Chile in 1918. She obtained little formal education and acquired no profession, but influenced by family, friends, and the conditions and political culture of the northern nitrate and copper zone, she affiliated with the Communist Party at an early age. She held numerous political offices from the city-council level to deputy and senator in the national Congress. As a senator in 1973, she was targeted for arrest, but managed to escape and spent the next thirteen years in a peripatetic exile.*

*Campusano returned illegally in 1987 by crossing the Andes from Argentina. She was one of several prominent leaders, including Socialist Clodomiro Almeyda, named in the lists of excluded persons who entered clandestinely in 1987 and 1988, appeared at a prearranged press conference, then turned themselves in to the authorities. This tactic was designed to expose the regime's weakness by defying the rules on exiles' return and to embolden the population to oppose the government in the upcoming plebiscite. Campusano's relatively mild punishment of short-term internal exile further exposed the regime's weakening moral authority to punish lawbreaking.*

In 1987, with Mireya [Mireya Baltra, another prominent exiled Communist leader], we spent January and February preparing to come back. We entered Chile from Bariloche [in the southern Argentine Andes] to

* The authors wish to thank Germán Palacios for sharing this interview with the late Julieta Campusano, who died in 1993. The interview was conducted between September and November 1991.

Puerto Montt. We were helped by many Argentines who couldn't accept that two Chilean women, born in Chile, with Chilean children, married in Chile, with Chilean grandchildren, would be denied the right to live in their country. They helped us to get across the border and then we traveled by cart—one piece by mule—by pickup truck, and by bus till we reached Puerto Montt.

We made the decision to announce our arrival on May 12. Our compañeros—given the fact that on other occasions other Chileans had returned to the country and they had made them disappear and afterward said that they had never entered Chile—held a press conference with all the international media. I was very moved to see the ability of the party, the ability of the Chilean resistance, to gather all the journalists from the international agencies, from the radio and the national press for an event. We went into the courts accompanied by our two lawyers, don Jaime Castillo Velasco and Enrique Krauss [both prominent Christian Democrats], who sponsored our cases. Then we went to the Commission of Human Rights. That was an important moment in ending the campaign the dictatorship had carried out to discredit the political leaders, against "the old causes of all the evils"—especially for the young people, to show them that even if there are politicians who have sold out and become corrupted, there are also revolutionary politicians who defend the interests of Chile and that they shouldn't lump all politicians together.

Later, don Jaime Castillo Velasco tells us that the government is not going to put us in jail, but rather sentence us to relegation (internal exile). Then they came to notify us from the Ministry of the Interior—Mireya to Aisén [Puerto Aisén, a small city some 1,650 kilometers from Santiago in the southern fjord region] and me to Sierra Gorda—and I protested: "Why are they are going to separate us, we have been together for such a long time?" But there was nothing we could do about it. After that, they took us out of there and said that they were taking us to Investigations, but they took us directly to Cerrillos [one of Santiago's airfields], and there were two little planes there, one to Aisén and the other to Antofagasta and from there to the interior of Antofagasta—to Sierra Gorda.

When they took me off the plane in Antofagasta, I felt the sea air and said: "It doesn't matter that I am in internal exile—I am in Chile," and that made me very happy. In Sierra Gorda, they turned me over to the carabineros. The carabineros asked me: "And where are you going to stay?" "I don't know, I don't know anyone—here in the barracks." "No," they said to me, "you can't stay here." "Then I don't know where to stay." "In the church then." In the church, there was a caretaker and I stayed there in the caretaker's house. The next day, I began to receive expressions of solidarity. First the leaders from Chuquicamata came, those from Calama; people came from the solidarity committee of Antofagasta, from the church; the telephone calls began (there was a telephone in Sierra Gorda) from England, from France, from Spain, from Italy, from Cuba, from the USSR, and the telegrams began to arrive from organizations worldwide, demanding our freedom, and people began to get organized. A delegation came from the El Salvador mine, others were university students from Antofagasta.

Then the government decided to take me out of Sierra Gorda. I was there for two and a half days, and at 1:30 P.M. people from Investigations in Calama came to get me, and they never told me where they were taking me. When I got to Antofagasta, I didn't want to get on the plane. They said: "But why are you suspicious?" "Because you have been known to throw people into the sea." I had to get on the plane and we arrived late at night — because it got late — at Iquique. It was dark and there immediately we were in a jeep heading toward the *pampa* [the plains], but I didn't know where they were taking me, and we got to Mamiña [a mountain village inland from Iquique]. In each of the places that they had me — Investigations or carabineros — there was always a doctor to verify that I hadn't been tortured, beaten, rather that they turned me over in good condition.

I had my birthday on May 31, and Radio Berlin International announced it. There were more cables and the women organized visits. My daughter had come to be with me, when at about 11:30 P.M. we heard noise outside and there were people singing. The compañeros had come, ex-prisoners of war from Pisagua [a concentration camp for political prisoners located in the north] who had an organized committee; they had come to wait with me for it to be my birthday. At about four in the morning, someone brought a cake with candles, someone a bottle of champagne. These were very nice moments, and the next day, at 7:30 A.M., we heard them singing "Las Mañanitas" [traditional birthday song] outside. It was a bus of women from Arica who had come to be with me on my birthday, and at four o'clock in the afternoon of the thirty-first, some women arrived from Santiago — it had taken them more than sixty hours to get there because the police created all kinds of problems for them en route. The women from Arica also brought a cake.

Since I had to sign in twice a day, when I went to sign in the morning the carabineros said to me: "So, it's your birthday and you are having cake." "Yes," I told them, "I am having cake." I went back to where my compañeros were and said to them: "I am going to send part of the cake to the carabineros." Whoa! Indignation. "But how can you even think of that, compañera, sending it to these dogs," etc. "But they aren't the ones responsible—let's not treat them the same way we would those who have tortured, those who have committed murder." It was difficult, but part of the cake got taken to the carabineros. A delegation went to deliver it and they invited the officer to come join us, and the officer said to them: "No, I can't do that—not because I don't want to, but because I want to be able to make it to retirement as a carabinero."

Later, the isolation in Mamiña was very great. It was a little town with a population of five hundred, very tiny. I couldn't even go to the hills above to see the other towns, nor down below. So I could only be in this one place. There was no telephone, no post office; there was a truck that came once a week. So the isolation was very great. I had the pleasure of being at the festival of fire. It had a great impact on me when a young man came up to me and said to me: "You are the person in internal exile." "Yes," I said, "you have come for the festival?" "No, I came to meet you."

Sometimes people are very introverted. There, in the boarding house, they sold liquor. So sometimes when they were half drunk, more than one of them came up to me and said to me: "I know who you are, I know." I said to them: "Tomorrow come talk to me for a little while." But no, they didn't come. But when they let me go, this town that did not show me any warmth when I arrived, I saw how they pulled back the curtains and they waved at me from inside, showing their happiness that I had been released. On the way down from Iquique to the port, the delegations from the solidarity committee were already there. They held some very nice activities, a great show of solidarity.

## Miriam Casanova

*The inhabitants of Santiago's poblaciones suffered a double repression: not only political but economic, as a result of the radical economic restructuring featuring shock treatments that produced massive unemployment while drastically curtailing services. By 1983, the poblaciones had become a battleground between the government and the opposition; along with the youth militias of the Frente Patriótico Manuel Rodríguez (FPMR), which pursued the armed struggle and figured prominently in the "national days of protest," were growing numbers of organizations and individuals engaged in a variety of projects among the pobladores. These agencies included the Centro de Estudios Sociales (Center for Social Studies, CESOC), for which*

*Miriam Casanova worked upon her return from exile in Italy in 1985. By this time, many Communists had broken with the party, formally or informally, over its adoption of the armed-struggle line. Miriam Casanova had done so, considering the "old guard left" to be out of touch with reality.*

*Casanova's political work in the poblaciones illustrates the critical role of the nongovernmental agencies (NGOs) that had been formed since early in the dictatorship to conduct human rights, social, and academic missions, and which expanded after the 1984 liberalization of return policy. Often financed by foreign governments, churches, and international political movements such as Christian Democracy and the Socialist International, these groups provided employment for returning intellectuals, professionals, and party cadres who otherwise would have had no means of subsistence. They published social and economic studies that pushed the limits of censorship, and organized and supported self-help and human-rights groups in the poblaciones. Although it was illegal and dangerous, they also conducted political education and recruitment at the grass-roots level in preparation for the 1988 plebiscite on extending Pinochet's rule for another eight years.** *

*Today, Miriam Casanova lives in Rome, where her husband is cultural attaché in the Chilean embassy.*

When I arrived in Chile in 1985, I saw that much had changed. Well, in the first place, I reacted strongly to seeing a country so totally controlled, with military everywhere, many policemen, many carabineros guarding the entrances to the universities, etc. One also reacted strongly to the level of poverty. When I arrived, I had never seen such a thing and I couldn't have imagined that there could be such misery. This is a country that, for as long as I have known it, I don't remember having seen so many people asking for handouts, so many barefoot children, so many people asking for anything, a phenomenon that really hit me. I bought everything offered to me. The number of people that got on the buses to sell things, now—because there is still some of this, some of it still happens—those selling candy, but it isn't a twentieth of what it was before. One got

* Jeffrey M. Puryear, *Thinking Politics: Intellectuals and Democracy in Chile, 1973–1988* (Baltimore: Johns Hopkins University Press, 1994), examines the role of private academic organizations. Philip Oxhorn, *Organizing Civil Society: The Popular Sectors and the Struggle for Democracy in Chile* (University Park: Pennsylvania State University Press, 1995), and Kenneth Aman and Cristián Parker, eds., *Popular Culture in Chile: Resistance and Survival*, trans. Terry Cambias (Boulder: Westview Press, 1991), discuss the impact of NGOs in the poblaciones.

off, another one got on and people said, "Please buy this from me," and you bought it. I always came home with things that I didn't need: combs, needles, thread, whatever. There were gentlemen, young people, men — the unemployed young men selling things.

The problem of drug addiction among the youth was overwhelming. Children who had become total idiots with neoprene and a huge amount of delinquency in the poblaciones, something that hadn't been seen before. Some pobladores even robbed others. I think that the terror that had been produced among the people in the poblaciones was greater than anyone can imagine. It was a strategy of the dictatorship to build houses in one area and then to move people there from all over and to take the people who lived there away and house them somewhere else. So that this way there wouldn't be any possibility of making contacts and it would mean that there would be conflicts among the different groups in the poblaciones, violence from one block to the next. Later, they put on guards to be sure that people didn't go out at night, using the delinquency as a pretext, but it was a way to control what was going on.

The CESOC program consisted of personal development and an initiative training people for work so that they would form economic units. The goal was to help women learn a trade and then organize them into a cooperative which would mean that later they could have a certain economic autonomy and be able to help themselves more. We knew that it would be very hard for people to solve their economic problems, but that they could — working at home — do some kinds of things that would allow them to earn a few pesos.

We went into the población through the parents and guardians of students at a new school that had been founded recently with the sponsorship of some international organizations. These women were very concerned that there be no talk of politics, because the subject of politics was something that they didn't want to touch, because they were terrified. This was a time in which the población was still very afraid, afraid to get involved. Women, especially, in those sectors had been greatly affected, not just by the unemployment but also by the repression, and there was great fear of the repression, of the carabineros, of the searches that were made frequently of the pobladores' houses.

The majority of us who worked in that program were people who had been out of the country. Some of us thought that we could do things more easily than, in fact, we could. I think that the truth was that you had to work patiently, slowly — only to the degree that you were able to achieve personal development could you then speak of democracy, which is what we wanted. We were really interested in what would make people aware of the importance of democracy, and indirectly, we began to express it more and more openly. Besides, the people – as they lost their fear – many of them were able to say more, because the women already knew that we didn't have anything to do with the government, that was clear. At first, there was doubt, but later then they realized that we were absolutely, clearly critical of the dictatorship, but the personal part also came into play: sympathy, trust, which meant that the women – some of them suddenly, with no warning – expressed their concerns. Remember that we had wives of carabineros among the parents or guardians of the children – wives of carabineros of the unit that lived in the población. So then we had to be careful with certain things that we said – we had to bite our tongues at times.

On the other hand, there was also a program for young people. Those kids were on the edge of danger; that is, they were involved right on the edge of violent forms of subversion; they were involved in protests. They were organized into cultural centers, but they were clearly involved in the subversive struggle. More than the Frente Patriótico Manuel Rodríguez, it was the militias, but anyway, they participated later. They were like children, and we also played the role of the mother in this story – because when they were taken prisoner more than once we went to the Vicaría [de la Solidaridad] to get help to get them out.

We didn't live in the población itself. Only the nuns did that, the lay workers. I had some good friends who were lay workers – there were even North Americans, British, but, well, we were really Barefoot Carmelites. They were more daring than we were, because it was the most socially committed part of the church which came there. It was very interesting, because they even had a very progressive idea of what had to be done, of how you had to promote organization, work, the kids, and politically. Besides, they were great workers in the sense that they mixed democracy with their Christian ideas – but it was a very committed Christianity.

What's certain is that in contrast with other programs carried out at the same time by other NGOs, we were constantly present in the población. We went every day and we had a little house – just to show you – that was open from Monday to Friday, and there were even activities on Saturdays. We would let people who wanted to do something use it.

The project lasted from 1985 until 1990. We had craft workshops, many for weaving. The women organized pretty effectively because they even began to export their weaving. They worked with natural materials, with dyes, and these are people that are still exporting, through a company. These weren't the famous *arpilleras* [tapestries made by women in the shantytowns, under the auspices of the Vicaría, that depicted the realities they were living during the years of the dictatorship]; that was another phenomenon. The arpilleras became known worldwide; they were sold and exported for the income this provided.

Besides the weaving workshops, the dyeing, I worked a good deal with the children in the artistic aspect – theater – for personal development, in order to promote creative activity. We invited them, we brought activities to them, we did many workshops on personal development, for growth. The most worthwhile part of this project is that the *Casa de la Mujer* [Women's House] still exists; it was a product of the work that we did there, that is, there are permanent results of this project.

We never lost sight of the fact that the work that we were doing there was leading toward democracy. We always thought that manual work was a way in which the women could learn something concrete, but at the same time, the importance of personal development. We had courses on civic education; we taught people how to vote in the plebiscite, "YES" and "NO." We had campaigns so that people would learn how to vote, so that they wouldn't be afraid – many were terrified that the military would know whether you voted "YES" or "NO," so we also had to overcome this fear and let people know that they could vote and that nothing was going to happen to them if they voted, and that they were not putting themselves in danger. We started from the premise that people had to get back their right to vote.

Women were very important in the overthrow of the dictatorship. What happened is that the women found a concrete space, that maybe the men didn't find. For economic reasons, for reasons of survival, women joined together – spaces the men didn't have access to. They joined workshops that also were sponsored by the Vicaría de la Solidaridad, that were sponsored by NGOs that were also working in that area. So then, the women organized themselves and the women's movement was born in this period. It was women who went out to struggle first. It is women that took to the streets first before the men in this country.

The women had already organized around the committees, wives of political prisoners, wives of the disappeared. Already in this period, women began to protest – even in 1980, there began to be some protests by women, where a group sent letters or delivered letters to Pinochet at the Moneda, to the Human Rights Commission. There was a great movement toward public action. It is the women who make things more interesting—they are closer to the masses, more visible besides. There was the demonstration in Santa Laura, "the women with the clean hands" [demonstrations in which women showed their hands to show that they were "clean" and not stained with blood like those of the dictatorship], and the marches that were held by Mujeres por la Vida [a series of protests in 1985 called "Jornadas por la Vida," or Days for Life, organized by the Chilean Human Rights Commission and led by the widows of three Communist leaders assassinated in 1985—the degollados]. There were groups of people who began to go out, and there were some of the men that came along behind, because there were always confrontations with the carabineros. They arrested a good number of people and they grabbed the women, they grabbed the youngest ones, the students; they left the older women alone and then the men who came, they grabbed them immediately. The carabineros ran straight toward the men, putting them in the vehicles and hitting them and everything, and afterward they put all of them on the floor of the vehicles and they began to walk on top of them, because that was their system.

Before the plebiscite, people began to talk, to lose their fear; there were large public demonstrations. The thing had gotten out of control for the dictatorship, and that is the most beautiful moment that we have had these last years in Chilean politics. When the plebiscite was coming, there was great energy and really, it was all of us against the same thing, all of us against Pinochet, all of us for ending the dictatorship. So that it was a very beautiful movement, because it didn't matter what political group you belonged to, everyone was working for the same thing—a very beautiful period in Chilean politics, very bright, full of hope. Well, and the Concertación [coalition for the "NO"] took shape then, but also those who were outside the Concertación were fighting for the same thing.

## Ana Laura Cataldo

*Journalism in Pinochet's Chile was a very tricky business. After initially squelching all media that were not certifiably pro-military, the regime offered slight and guarded openings when it felt it had secured complete control, circa 1977, but was quick to crack down on both print and broadcast media in times of tension, such as the 1983–86 protests and the aftermath of the assassination attempt on Pinochet in 1986. Even in less turbulent times, any reporting that went beyond the limits of prudent self-censorship led to threats or closures. And of course opposition media found it extremely difficult to sell advertising. Despite all the restrictions, journalists took advantage of the limited space allotted them to work for the dictatorship's end. Ana Laura Cataldo (introduced in chapter 3) carried out her post-return political mission from behind a microphone at Radio Cooperativa, a national network owned by a group of Christian Democrats. This was a powerful position in that Radio Cooperativa was perhaps the most credible news source in Chile.*

*Cataldo's story culminates on October 5, 1988, the day of the plebiscite on Pinochet's continuation in power for another eight years. In contrast to the plebiscite on the 1980 constitution, in 1988 the government allowed the opposition to organize and campaign, although with restrictions that did not apply to the pro-"YES" side. The presence of international observers and the access obtained by the "NO" forces to the electronic vote count seemed to assure a fair tally, but the danger was that if Pinochet lost he would conjure up plots or threats to public order to justify nullifying the plebiscite. Indeed, using selected districts, the government announced twice during the day of October 5 that the "YES" was ahead, while the "NO" was really winning. Moreover, when told of the actual results, late at night, Pinochet did threaten to override the vote and was only dissuaded when his colleagues, the commanders of the navy, air force, and carabineros, refused to cooperate. Thus the extreme tension that Cataldo describes inside the "NO" headquarters and the significance of Air Force Commander Fernando Matthei's acknowledgment of the "NO" victory.\* In the final tally the "NO" won, 55 to 43 percent (the other 2 percent were void or blank).*

Radio Cooperativa welcomed me and I began to work there in March of 1985, almost a year after having returned, and, little by little, doors opened for me. I began as a substitute; I worked Saturdays and Sundays. I worked until midnight, then sometimes I took another shift and was the one who opened at six in the morning. Then again there would be a week when I didn't work all week long, but, bit by bit, I began making a place for myself and, little by little, I was getting ahead, until I got to be one of the best-known journalists in radio, and I played an active role during the five years that I was there.

Once I had a stable position at the radio station, I reported on education. Thinking about the historical development of this country, I knew

---

\* Mary Helen Spooner, *Soldiers in a Narrow Land: The Pinochet Regime in Chile* (Berkeley: University of California Press, 1994), 238–45, captures the tension of the vote count and subsequent machinations described by Cataldo.

that it had always been through the university, through the student movement, that a good many changes had been achieved in Chile. So I told my
boss that I wanted to cover education, and that was one of the spaces that
we had where we could talk about changes, where we were able to tell
people what was going on, what concerns the youth had, what the professors of this country expect, what is happening with the universities, and
finally, what were the concerns that were moving Chile in that moment.

Being an education reporter, you could get around the restrictiveness
of the prohibition on politics a little. What was happening in the student
movement at that point was very strong—they wanted to end government
control of the university. They wanted to prevent municipal control of
primary and secondary education. There was a strong movement among
the teachers, you could present social concerns, and even though these
were the concerns of only one segment of the population—that's not true,
at its heart this group represented the entire country.

Now I tell you, the other thing, the family thing; during all those years,
my work as a journalist on the radio station that was the voice of the opposition was difficult. Next to my apartment, there was an administrative
office of the CNI [Central Nacional de Informaciones, the secret police
formed to replace the DINA in 1977], where they knew all the people who
lived in that building. I had, at that time, a preadolescent son and he had
to go to school every day. We would get calls at the radio, in which they
said that they had chosen three of us, that they were going to cut our
throats—they said "We are going to kill you, you Communists." Obviously, this didn't happen every day, but sometimes it was worse than others. So you worked under a good deal of tension, with a good deal of fear,
because, besides something maybe happening to you, that not only maybe
were they going to suddenly crash into the car you were in—the mobile
radio—it was also what might happen to your son, or what might happen
to your home. It was hard.

I think that the radio station accomplished an important task, that it
saved many people, because beginning when someone was picked up, the
relatives, the friends, called us at the radio, and then whoever answered
the telephone took charge—and more than once it fell to me to answer.
They would say to me, "Look, so-and-so, who is a student at such-and-
such a place or is a party leader or is a union leader, has been taken prisoner. They came to his or her house to get him or her, or they took him
or her out late last night or they took him or her from work or they got
him or her in the university"—I don't remember the exact words—then
we announced this information immediately. This way, then, we saved

many people, because we said "carabineros took them prisoner, the military took them prisoner, they took them to such-and-such a place, and
they must be there right now." Do you see? That is, we kept track of
where people were. People often came to the station — they put a lot of
faith in the radio. So, because of this I tell you, it was not just the area
you covered — you did that, but also, you did other things. Suddenly, one
weekend you had to cover your area, but also you had to cover what the
rest of your colleagues who had the weekend off couldn't cover, don't you
see?

Radio Cooperativa belonged to factions of the Christian Democrats. I
think that it was one of the important contributions that the Christian
Democrats made toward ending the dictatorship and keeping the dictatorship from committing even more atrocities than it already had. And I
think that the station played an important part, don't you see? I think that
all of us, all of us, that is, from the errand boy to the manager all played a
role that was truly extraordinary. Remember that in the first years of the
station — the years 1980, 1981, 1982, when the station began to be what it
is now — at that time it was economically strangled because it didn't have
ads, because it didn't have financing. So, really, the people who worked
during those years, many times worked without thinking about whether
they would be paid a salary or not. Many times. So then, the radio station
played a key role, yes, it did.

We worked on the plebiscite many months in advance, preparing people, being sure they knew that a "NO" vote was everyone's salvation, that
we had to be united, but that we couldn't give them any excuse for repression. And the long-awaited day arrived, October 5 [1988], on which I
was assigned to be at the "NO" headquarters the whole day and do the
sign-off. The station created a link with fifty-four stations around the
world. And the day after the plebiscite, or the day after that, when I was
asleep at about five or six in the morning, a call came from Australia, from
some friend who had heard me in Australia — some friends with whom I
had lived in Lima who had heard me. And later, a friend who had heard
me in Barcelona — so that it was really nice, I can tell you . . .

There at the "NO" headquarters, there was a computer center where
we began to get information between 4:30 and 5:00 P.M., approximately.
We knew that we were really hoping that "NO" would win because of that
gigantic march there was, where people and delegations came from all
over the country. It was a march that took place on the North–South
highway [on October 1]; there were more than a million people in that
march. And I can tell you that when I speak about how we saw the situa-

tion—"we" were the journalists of the Cooperativa—but when I speak of "us," I think that really it was all Chileans at heart, or at least 80 percent of the Chileans. In that moment, having the opportunity to have a micro-phone and speak to the whole country—because the station was and is still a station that is listened to all over Chile, then one obviously was rep-resenting the concerns of many people.

That day at the "NO" headquarters went by in great hope, but also with great fear until very late that night, until a celebration started in this whole part of the Alameda [the main avenue of downtown Santiago]. The "NO" headquarters was a very tiny thing, right in front of the Diego Por-tales building [a huge edifice built under the Allende government as a cul-tural center; under the dictatorship it housed government offices, in-cluding Pinochet's], where the whole computer system of the Pinochet government was housed, and we were in a very small area that was filled with Chilean journalists, full of foreign correspondents, and we got very, very encouraging news as the night went on. We already knew that we had won by a big majority. So then when Genaro Arriagada [Christian Demo-cratic manager of the "NO" campaign] made the last calculations in the "NO" headquarters, the truth is that there was a general weeping, I tell you. That is, everything that you had stored up all those years—the fact that all of Chile had said, "No, Mr. Pinochet, it's time for you to get out"—the emotion was tremendous, very difficult to describe to you at this moment, but I think that I made more than one report with more than one tear in my eye.

Of course, at this point, we didn't know the official results. Then, it was around two o'clock in the morning, wasn't it, when Matthei [General Fernando Matthei, air force commander and a junta member since 1978] was the one who acknowledged it, and he acknowledged it on Radio Co-operativa too. He acknowledged it to Gema Contreras [another radio journalist at Radio Cooperativa], when he said, "Yes, in fact, the 'NO' vote has won." So then the tension was really great. We had carabineros stationed in front, we had carabineros stationed all around us. That is, the headquarters was surrounded by special forces, and there was military too, but I can tell you that there was a lot of effervescence, a lot of emo-tion, I don't know, it's hard to explain the combination of feelings that one had at that moment. I think that it was much more moving than knowing that Aylwin had beaten Büchi [Concertación candidate Patricio Aylwin defeated military-backed Hernán Büchi in the 1989 presidential election]. Much, much greater. The next day, the way the young people went out to celebrate. The best thing, maybe, is knowing that one way or another, the media where I worked contributed to keeping the majority of people at home, not out on the streets, to avoid confrontation, so that there would not be any excuse for any further killing. Look, we presented, more or less, a social chronicle, and at the end we said, "Don't forget October 5, get up early, go vote and then go home and celebrate at home, no one ought to be out on the street."

I tell you that our tears on the night the "NO" won released a great deal of tension, saying that "Well, finally, finally, we are going to be able to breathe."

## Sergio Buschmann

*While most returning activists engaged in political work in anticipation of the 1988 plebiscite, members of the MIR and the Communist Party returned for that purpose as well as to lay foundations for an armed struggle against the dictatorship. In order to resuscitate its decimated underground resistance, the MIR in 1978 had adopted the policy of ordering members to enter Chile clandestinely. Although challenging the military's seemingly absolute control appeared to be a suicide mission, substantial numbers of MIRistas did return after 1978 to rebuild the party. The MIR also began building a base for guerrilla training in Neltume, a remote site in the southern Andean foothills. Discovered in 1981, the unfinished Neltume camp was destroyed and its operatives liquidated.*

*In a radical change from its historic policy of gradualism, the Communist Party in 1980 endorsed the armed struggle as one of several tactics to employ against the dictatorship. Sergio Buschmann (introduced in chapter 2), exiled in 1977 after underground resistance, returned to Chile in 1983 to establish the Communist Party's armed wing, the Manuel Rodríguez Patriotic Front (FPMR). The FPMR was a central component in the 1983–1986 popular protests, particularly through its affiliated "militias" of alienated youth from Santiago's poblaciones, who, feeling they had little or nothing to lose, threw themselves repeatedly against military and carabinero forces and paid a large price in casualties. The FPMR's most spectacular action was a September 1986 assassination attempt against Pinochet, in which several bodyguards were killed, but the general escaped unscathed.*

*Buschmann was arrested with other Front members a month before the assassination attempt, for illegal importation of arms through an isolated cove on Chile's north coast. The following year, with three companions, he*

*escaped from prison in Valparaíso and made his way abroad. Like hundreds*
*of individuals charged with armed resistance to the Pinochet government,*
*Buschmann could not return to Chile without risking detention and prose-*
*cution by military courts, despite the return of civilian government in*
*1990.\* In a highly publicized move, Sergio Buschman returned in June*
*1994 and, after eighteen months of detention, was released. Rather than*
*being pardoned for his role in opposing the dictatorship by force of arms, he*
*was sentenced by a military court in August 1997—eighteen months after*
*this interview—to ten years in prison.*

In exile, we had formed the "Zero" Front, which was the embryo of what later became the Manuel Rodríguez Patriotic Front, and I came for the founding of the Front in December of 1983. I was lucky that around that time I appeared on the last list of those who could return legally, so that I came in legally and immediately I join the underground struggle. We form the Front—we begin to develop an armed front against the dictatorship. I participate in getting arms for our liberation from Carrizal Bajo [a cove near the northern town of Vallenar], and I am arrested again there in August of 1986. I am tortured again.

Those movements from Carrizal Bajo were detected by spy planes that flew over the continent constantly. What happened is that since we only operated at night, they detected something but didn't know what it was. They discover the arms cache through the torture of compañeros who broke down. They torture all of us for being in a "school of guerrillas," because they were sure that what they had found was a school for guerrillas and not a cache of arms for liberation. So they tortured me savagely, but again were not able to get anything at all out of me, and I was transferred to the penitentiary in Santiago. Then, through orders from the military prosecutors, they take me to Valparaíso. I tried to escape from the penitentiary in Santiago without any luck, but the attempt in Valparaíso was successful. Four of the members of the FPMR escaped in August of 1987.

In the following days, I integrate into the clandestine struggle, and the next year I leave the country to carry out an international task of explaining to the world who the FPMR was, why it had been formed, why we had taken up arms, and what our role was. And I travel through a good part of

---

\* Estimates of the numbers of Chileans facing charges of armed resistance range from three hundred to over one thousand (*La Epoca*, June 26, 1994, and *El Mercurio*, June 26, 1994).

the world explaining this, and the Americans even mess up, because they kidnap me from a plane when I was going from Australia to Amsterdam at a routine stop in Anchorage, Alaska. The CIA just gets on the plane, twists my arms behind me, and takes me off the plane. Now they make a big mistake, because they think that I am traveling with false papers. But no, because the United Nations had recognized my status and I was traveling with a UN passport.

There was a great international protest and they made the U.S. government responsible for what might happen to me. So then the UN comes to Alaska and they have to admit that they have me prisoner. Of course, if I had been traveling like I did many times with false papers, I would have never been seen again. Later, we sued the U.S. State Department and we won. They had to pay 150,000 dollars in damages. Half of that went for costs, and I got 65,000 dollars, which I gave to the Chilean left.

Even after Aylwin's government took office in 1990, I was outside the country and those who killed and murdered their own people were still able to keep me out of my own country. In spite of the fact that they had had me in their torture chambers, to further complicate my life they put out an extradition order once a year. It was crazy because each time it was more ridiculous. They had told them no in Sweden, in the U.S., in Germany, in Australia, in Nicaragua. I think that this was a way to tell me "Don't even think about coming back here because we will arrest you." All the military power is still intact through the military prosecutors. Those who tortured and murdered continue to be those judging the people that they murdered, tortured, or made disappear. They are their own judges through their military prosecutors — none of this has been changed in what we call this "small democratic space."

So I didn't have any other alternative than to come back and go to jail. What other path did I have? We are not working underground today, that doesn't make sense at the present time. While there is an alternative to being killed, don't give up your life — we have always looked at it that way. The gun appears when they kill you, when they come after you, when they don't let you express yourself. But given that there is a small democratic space, being underground doesn't work any more. Being underground is foreseen for the day when the right tries again to order the military to stage a coup, and yes, then we would go back into hiding and take up arms again. I hope that it will not be necessary, we hope that we can enlarge the democratic space.

They have charged me with illegal arms possession; the only charge that they have is illegal possession of arms, violation of the arms-control law. So that was why I spent a year and six months in jail before they re-leased me November 14, 1995. That is when I have to, let's say, integrate once again. Of course, the attitude of people on the streets is great, the admiration and affection that people show at all times, from the first day and still today. And of course, here comes the other thing, the black part, which is that the dictatorship continues to control the job market and all the rest. In this aspect, I haven't been able to find work. This is such a great injustice, and there is so little that people can do, that it makes me really angry. The former prisoners that fought against the dictatorship don't have a right to anything. To give you one example: I couldn't renew my driver's license. I went to renew it and they turned it down.

I had a possibility of working with a vehicle, but I couldn't do it, be-cause with my record I can't get a driver's license. And why even mention the compañeros who have managed to start little businesses here and there, getting checks from their in-laws, everything in friends' or in cousins' names. The man who fought against the dictatorship and was a prisoner has no legal rights. This is something that is maddening and humiliating—it is something that we aren't going to put up with any longer.

We just formed a committee of ex-political prisoners and we will go to international organizations and we will have signs and we will tell the whole world how shameful it is—how shameful it is that it is even possible that still today we tolerate this kind of control by the murderers of the people who were the shame of modern international politics. Nothing, a political prisoner can't have anything—not a bank account, not a savings account, nothing, he can't have anything legally. And we have had—we have to say this too—five years of a democratic opening. How can you jus-tify that the national shame of the military prosecutors continues? No one can give me work, I don't have work, so then they still have their power everywhere and add to that the fact that you can't have anything legally if you went to jail for having fought against the dictatorship.

# NINE

# Return to a New Exile, 1988–1994

The military government's liberalized policy on return, adopted under pressure in 1984, formally opened the doors for most exiles to go home. For the great majority, however, the new policy meant little because of the continuing impediments to their return. Most exiles were leery of living under the same dictatorship that had forced them out of their country. Furthermore, the government's new return policy was adopted at a time when both political and economic conditions were uninviting.

On the political front, the government faced the outbreak of popular opposition beginning in 1982. On one hand, this awakened hope among exiles for an earlier end to the dictatorship than that which might result from the scheduled 1988 plebiscite. On the other hand, the regime's responses to the rising opposition clearly demonstrated its willingness to use as much force as necessary to retain control, as reflected in the internationally reported 1985 murders of three Communist leaders (the degollados), the 1986 burnings of two children by a military patrol, and a dramatic increase in the number of political exiles. In the economic realm, the boom of the late 1970s had given way in 1982 to Chile's worst economic crisis since the Great Depression, and a sustained recovery did not begin until 1986. This made the prospect of finding employment even bleaker for returning exiles, who already faced the blacklist as well as negative attitudes of the business sector toward hiring them.

The 1984 repatriation policy, moreover, was narrowly juridical. It was a concession wrung from the regime under duress. The government continued to discourage return by offering no incentives or services for returning exiles, in contrast to the generous terms it had offered the few Chileans who had left during the UP government. Moreover, it was not uncommon for returning exiles to be turned back upon arriving, on the pretext that their papers were not in order, and for those admitted into the country to face harassment in various forms. News of this kind of reception certainly discouraged many of those inclined to return.

In the absence of governmental support, a host of nongovernmental organizations attempted to fill the void by developing a variety of services designed to promote and facilitate return. Some of these agencies were the same ones that earlier had fought to get the persecuted safely out of the country: the Vicaría de la Solidaridad, FASIC, the OIM, and the World University Service (WUS) prominent among them. Foreign governments and private foreign agencies also helped. These organizations offered information on return, free or subsidized passages, short-term living allowances, employment services, low-interest loans to establish small businesses, psychological services for adults and children, and other forms of aid.

With the approach of the October 1988 plebiscite on Pinochet's continuance in power, the pace of return picked up. By now the economy was booming again, and the periodic lists of excluded persons continually shrank until the government, seeking to legitimize the plebiscite it expected to win, formally lifted the ban on return on September 1, thus allowing even its worst enemies to return. The opposition victory in the plebiscite was followed in December 1989 by the victory of Patricio Aylwin, representing the broad antigovernment coalition Concertación de Partidos por la Democracia, over the military's candidate in the first presidential election since 1970.

The civilian government inaugurated in March 1990 acted quickly to promote exiles' return. Among its first acts were the establishment of the Oficina Nacional de Retorno (ONR) and the passage of laws creating a commission to validate the degrees and professional certificates of returning exiles and exempting up to twenty-five thousand dollars worth of their belongings from customs duties. The ONR had a modest budget, limited powers, and a four-year life span. It acted primarily as a coordinating and referral agency, relying on the existing private agencies to provide most of the concrete assistance to *retornados*. Although largely symbolic, these measures in conjunction with the end of the dictatorship stimulated a wave of return from exile. During the four years of its existence, through August 1994, the ONR served 56,000 persons.[*]

For most exiles, the return to Chile has been a disappointing, even a bitter experience. They have faced numerous and varied problems: unemployment; discrimination; bureaucratic indifference to their needs; rejection; and alienation in a country that, many feel, is not the same country they left fifteen or twenty years earlier. Almost without exception, those who have returned report frustration, malaise, despair, and a feeling of being strangers in their homeland. They sense little attempt at reconciliation on the part of most Chileans; rather, they feel frequent reminders that they were the losers in 1973, and believe they are treated as such. To some, return is a new exile. Against this backdrop, it is not surprising that some retornados have gone back to their adopted homelands, often exacerbating the fragmentation of families initially sundered by exile, later by return to Chile. Nor is it surprising that a majority of exiles had not returned by 1994, when the closing of the ONR symbolically marked the end of Chile's era of mass exile.

## Padre Luis Caro

*Father Luis Caro (introduced in chapter 6) spent ten years in Western Europe as a missionary to the Chilean exile community. Beginning in the early 1980s, he was active in the pro-return movement and worked closely with return committees in several countries. He returned to Chile in 1990 to serve his order, and has continued his involvement with issues of exile and return. With his firsthand knowledge of the phenomenon of repatriation, Father Caro offers the perspective of a participant observer.*

---

[*] Oficina Nacional de Retorno, "Informe Final" (Santiago, 1995), 5. Note that this figure includes returning economic as well as political exiles.

What we always intended in the Exile Pastoral work was to have the right to live in our own country. That was our struggle. Then that had to be accompanied by a job in order to have that right, to reach that objective. It was not the goodness of Pinochet, the goodness of the dictatorship. Now, how many people did this work? They were a minority. I would go to a meeting of some pro-return committee and it was always the same people. And later, you ran into people and heard: "But they don't do anything." "But how can you say 'They don't do anything?,'" I said to them. "We have to do it together." So then I said to them, "But you, tell me what are you waiting for? For others to do things for us?"

As far as the return of Chileans to their country, there was willingness on the part of the majority of the European governments — some more, others less. Many local organizations, churches, political parties, humanitarian organizations were always ready to help Chileans with their plans to return. I think that, in this sense, we can say that the Chileans enjoyed a certain advantage: they always had local support, as great as when they arrived, later when it had to do with going back.

We put forth great effort to try to make returning easier. We went to the German Parliament, to different ministries, trying to find some way to get the funds that had accumulated in retirement contributions transferred to Chile, for example, but we didn't succeed in that effort. So then one could ask: "What support did they give?" Of course, there was moral support.

There were countries that didn't really want the Chileans to leave. For example, Sweden did not really want the people who had been trained to leave because you have to remember that Sweden provided training for people. They paid for their language classes, they made a series of investments. When you say, "Oh, how good the Swedes were!," yes, but also they did it with the idea that they would have manpower, that they would have certain things guaranteed in the future. It was much cheaper for them to train an exile than a Swedish child. Now they don't want the Chileans to leave, because it would mean that they would have to bring Romanians, bring people from the east, and have to invest all over again for them to learn the language.

Some say that if they help the Chileans go back they would have to do the same thing with the Turks, and with all the Turks that there are in Germany, for example, this would be hard for them to do. If they give the retirement funds back to the Chileans, then they would have to do that with all their immigrants and they have an enormous number.

In France, for example, there were organizations that put out a good deal of publicity about going back. But when it came to concrete help, there wasn't any. So then, if I have to go to Chile a shipping container would cost me five thousand dollars. So then I have to know: "Am I going to take the armchairs that I have? Am I going to take the refrigerator? Should I take them or not?" In those countries they reuse things, but if you sell a refrigerator second hand they aren't going to give you anything for it. And in Chile if I am going to buy one, it will be very expensive. The pro-return committees saw all of these practical details. What happened was that the Chileans began to look for help on their own. For example, some of them got together and rented a container among two or three families.

I think that those who were prepared for their return did not have major problems. That is, those who thought "I am going back to Chile under such and such conditions" and saved, they haven't had problems. Those who have had the greatest problems are those who didn't look ahead, or couldn't plan ahead, and who thought that in Chile someone would help them. For example, the people who have returned from Argentina, or from other Latin American countries.

In general, the people who came from the richer countries could perhaps save ten thousand dollars that would allow them to get settled, or they simply sold their car and their house—if they had managed to buy them—and with that in Chile make a down payment on a house, do certain minimal things. But the people that come from Argentina, Brazil, or even some countries of Europe in which it was hard to get good jobs—like France—come with nothing. Also, there are those who never worked in exile, who lived on social welfare or the unemployment systems of those countries. Those people expect to get everything from the Oficina de Retorno. And we know that the office doesn't give economic assistance. This office is for orientation, nothing more. The office refers, registers—administrative things—provides orientation.

Because of this, I say that those who prepared for their return are going to find it much easier to reintegrate into the country. When they have a place to come to, a concrete place to live—but, if not, you have to go to relatives. The first week, the entire family is happy to have you back, but after a week, "Well, and how long are we going to have them here?" It can be very uncomfortable if people don't become independent; there will be family conflicts. Women come back with a different way of thinking, then they get here and they clash with their family, with their mother—because of how they act, how they raise their children, how they dress. There are several things that changed her while she was away and that seem normal to her now.

I came back with the idea of starting a home for young people, a place where young people can be taken in. The idea was that then the young people could do something more than just come to Chile to visit their families, between December and March [summer vacation in Chile], go to the festival in Viña [del Mar], the beach, and vacations, and then return to Sweden. It is not the same thing to come for vacation as to come to stay. But no one supported me – no one – but everyone said that it sounded like a very good idea: "This is excellent, it's the best thing you could do, with your experience, this will be very positive," but "We don't have any money to help you." Tell me, then, "Where can I go?" There isn't anywhere.

We need to be aware that a young person who comes from Sweden, from Canada, from England, Germany, France cannot be expected to know the history of Chile, nor to speak Spanish, nor anything. So we need to find a way to help them get into the university. There are so many barriers that exist and which haven't been dismantled. Those who return also are going to find problems with health care, with housing, a number of things. The degrees that they received in foreign countries – here there is a serious problem because many arrive desirous of working in their country and their degrees aren't accepted and they can't work.

One is aware that there are different economic problems that we know that everybody in Chile has, but there are other things that can be fixed. Even the service of the Oficina de Retorno is awful. Every day, people lined up in the street. So then, there is a difference between their arrival in exile and their arrival here. The difference is very great. Here, in order to let them know that I have arrived, I have to stand in the street, in the Alameda, waiting for them to give me a number and then waiting with this number for them to schedule me for an appointment a month later. Why can't they just say by telephone, "Come such and such a day at such and such a time?" Now the Oficina de Retorno isn't open any longer.* Even though the help that it gave was small, they could have waited a little longer before closing it.

I think that the reception that the Chileans who have returned have been given has not been ideal. But if one compares it with so many other

---

\* The Oficina Nacional de Retorno was technically still open at the time of the interview with Father Caro, but it had stopped accepting new clients in anticipation of its closing in August 1994.

things that have happened in the country—the violation of human rights, the disappeared, impunity for crimes, the serious economic crisis that was experienced under the dictatorship—then compared to that, this, the situation of those returning, is only one more.

## Francisco Ruiz

*Pancho Ruiz (introduced in chapter 3) spent fifteen years of exile in Canada. He considered himself well adjusted to his adopted country, but could not resist returning to Chile when the opportunity arose. Today, he is a businessman in Santiago. Although economically well off, Ruiz tells of the social and psychological problems that affect exiles upon their return.*

I arrived in Chile in a fairly good situation. But, in general, I think that many Chileans have had a hard time settling in with any comfort. Those of us who were in Canada have found it very hard to reintegrate here in Chile. In Canada, from the very first day, someone brought you an armchair, another an old refrigerator, clothing for the children. There was a good deal of help. This has not happened in Chile. In general, you can say that no one helps you.

When you get here, there is not one Chilean who asks you, "What do you need? What was it like? What was your experience like? What did you do?" It is as if there were a collective conspiracy to say that those years that you lived in another country—and they are more than a few, fourteen or more—didn't exist for you. They don't want to know anything: "Don't tell me; I'm not interested." So then, it is so strange—you feel that part of your life exists only for you.

Abroad, I got divorced, I got married, I had another son, I adopted a Canadian daughter. I spent fifteen years there, I spent my whole life there, and there is no one who will ask you, "What did you do? What was your life like? What happened to you?" Nothing, and you ask, "When will the vast majority of Chileans feel the need to talk?" This is what we talk about among ourselves, those who have returned. With foreigners there is a sympathy, curiosity: "Well, tell me, what is the food like there?" There is a thread of conversation. But in general, the people are not even interested in talking to us.

I know that there are people in my family who love me a good deal, but I don't think that anyone knows what work I did, how I made a living, or what it was like. They have no idea. I have never understood it. Why? I have no idea. It is something that I talk about with Chileans who come back and when I bring this up, they feel the same way. It seems to me that those ten or fifteen years can't just be tossed out as if they had never existed for you and your family. You can't talk about it or share it, nothing.

We have found there to be a strange mentality. If you come back and you are relatively well off economically, they are going to be jealous of your "golden exile." If you come back in bad shape, they tell you, "I would have done better." It's like there's no way to escape this.

I go to Canada frequently and what I talk about with my friends for years has been: "Pancho, what can you do with thirty thousand dollars in Chile?" or "What can I do with so much money in Chile?" It is always the same friends with the same thirty thousand dollars. I tell them that I can't give them any advice, nothing. The only thing that I can tell them is: "When you get to Chile go in through the window, be quiet and begin your life. Find some of the friends that you had before and if you are not able to meet new people now, it's better that you don't go back, because you will not be able to recreate a world that doesn't exist any longer."

Before I went back, I thought that I had many friends in Chile. In general, there are a lot fewer than I thought. I always said that I had a million friends in Chile—when you go back you realize that they are very few. I was lucky to put in a café and through the café had contact with many people who have returned. Also people from the artistic world, musicians, TV people—new friendships were born, but it was because I created a place to meet people who would talk. But that is a unique situation.

Sometimes I think that we are tearing down the barricades and the truth is that we are not doing anything. The other day I went to see *The House of the Spirits* [movie based on Isabel Allende's novel]. I cried halfway through the tape. You think that you are under control—that's not true. They show you an image that makes you remember people close to you that died or situations that you experienced and there is nothing that you can do. You totally fall apart. I think that we have to learn to live with that. There are sorrows so great that they will always be there and there is nothing that you can do to change that.

We came with two adolescent children, thirteen and fourteen years old—when they were just entering adolescence—and the little Canadian girl. Now, again, I tell you that I am in a privileged situation. I came back to a kind of condominium, a neighborhood consisting of a group of houses in which all of us who live there think more or less alike. In this group, there were many children, so we got there one day and two days later my children had a social life. Within a week they had a school. So then, with a school, life in the neighborhood, being well off economically, it wasn't hard. Even now that they are going to go to the university, I gave them the choice of going back and the answer was "outside the country, nothing doing." There was no scene. They don't miss anything. In their cases, it has been easy.

On the contrary, I have had friends who, at night, their children of the same ages as ours left lists for their parents on the table: "We had such and such for breakfast in Canada; we have this now." The pressure has been so great that they have had to go back. A complete crisis, a great deal of conflict because of the image of Chile that the children got from their parents and it doesn't exist any longer. We had such an incredible Chile, that is, we were constantly remembering things. Exile makes you have an incredible imagination and fantasies. For many other children, it has been traumatic, especially for the people who came from richer countries.

My compañera is a different case. She is Canadian, she is active intellectually, doing things, the kind of things she did in Canada. I always thought that it would be a problem when I returned; I didn't want to have to get another divorce to be able to live in my country. So that it was something that made me nervous. But not her; she was very willing to come. I always tried to play down the image of Chile, so that the blow would not be so hard for her. She said one day, "I have to integrate," and she began to give a monologue about what it meant to be married to a Chilean exile who had lived in Canada and who returned to his country. Something funny. She began to work with a very well-known comic here in Chile and had a run of a year and a half and toured all over Chile; she went to Canada, New York, Washington, with this piece. So I think that she resolved all her problems by putting them in the show.

Now, I came back, not because it was a problem for me to live in Canada, but I needed for my children to live this life, to raise them here. I was moved by the concern that my children be in Chile in this period of adolescence. That was the principal reason.

It is very frustrating. Through psychoanalysis, I got through it or I probably would have carried this frustration to my grave.

## Eduardo Olivares

*After fourteen years in Paris, where he worked a series of blue-collar jobs, Eduardo Olivares (introduced in chapter 3) returned in 1989 with his wife and family. He works in the human resources department of the Compañía de Teléfonos de Chile. Having approached exile in as positive a manner as possible, he faced repatriation with low expectations. As his testimony reveals, he reintegrated into Chile with fewer problems than many returning exiles precisely because he came home without illusions.*

Return has been like I expected, because I always had the following idea: if we were here in Chile, trying to change the country, it was because the country wasn't perfect. Chile is your country, but you have discovered that there are other countries, other people, and that, somewhere else, you begin to live with the people, and it doesn't matter where those people are from. You begin to discover identities beyond the different cultures and the different nationalities. You discover that behind all this there is a new man and a new woman; there are hopes that are the same, love stories that are the same, houses on the beach that are the same, vanities and sorrows that are the same. Now, each one expresses them, some with the blues, some with a *bolero* [a popular Latin American musical form], others with Piaf [Edith Piaf, French singer]. But, finally, there is one thing that you have in common, and one discovers that, and that makes you feel not so far from home in another place.

So, I tell you that I didn't have the idea that I had left behind a perfect country, and I also thought that there was no reason to think that the dictatorship had improved it—on the contrary. For those reasons, I didn't have any illusions about arriving in an earthly paradise. I didn't come with expectations.

On the other hand, I also was very sure that there would not be an overwhelming reception. With all the propaganda that the dictatorship disseminated against the exiles, it could be supposed that the exiles were not only terrorists, violent people, Communists, but also that they were people enjoying some long vacation and a trip around the world. So that they were unsympathetic rather than sympathetic characters. Besides, the people in Chile during the dictatorship had a very hard time. They lived through a difficult situation regardless of what their political ideas were. There are even people on the right who were very unhappy about not being able to go out at night when there was a curfew, for example. That is, this means one thing: they didn't feel that they were living in a marvelous situation either, and therefore had the impression that those who were on "vacation" outside the country were having a better time.

So there was no reason to expect that you would get here and they would say to you, "Poor thing, come, we will take care of you." No. I think that the most logical thing was for the opposite to happen. So there was no reason to think that they would throw open the doors for you, nor that they would take care of you, nor expect that they would solve your problems, rather that you would relearn how to live together in a country that wasn't the same. In all these years, I haven't stayed the same, other people have also changed. Your friend or your brother, however close he may be, if you cut yourself off from him for fourteen years that changes the whole relationship for both of you.

I came back with two children who were born there, and I wouldn't have allowed myself to impose a reverse exile on them — because Chile was their parents' history, not theirs. In France, they talk a lot about your primary residence and your secondary residence, when you have a house in the country or at the beach. I told them: "What we are going to do is change our principal residence."

If someone asked me, "Will you go back?," I would answer them, "No, I won't go back. The world is round, so I will get to Chile again, and maybe I will stay." But I don't think that this structure of reasons and feelings is what will allow you to arrive here in a relaxed state, without being afraid, without judging, without saying, "Oh! I didn't get the reception that I thought I would." I think, finally, that this has meant more pleasant surprises for me than the opposite. I wasn't expecting anything and the little I have gotten is enough for me.

People, in general, are not interested in how you lived there. They ask you, "What are you doing here? What have you come for? Did you come with anything? Did you bring a little money?" So, then, this whole story is an unresolved subject, not talked about like so many other things in this country; that is, there is a strong tendency in this country to sweep the dirt under the rug.

Evidently, the subject of the exiles and those who have returned, in the order of priorities, is very far off, is way back. What I get passionate about, and I am determined in this, is to look for ways in which the exiles can contribute what they have brought back. This is like when an uncle comes to visit and brings chocolates, pencils, toys. Well, we brought things that we learned, ways of life, windows open to other realities that could get this country out of its insularity, its provincialism. It would be good to be able to make these possible contributions in some systematic way, but, up till now, they are contributions that people make individually. I start from the premise that we have more possibility than those who stayed here of understanding the complexity of the subject, because I believe that Chile allows little; other realities allow more, other confrontations, other, more open dialogues. Countries like France, like the United States, that is a country that currently has exiles living there. This country lived a dictatorship, with a communications system that put forth these and those ideas. Then a democracy came along which has fought against the dictatorship only in certain areas.

I think that the saddest situation is that of those who had harbored a lot of illusions. The people who spent all the years of exile resisting the idea of integrating into the countries where they were, out of a fixed idea of loyalty to Chile and being Chilean. Thinking that you should only speak to your children in Spanish, dance cuecas [traditional Chilean dance], eat empanadas. Resisting the richness of a different place—you don't have to stop loving what is yours to be enriched by new things. And the people who came back with this problem, those people, I think that for them it has been a great tragedy, because those people didn't integrate well there, expecting to return to the Chile of 1973, and find that today's Chile is nothing like it, nothing like it, nothing. So that it is very tragic for them, because this Chile is very hard, very, very, hard.

And besides, exile, with all its institutions, solidarity, made many people very dependent. Solidarity is an extremely dangerous drug, and the dependency on it is hard to break. Think about what happened here. The person who worked to earn a living, normally, with a good deal of effort and from one day to the next, there is a coup d'état and he finds himself in an embassy. Evidently, it is a situation in which there is a loss of freedom, but seen from another perspective, compared to ordinary people, he doesn't work, they feed him, he is housed, they put him on a plane—people who especially in 1973 didn't travel much—and he travels to Europe, a continent that he had never even dreamed of visiting. And all this "free"—at least in some cases. You get there and you are housed somewhere, people come that you don't know and they tell you: "I brought you this for your baby, I brought a toy, I have an old car that I can give you if you want," and this creates dependence.

I know people who, in fact, said, "This is the opportunity of my life." Truly, there are people who got used to there always being someone who was going to give them a hand, and they get to Chile and here it is different. No one gives you anything. They can't. So that it is a rather big difference and that has been extremely difficult for the vast majority of those who have returned.

## Eduardo Saavedra

*Eduardo Saavedra (introduced in chapter 5) came back to Chile in 1988 with his wife, but without his children. Although his circumstances in Brazil, where he spent most of his exile, were far from optimum, he is bitter about having returned. He criticizes Chileans for what he considers their materialism, philistinism, and lack of political concern, and resents the changes that occurred under the military dictatorship—changes that made adjustment very difficult for many returnees. Unemployed for six years after his return, Saavedra now works for the Ministry of Health in Concepción.*

I am not glad that I came back. No, not at all. I don't know if I would prefer to be in Brazil, but, in all sincerity, I would rather be in Europe. I think that is an experience that I ought to—at this point in my life—have, before my final departure. I think that it is good for anyone who can do it.

Now, speaking in journalistic terms, I would really like to have an experience of that kind also in Spain, for example, working on a newspaper like *El País* [one of the leading Madrid dailies, founded after Franco's death]. Of course, I am a dreamer, at sixty-five, I know that. I had a chance at *La Época* [one of the most important Santiago daily newspapers], but unfortunately I got sick. I had recently been operated on for prostate and I had complications, so that it wasn't possible for me to work at the pace that the paper demanded.

Upon our return, we have found a country so different that it has no relation to what we expected. The people—the people are so selfish, so individualistic, so self-centered, and what worries me most is that they have no illusions, no hopes. Also, there is still this cultural blackout. You live to have a few pesos to buy foreign magazines, to see that elsewhere there are things you would like to know about. I would like to have nine thousand pesos (twenty-five dollars in U.S. currency) in order to have cable TV, to see Spanish television, and to know that there are still things going on and that you are still interested. We live in cultural mediocrity. But finally, what hurts me most about living in this country is the hypocrisy that we are sunk in.

I cannot understand the calmness with which people accept or don't talk about so many shameful situations. We weren't like that, we didn't accept that kind of thing. I don't know whether to call it indifference, lack of interest. I have not had the opportunity to have conversations on the level that I am having now for this project. In Santiago, you don't talk to anyone, because no one is interested. They are all worried about what time it is, because tomorrow they have to go to work at seven o'clock in the morning and my *pituto* [connection needed to get a job] this and my pituto that; that is, no one is concerned at all to know what is happening in the world nowadays, they are wrapped up in themselves, that's all.

For example, I had a very interesting family and they were all active in political parties until 1973. Now, they are people concerned only with get-ting together enough money to go to Iquique to buy things. They all stopped being active politically, being concerned about their politicians — they voted for Frei so that Alessandri wouldn't win [a reference to the 1993 presidential election won by Christian Democrat Eduardo Frei, in which conservative Arturo Alessandri finished second in a field of six] — to such an extreme that they don't want to see the difference between a govern-ment that will maintain the status quo like that of Frei and an alternative like that of Max Neef [candidate of the new Humanist Party, who placed fourth with 5.5 percent of the vote] or any other. No, none of that, and I am telling you this because my sisters were political and they have lost it — they don't want to hear anything about it. And so, then, they exchanged it for things, like, for example, having a car. Even our daughter also is con-cerned about having a car with a catalytic converter, living the "mall lifestyle," and she who was a leader of the Socialist Party and doesn't talk about that at all — she doesn't want to hear anything about politics, she's not interested.

Something positive about coming back has been the satisfaction of being in the country, of being with your friends, your relatives, and more importantly, trying every way you can to integrate yourself into this struggle and try to do something more. We have been trying to integrate for six years.

## Mario González

*Mario González (introduced in chapter 2), a former flight mechanic in the air force, spent his exile in England. Upon returning in 1989, he en-countered the practical problems of discrimination in employment, unaf-fordable education, and the general indifference of society. González's testi-mony also brings out the common problem of having one's retirement or*

*unemployment funds stolen from public agencies during exile. Subsisting on
a small pension and part-time work, González lives with his family in
Santiago.*

Coming back has been very hard. Hard in the sense that Chilean society
has almost no interest in looking back at what happened, making a critical
analysis, and being able to see the reaction and being able to look at our
experiences in the positive sense of trying to make this better and so that
this never happens again. You don't see this in Chilean society nor in
the Chilean people, except for the groups that are in solidarity with the
political prisoner, the disappeared, the prisoners who were executed. We
find that this country, this society, has no warm welcome for those who
have returned. It's a society that is not interested in learning from our
experience — in the sense of giving something back to us for what we, at
least, tried to do to end this — people don't see it that way, they have no interest in learning about our experience. In England, yes, there was great
interest, unselfish, open, a hunger to know what our country was like —
here, no.

I think that it is the way it is because of the way that society was
changed during the dictatorship. They presented us in a certain role, the
role of frustrated guerrilla or frustrated terrorist, and like people who
would never be useful in this society. That was something they did
throughout the entire dictatorship. Now what has been imposed on people is this economic system, practically alienating people, of having this
attitude of living for today in the sense of unrestrained consumerism.
That is, who is it that is considered successful? The person who has more
money and not the one who is able to think or analyze, or develop as a
person. I see this ignored in the schools.

I have a very vivid memory of when I returned, because I couldn't get
work: first, because I was an exile and had been expelled from the armed
forces, and also because I don't have a high school diploma; I received a
military education and a military humanities formation. I had to get my
high school equivalency in order to be able to work or to go on with my
studies. My decision was to continue studying public administration and
political science, so then to get my diploma I had to pass an exam of first
to fourth year of secondary school, which was very hard. The other alternative was to study a year and do the third and fourth years of high school
and get my high school diploma. Since I had time — I wasn't working — I
went to a school for adults and began to study with boys who were eighteen, nineteen, or twenty years old. There, I began to have contact with

Chile again, the Chile of today. They didn't know where I was from, but they thought I talked a little funny and someone said to me, "You are from somewhere else, you come from another country," and I told them, "Of course — I was in such and such a place," and so they began to find out. They learned a lot from me, and I learned from them in the sense that I talked with them about things that I had seen in Europe, that I had known in Europe that they thought of as something very far away. So then, the history, math teachers realized that I was one of those who had returned. The history teacher, with great solidarity, said to me: "Your experience is very good, very rich. I want the young ones to learn from you and you can tell them about the things that you saw. I'm with you, I am very sorry about what happened to you, and we are going to help you in every way we can."

I managed to get my diploma and I decided to take the academic aptitude test. I got enough points to get into the University of Santiago in public administration and political science, but I don't have money to study. I was studying political science in the Academy of Christian Humanism for some six months, but it was very expensive. I asked for a reduced tuition rate and they didn't give it to me, only a discount of 2 percent. I had to pay some 50,000 pesos a month [about 125 U.S. dollars], and I couldn't manage that. My daughter is studying at the University of Chile, and we can't pay for two university tuitions.

I think that there is a blacklist that is distributed among the business owners and it keeps many exiles from working in certain companies. And, in our case, the Defense Ministry isn't going to give us work. We can't get in to the units of the armed forces to ask for information or documents. They ask us for our ID card, they check it, and, in a bit, the officer comes with two guards. "Sir," they tell us, "we can't help you. You cannot be here, please leave." "But why — we have a democracy now, it's all over." "No, you have to leave here."

I went to apply for work. They thought that I had a very good résumé, excellent for work in the metal mechanical industry, able to speak English and everything. I left the application, I signed, and I never heard anything else. I went to LAN Chile; I sent letters to Ladeco [LAN Chile and Ladeco are Chile's major airlines] with my résumé, to Fast Air. I even have a friend who is manager of maintenance, a former engineer with the air force. He hugged me when I arrived. I presented myself, left my résumé; he said to me, "I'll let you know, I don't foresee any problem," and nothing happened.

Now, I do translations on a computer that I have, and I work in auto mechanics. In England, I did that with friends and now I work in this, on my own. I live on an air force pension that I have the right to, according to the law, and because of that, I was able to survive the jail time and my family too and this house could be paid for while I was there. When I returned, I went to the Caja de Previsión to get my severance pay that they were required to pay me since they threw me out of the institution. They told me, "It isn't here." I told them that I have never collected it. I am waiting for an answer from the government, and if I don't get it I am going to have to write to the National Comptroller to ask for an investigation into my severance pay. I have been told that these monies were paid to the intelligence services; the DINA took this money.

Now, I worked in England, and my pension fund money is there. There is no way, no agreements with Chile, to transfer those funds. No one will help with the problem — neither the British nor the Chilean government here. There is no political will on either side, because to resolve all this takes a political will.

## María Inés Ruz

*María Inés Ruz (introduced in chapter 2) left Chile under duress after the execution of her compañero. She lived in Cuba from 1975 to 1991, where she worked for the MIR and eventually married a Cuban. Distressed by the declining economy and erosion of morale in Cuba, she returned to Chile, facing the usual problems of unemployment and alienation. She eventually found employment as a journalist at the daily* La Nación, *where she works today. Her sister, visiting from Cuba in 1994, told the authors that despite the economic hardships on the island she still had the security of a subsistence there — something that María Inés Ruz had not achieved in Chile.*

We always had the idea of coming back. There were very concrete things. First, you hadn't left with the idea of staying away. But I wasn't nostalgic about coming back either — nostalgic about the empanadas, the red wine, and the Andes Mountains. But I also never thought that I would live the rest of my life somewhere else. Later, when there was the opportunity someone offered to help me go back, then I decided to come back. Before, I had the logical question of how was I going to come back if all my family was in exile? I didn't have a profession, how would I get settled? But when some friends came to Cuba, they said that they could help me, so then I began to think about coming back.

It also had to have been a factor that I had begun to feel bad in Cuba — not just because of the everyday reality that was becoming more difficult — but also because politically I had begun to feel bad. The MIR was born under the auspices of the Cuban Revolution, which was its light and its guide. So that in the measure in which I began to see that it was a dream and that I felt the impossibility of being a political actor inside this process, I began to feel I wasn't being honest with myself. For example, the first time I decided to buy a chicken on the black market was hard. After that, you get used to it.

But you feel bad because, on the one hand, there is the official discourse, and on the other hand, in your everyday reality you do something different. Certainly, the time I felt very bad was one time in a meeting of the CDR [Committee for the Defense of the Revolution, neighborhood or block committees whose primary functions are to generate support for the Castro government and to suppress dissent]; they said — at this time we had begun to see some posters against Fidel — that they had seen those posters and that by order of the head of the party for the province, if someone spotted a person doing something of this kind, that person was to hit them with whatever came to hand, that later, he or she was to call the Policía Nacional [the National Revolutionary Police, PNR] and that they should not worry, that the PNR would not do anything to the person who had hit the other.

I was able to see that was very bad, very negative, but I didn't dare say anything. So then I had a very guilty conscience because if I — who was Chilean, who was allowed much greater leeway in what I said — could not be consistent with my beliefs, could not say what I thought, say that this did not seem right to me, that it wasn't right to do that, how could I continue to live with this double weight on my conscience? And I think that was one of the deciding factors for me.

My arrival here wasn't easy. Not finding work — I think that is the greatest difficulty everyone who comes back from exile faces. Now I think that in my case it was easier, first because of the attitude I had when I came. I came expecting to find this reality and not another, with the idea that I was going to find people who were concerned with their own survival and not with being in solidarity. Even then, I think that I have received a great deal of solidarity. This table that we are at, this chair, the beds, the sheets, the towels at my house are from people who gave them to me, and the clothes that I have on too—so then this is a concrete manifestation of solidarity. I have found a great deal of solidarity.

I have been lucky, but I tell you that it also depends on the attitude you have when you come. If you come with the idea that here I am, and I have an important story, and I have to find someone who will recognize the importance of this story—well, it's not like that. You get here and you feel like no one knows you, no one knows who Fernando Krauss [her compañero, executed after the coup] was, it doesn't matter to anyone what happened at the time of the coup, nor the repression, nor anything. You are another number and what you went through is no more valuable or tragic than what happened to those who lived through the dictatorship here. Many times I have thought that the people who stayed in Chile suffered more than those of us who left. Those of us who left received at some point political and social recognition from the people who took us in. Those who stayed here had to hide and swallow their ideas and their feelings for a long time, and this is more damaging than what we could have suffered.

So then if you get here and you say, "Look, recognize me—I was exiled such and such number of years and now you have to help me"—that compañero who stayed here or that ordinary family without work, humiliated, that had to swallow its ideas and its emotions says to you: "What right do you have to arrive here from somewhere else and ask me this when I have suffered more and there isn't a return law [the 1990 law establishing benefits for returning exiles] for me and I don't receive compassion or any help at all?"

Because of this, I think that the attitude you come with is very important. It is basic, and we, since we arrived—and we arrived pretty much with the clothes on our backs, with our suitcases full of books—we found solidarity because Felo, my Cuban husband, within fifteen days was working at a center run by former MIRistas. Of course, I didn't arrive in the conditions that a family would that has no political connections. I had broken with the MIR, but my political relationships continued, so because of that I had friends, I had people here and there and you start to look around.

I found a job doing surveys, later I started at an NGO. With this, plus what my husband brought in, we never went hungry. But we don't buy a single Coke, nor a chocolate bar, we never permit those luxuries at our house, never. We knew that we were coming to a society where all these things existed, but we continue to have the same level of consumption that we had in Cuba. We always manage, first with what the United Nations gave us, later with Felo's small salary, with what I got from the WUS scholarship—I applied for a WUS scholarship. The worst moment was when I replaced someone for three months at *La Nación*, and after that, when the replacement job ended, I didn't have the scholarship any longer, I didn't have the job with the NGO, Felo was out of work, and we were totally up in the air. That was some two years after we came back, there was no longer any solidarity and we had to do something. I started doing polls in Valparaíso.

When I started at *La Nación*, it was the first time after I came back that I worked in a job with a lot of people, in a workplace, so I had to muster my courage, and at the same time be modest when I told a girl twenty-five years old, who was my boss, when I was forty-four, "I don't know how to do this," and have her say to me, "You do it this way," and recognize my shortcomings, my lack of experience. I took it very calmly—I was very sure that this was what I had to do. It wasn't easy because at this moment here in Chile, people are young—wherever you go, you are the oldest, that is, you go into a workplace and the people are twenty years old and up, the average is thirty and below, so then when a gal of forty-plus comes in and, on top of that, doesn't know how to do things, it isn't easy. So then, as I told you, I accepted it stoically.

And besides, we were used to being key figures, we were leaders—I spoke at assemblies, I led party meetings. We thought that we were, in some way, people who had something to say to others, to show others the way. So then you get here and your real condition is that of one more in the crowd, and I think that having realized that I am just one more in the crowd was still valuable—even so, I don't have to forget my experience. My experience still helps me to face life, but I don't have the right to tell anyone anything.

## Ramiro Arratia

*Ramiro Arratia was born in Santiago in 1951 and brought up in a middle-class family. He studied in public schools and the University of Chile, where he was enrolled in the Faculty of Chemistry at the time of the coup. Although supportive of the UP government, Arratia was not a party member nor an activist, being dedicated rather to finishing his studies. Nonetheless, he was interrogated extensively following September 11,*

*along with faculty and other students. Following his graduation in 1976,*
*neither he nor his classmates could find employment owing, he believes, to*
*the blacklist. After four years of unemployment, he received a Fulbright*
*grant and a teaching assistantship for graduate study at the University of*
*California, Davis, where he finished a doctorate in 1984.*

*Arratia was one of the lucky exiles to be offered a job in Chile while*
*still abroad. After teaching stints in the United States and Canada, he*
*was contracted in 1989 by the Pontífica Universidad Católica on the basis*
*of his research record and growing reputation. Despite what might be*
*called, paraphrasing the term applied to exiles, a "golden return," Arratia*
*soon discovered that the realities of being a returned exile applied even*
*to persons such as himself who had had no active involvement in leftist*
*politics. Today, he teaches at the Universidad Austral de Chile in*
*Valdivia.*

I settled in at the Catholic University, having been hired at the lowest
rank, with no credit for my successful academic performance in the U.S.
and Canada. Nevertheless, I was so happy to have returned to my country
that these economic details were of secondary concern. I directed research theses and my students graduated with high honors and then were
accepted at Canadian and American universities. I carried out research on
an international level, as a result of which I got funded for numerous national research projects and also some from the European Community —
I was the only staff member in the Chemistry Department who had received international grants with budgets that were very high by Chilean
standards. This obviously generated a great deal of envy among my colleagues and I was constantly excluded from positions of power in which I
could bring all my experience to the service of the academic community.

Having funds for the training of students, I invited and financed the
visit of a Cuban academic to do his doctorate under my direction, and
thus brought the first foreign student into the Chemistry Department.
The director of graduate studies at the time manipulated the applications
of the doctoral students in such a way as to give scholarships only to Chilean students, even though their records were inferior to that of the Cuban
student. This open arbitrariness and discrimination against the Cuban
and against me led me to take the problem to higher authorities in the
Catholic University, who decided against me, saying that I was a conflictive person.

In the story that follows, it could be that other factors have influenced
the attitudes and actions of my ex-colleagues and the university adminis-

tration. But one thing is clear, and it is that as someone returned from exile, I never received the same consideration, the same treatment, that the other academics at the Catholic University receive. This could be seen from the beginning, personally as well as professionally. It was as if, having returned, I didn't have, because of this fact, the same rights as the others. In addition, I had to make a greater effort to prove my abilities, and, in return, received even greater ostracism and discrimination. There was no way to be successful in that bastion of conservatism. Perhaps in a state university it wouldn't have been that way.

Well, the story is that in a secret meeting among five members of the department and presided over by the dean at that time, they decided to end my academic functions. All this was done in complete violation of the academic statutes of the university, and the rector signed my firing September 30, 1994. The rector later saw me and explained to me that a group of "distinguished academics" had asked that I be relieved of my duties, to which he had agreed. I told him that according to university rules, the Faculty Council was the only group legally allowed to terminate academics' contracts. He argued that many times Faculty Councils don't act in accord with the university's interests. This statement amazed me and I understood that his decision had been completely arbitrary and in flagrant violation of the existing rules. All of this confirmed my worst fears in dealing with a rector appointed by decree of the military government in 1985.

My firing even inspired the dean of the School of Chemistry to order the confiscation of all the materials from the research I had carried out in my five years working there, and they even violated my e-mail. Fortunately, my lawyers presented the case to the Appeals Court and the Labor Board, who after months of deliberation found in my favor, and it was even confirmed by the Supreme Court, ordering the immediate surrender of all the research materials belonging to me. In retaliation, the university authorities interceded with other universities so that they would not hire me. Fortunately, after four months without work, the Universidad Austral de Chile in Valdivia hired me at the highest academic rank. The solidarity of the academics at the Universidad de Chile and of some ex-colleagues from the Catholic University helped me enormously to get through those terrible moments, and I am very grateful to my lawyers, the colleagues who showed their solidarity, and the administration of the Universidad Austral for giving me the moral support to be able to stay in my beloved country and thus be able to give the best of myself to contribute to the consolidation of democracy in Chile.

# Julio Pérez

*Julio Pérez (introduced in chapter 3), a journalist and member of the MIR, lived fourteen years in Montreal. Today, Pérez lives with his Canadian wife and their daughter in Temuco, where he is director of communications for the Universidad de la Frontera. His return in 1988 has been marked by the usual problems, exacerbated by the frustration of official indifference toward the certification of his wife's credentials to practice her profession in Chile. His critical views of post-Pinochet Chile underscore the feelings of many retornados that the country to which they returned is not the same one they left.*

I had many reasons to return to Chile. One of them was to be with my parents again. They had immigrated to Canada in 1980, in September, at the beginning of the Nordic winter. They had come before to visit, separately, and they were enthused about the idea of coming back again to live with us—my wife and my daughter. They did the necessary paperwork and came as immigrants.

My father, a railroad worker with little formal education, had serious difficulties when it came to learning the language. On the other hand, my mother adapted easily and learned French quickly. I think that my father lost his independence and came to depend on my mother for even basic communication. This was one of the reasons for their decision to return to Chile seven months later. Also, my sister was still here; she had not been able to get permission to come to Canada. It was very painful for my mother, since she was happy in Canada. For her, as a woman, it was the discovery of another world—things that she hadn't had in Chile, the possibility of having a social life through organizations for those in the "third age" [used in some countries instead of "senior citizens"], which had many trips, parties, and meetings constantly.

Well, we arrived here in January of 1988. We came to my parents' house. I think that this was exhilarating for many of the exiles: coming back to the home of some family member. After fourteen years of absence, it was all wonderful the first two months; then living together got harder.

These were very hard times, with no friends, without contacts, without knowing the city. Before I went into exile, I had always lived and studied in the south. The first great difficulty was trying to find a school for my daughter. The school year was beginning and it was urgent. Choosing among a jungle of schools—the majority of them private—was very complicated and especially without having much information. The Pinochet government allowed the indiscriminate creation of private schools, institutes, and universities, many of them of dubious quality.

Then, looking for a place to live without much money was not an easy task either. Finally, I found a place where I began to work as foreman for a construction firm in a housing complex; I had a house there. At least, I think that my experience in Canada of working in any number of things and different occupations helped me to find work in Chile. For my daughter and my Canadian wife, it wasn't easy. The difference in the conditions of hygiene in Chile, so different from that of her country, caused my wife to catch typhus, which confined her to bed for three months. Fortunately, during this period, we were living in the same place where I worked, which allowed me to take care of her. Typhus is an illness that keeps sufferers off their feet for at least two months. Also, I had gotten a job doing commentaries on videos for a specialized journal. This meant that we watched an average of three or four videos a day for almost a year.

In October of 1988, the first elections took place in Chile. Without a doubt, having experienced this period was very interesting for me. I managed to get a job for a year in a press agency, France Presse, which allowed me to have a position of privilege to witness the electoral process and the transition from dictatorship to democratic life. I also worked on the first leftist magazine, *Página Abierta*, that opened up that space at the end of the Pinochet era and did very interesting work from a journalistic perspective. Such activity in a situation leading to an eventual return to democracy made our work something very special. Seeing the huge demonstrations with the hope that people had for better days was really moving. A people who had lived sixteen years under the military boot had the right to dream. It was a wonderful period in which everyone said, "Happiness is coming!" The day that the "NO" won, people came out by the thousands to celebrate the arrival of democracy.

What hurt me most when I arrived in Chile was to see the lack of solidarity on the part of the majority of Chileans with those who returned. There were very few who offered a hand or were interested in our past. Even worse, if you have come back with a little money, they look at you with envy. If you have studied and gotten a Master's or a doctorate, that is another sin. They conclude that you have had a "golden exile."

Another factor that contributes to the frustration is the fact that my wife, who worked shoulder to shoulder with the exiles in solidarity work with Chile in Canada, helping those who came to Montreal get household goods for their homes, looking for apartments, acting as interpreter, doing translations—today in Chile, she is not allowed to work. They won't accept her degrees. She is a sexologist. Since in Chile this profession doesn't exist, they won't recognize it. Four years of paperwork and more paperwork without any possibility of her working. Perhaps in Chile, there aren't any sexual problems, we say to ourselves. Also, connections with political parties, the church, personal connections [*pitutos*] are essential if you want to find a job. These count more than any degree or experience.

It was difficult for me to find steady work. At one point, I had five different jobs: university professor from 8:30 to 9:30 in the morning; teacher at a professional institute from 6:30 to 8:00 at night; reporter at a newspaper during the day; press advisor in a university; and, at night, editor of a scientific journal. Fortunately, this last job could be done at home. Every day, for a year and a half, was a marathon for me that with luck I managed to endure.

Those of us who dreamed of a different Chile suffered great disillusionment. In general, people are concerned with consumerism and their personal problems. Twenty-five years ago, the price of public transportation went up and people took to the streets in protest. Today, the pollution kills children and old people during the winter months. Public transportation has become a jungle where the survival of the fittest rules and the pedestrian is the one who suffers. The work week is fifty hours a week. Faced with these — which are some of the most dramatic situations — Chileans don't react. Everything is normal. This is very difficult for me to accept.

All of this and many other things merely reflect the fierce capitalism that rules in this country, something that really impacts those who return — be it from socialist or capitalist countries. Everything is privatized: public transportation, the schools and the universities, the pension funds and health insurance. If you want to play a sport, enjoy life, you have to have a great deal of money. The free-market economy really rules with the complicating factor that of thirteen million people, which is the population of Chile, almost five million live in poverty, and of the eight million left, I think that five million live in a permanent state of anguish in order to be able to survive.

And there's another thing that's not talked about, but is real. Everyone uses the term "democracy" as if it applied to Chile, but all you have to do is look at the constitution and the electoral law to see that this country is a long way from a democracy where everyone's vote counts the same. What do I mean? The appointed senators, the system of electing congress — these and other things that give the right a veto power and make a real change impossible. There's no doubt that Pinochet's advisors were

very smart; they thought the whole thing through and left us with the fa-
cade but not the substance of a democracy. We'll be living with the legacy
of the dictatorship for a long time.*

## Viola Carrillo

*Viola Carrillo (introduced in chapter 5) left Chile at eight years of age for
the Soviet Union, after her coal-miner father was executed. The collapse of
the Soviet Union in 1991 ended the subsidies and privileges that foreign
refugees, including Carrillo and her family, had received from the Communist government. When the Aylwin government sent an air force plane
to Moscow in April 1993 to pick up Chileans stranded without resources,
she joined some sixty Chileans, many with spouses and children from the
former Soviet Union, who made the trip. The irony of her rescue by the
same military that had caused her exile was not lost on her. Arriving in
Chile, Carrillo faced the usual difficult problems of reinsertion: little support, no job, few prospects for improvement. Today, she works part-time in
a family owned, not very successful restaurant.*

When the system changed, no one cared any longer about us, the Chileans. No one was responsible for us nor helped us to get work papers. So
then, with the changes in the government in both countries, there was an
embassy now, and we went there to ask for help. After some time, they
sent a FACh [Chilean Air Force] plane.

I had never wanted to return to Chile that way, in spite of the fact that
we were well treated during the flight, and the flight itself was excellent.
Of all my brothers and sisters, I was the only one that had my travel papers up to date; because of visa problems, many people couldn't go. It was
terrible because many of them had been waiting for a year to be able to

* The 1980 constitution and the electoral law, both dictated by the Pinochet government, remain in force today. Between them, these two documents establish
mechanisms, such as the nine appointed senators along with thirty-eight elected
ones, that drastically overrepresent the right and prevent the country's political majority, the center–left Concertación, from amending either the constitution or the
electoral law. These continuing constraints on democracy, which preserve a strong
military power in government, had become a source of growing political tension by
1997. Tomás Moulian, *Chile actual: anatomía de un mito* (Santiago: ARCIS Universidad: Lom Ediciones, 1997), refers to the institutionalized obstacles to democracy as
"the iron cage."

leave. I was unsure about returning, but I got my papers ready because I had seen that it took some people so long that I thought that when I wanted to come I would have to wait much longer. Right when I had decided and I had my papers up to date, they notified us that they were sending the plane. Even though they said that it was from the FACh, I said, "Well, even so, I am going to Chile," and I came with my son.

On the plane, people were very worried. There had been many marriages of Chilean men or Chilean women with Russians. Some had gone to study in the ex–Soviet Union before 1973 and the coup caught them there; so then, they had been there for more than twenty years. At the Chilean embassy they had promised us many things, but people were worried because they didn't know what arriving there would be like. And they were right.

I have run into some of the people who came on that flight, and they are thinking about going back. Some families are very badly off economically. At first, they gave us a little of this and a little of that, some money—to a certain extent to keep us quiet. I, unfortunately, many times, protested in the Oficina de Retorno; one thing that I have is plenty of dignity and I don't like having to beg anyone.

They offered me a house on loan for three months. I took it at the beginning, but I didn't even have money to buy any furniture, besides which, it was over there near La Pintana [a Santiago población, extremely poor and considered very dangerous]. I didn't have any money. At first they said that they were going to give us the money for furniture, and then it turned out that there wasn't money for anything. People got tired of that. There were Russian women who cried, who were in really awful conditions. The worst part was their children. Some had children who were eleven, twelve, and I know of specific cases who have gone back.

Only recently, with the help of Vasily [her brother, a former member of the FPMR, who participated in the 1986 assassination attempt on Pinochet], who is working, I have been able to get together enough money to move. Then they told us that they would give us the opportunity to present a proposal, possibilities of scholarships, but up to the present time they haven't given me anything. I applied for a scholarship from WUS three months ago and I haven't gotten an answer. And as far as my brothers and sisters, none of them have gotten anything, except Vasily because he is Vasily Carrillo.

Those of us who came from Russia didn't bring anything, absolutely nothing. The only treasure that we brought was our education. I didn't bring any money, but I came with a degree. And what good does it do us now if they won't recognize our degrees here? The bureaucracy insists on stamps—and stamps from the ex–Soviet Union—before they will even look at our papers. Now, there have been many changes in the ex–Soviet Union and to get papers is a story in itself. The Chileans who have come from the Soviet Union are principally people with a profession, many of them agronomists. People that are being wasted, because they have knowledge and experience because they worked there for a long time, they were qualified specialists. Here, they don't accept any of that.

What I would like is some day to get work and have money I can save for a ticket. I would like to go back and visit Moscow, walk through the streets, go back to the university, go to the school where I studied. But, even more, I would like to have my family together—half is here, half there. My mother is still in the Ukraine. She is retired, but her pension isn't enough.

# Selected Bibliography

BOOKS ON CHILE DURING THE ALLENDE PRESIDENCY, THE MILITARY
REGIME, AND THE TRANSITION TOWARD DEMOCRACY

Alexander, Robert J. *The Tragedy of Chile*. Westport, Conn.: Greenwood Press, 1978.

Allende, Salvador. *Allende: su pensamiento político*. Santiago: Editorial Quimantú, 1972.

Almeyda, Clodomiro. *Reencuentro con mi vida*. Santiago: Ediciones del Ornitorrinco, 1987.

Aman, Kenneth, and Cristián Parker, eds. *Popular Culture in Chile: Resistance and Survival*. Translated by Terry Cambias. Boulder: Westview Press, 1991.

Angell, Alan. *Chile de Alessandri a Pinochet: En busca de la utopía*. Santiago: Editorial Andrés Bello, 1993.

Arriagada, Genaro. *Pinochet: The Politics of Power*. Translated by Nancy Morris. Boston: Unwin Hyman, 1988.

Bitar, Sergio. *Chile: Experiment in Democracy*. Philadelphia: Institute for the Study of Human Issues, 1986.

Campero, Guillermo, and José A. Valenzuela. *El movimiento sindical en el régimen militar chileno, 1973–1981*. Santiago: Latin American Institute of Transnational Studies, 1984.

Cassidy, Sheila. *Audacity to Believe*. London: Collins, 1977.

Cavallo Castro, Ascanio, Manuel Salazar Salvo, and Oscar Sepúlveda Pacheco. *La historia oculta del régimen militar*. Santiago: Editorial Antártica, 1990.

Caviedes, César. *Elections in Chile: The Road to Redemocratization*. Boulder: Lynne Rienner, 1991.

Chile. Comisión Nacional de Verdad y Reconciliación. Report of the Chilean National Commission on Truth and Reconciliation. 2 vols. Translated by Phillip E. Berryman. Notre Dame: Notre Dame University Press, 1993.

Constable, Pamela, and Arturo Valenzuela. *Chile under Pinochet: A Nation of Enemies.* New York: W. W. Norton, 1991.

De la Maza, Gonzalo, and Mario Garcés. *La explosión de las mayorías: protesta nacional, 1983–1984.* Santiago: Editorial ECO, 1985.

Délano, Manuel, and Hugo Traslaviña. *La herencia de los Chicago Boys.* Santiago: Ediciones del Ornitorrinco, 1989.

De Vylder, Stefan. *Allende's Chile: The Political Economy of the Rise and Fall of the Unidad Popular.* Cambridge: Cambridge University Press, 1976.

Drake, Paul, and Iván Jaksić. *The Struggle for Democracy in Chile, 1982–1990.* Rev. ed. Lincoln: University of Nebraska Press, 1995.

Fernandois, Joaquín. *Chile y el mundo, 1970–1973: la política exterior del gobierno de la Unidad Popular y el sistema internacional.* Santiago: Ediciones Universidad Católica de Chile, 1985.

Furci, Carmelo. *The Chilean Communist Party and the Road to Socialism.* London: Zed Press, 1984.

Garcés, Joan. *Allende y la experiencia chilena.* Barcelona: Editorial Ariel, 1976.

Garretón, Manuel Antonio. *The Chilean Political Process.* Boston: Unwin Hyman, 1989. Translated by Sharon Kellum.

Gil, Federico, Ricardo Lagos, and Henry Landsberger, eds. *Chile at the Turning Point: Lessons of the Socialist Years, 1970–1973.* Philadelphia: Instutute for the Study of Human Issues, 1979.

Hojman, Eugenio. *Memorial de la dictadura: 1973–1989.* Santiago: Editorial Emisión, n.d.

Jaksić, Iván. *Academic Rebels in Chile.* Albany: State University of New York Press, 1989.

Lowden, Pamela. *Moral Opposition to Authoritarian Rule in Chile, 1973–90.* London: MacMillan Press, 1996.

Moulian, Tomás. *Chile actual: anatomía de un mito.* Santiago: ARCIS Universidad: Lom Ediciones, 1997.

Muñoz, Heraldo. *Las relaciones exteriores del gobierno militar chileno.* Santiago: Ediciones del Ornitorrinco, 1986.

Oppenheim, Lois Hecht. *Politics in Chile: Democracy, Authoritarianism, and the Search for Development.* Boulder: Westview Press, 1993.

Orellana, Patricio, and Elizabeth Quay Hutchison. *El movimiento de derechos humanos en Chile, 1973–1990.* Santiago: Centro de Estudios Políticos Latinoamericanos Simón Bolívar (CEPLA), 1991.

Oxhorn, Philip. *Organizing Civil Society: The Popular Sectors and the Struggle for Democracy in Chile.* University Park: Pennsylvania State University Press, 1995.

Pinochet, Augusto, *El día decisivo: 11 de septiembre de 1973.* Santiago: Editorial Andrés Bello, 1979.

Pinto, Myriam, Rody Oñate, and Diego Vergara. *Porqué fuimos médicos del pueblo: Los médicos asesinados durante la dictadura militar en Chile.* Santiago: Ediciones ChileAmérica CESOC, 1993.

Politzer, Patricia. *Fear in Chile: Lives under Pinochet.* New York: Pantheon Books, 1989. Translated by Diane Wachtell.

Prats, Carlos. *Memorias: Testimonio de un soldado.* Santiago: Ediciones Pehuén, 1985.

Puryear, Jeffrey M. *Thinking Politics: Intellectuals and Democracy in Chile, 1973–1988.* Baltimore: Johns Hopkins University Press, 1994.

Reszczynski, Katia, Paz Rojas, and Patricia Barceló. *Tortura y resistencia en Chile: estudio médico-político.* Santiago: Editorial Emisión, 1991.

Rojas, Carmen. *Recuerdos de una MIRista.* Montevideo: Ediciones del Taller, 1988.

Roxborough, Ian, Philip O'Brien, and Jackie Roddick. *Chile: The State and Revolution.* New York: Holmes and Meier, 1977.

Schneider, Cathy Lisa. *Shantytown Protest in Pinochet's Chile.* Philadelphia: Temple University Press, 1995.

Sigmund, Paul. *The Overthrow of Allende and the Politics of Chile, 1964–1976.* Pittsburgh: University of Pittsburgh Press, 1977.

Smith, Brian H. *The Church and Politics in Chile: Challenges to Modern Catholicism.* Princeton: Princeton University Press, 1982.

Spooner, Mary Helen. *Soldiers in a Narrow Land: The Pinochet Regime in Chile.* Berkeley: University of California Press, 1994.

Valdés, Juan Gabriel. *Pinochet's Economists: The Chicago School in Chile.* Cambridge: Cambridge University Press, 1995.

Valenzuela, Arturo. *The Breakdown of Democratic Regimes: Chile.* Baltimore: Johns Hopkins University Press, 1978.

Valenzuela, J. Samuel, and Arturo Valenzuela, eds. *Military Rule in Chile: Dictatorship and Oppositions.* Baltimore: Johns Hopkins University Press, 1986.

Valenzuela, María Elena. *La mujer en el Chile militar.* Santiago: Ediciones ChileAmérica CESOC, 1987.

Verdugo, Patricia. *Los zarpazos del puma.* Santiago: Ediciones ChileAmérica CESOC, 1989.

Winn, Peter. *Weavers of Revolution: The Yarur Workers and Chile's Road to Socialism.* New York: Oxford University Press, 1986.

### BOOKS ON CHILEAN EXILE

Arrate, Jorge. *Exilio: textos de denuncia y esperanza.* Santiago: Documentas, 1987.

Celedón, María Angélica, and Luz María Opazo. *Volver a empezar.* Santiago: Pehuén, 1987.

García Márquez, Gabriel. *Clandestine in Chile: The Adventures of Miguel Littín.* Translated by Asa Zatz. New York: Henry Holt, 1987.

Kay, Diana. *Chileans in Exile: Private Struggles, Public Lives.* Wolfeboro, N.H.: Longwood Academic, 1987.

Montupil I., Fernando, ed. *Exilio, derechos humanos y democracia: el exilio chileno en*

*Europa*. Brussels and Santiago: Casa de América Latina and Servicios Gráficos Caupolicán, 1993.

Olea Guldemont, Mario. *Recuerdos de un exilio en Suiza*. Santiago: Imprenta Arygo, 1992.

Rivano, Juan. *Epoca de descubrimientos*. Furulund, Sweden: Alhambra de Lund, 1991.

Rodríguez Villouta, Mili. *Ya nunca me verás como me vieras: doce testimonios vivos del exilio*. Santiago: Ediciones del Ornitorrinco, 1990.

Vásquez, Ana, and Ana María Araujo. *La maldición de Ulises: Repercusiones psicológicas del exilio*. Santiago: Sudamericana, 1990.

Vergottini, Tomaso de. *Miguel Claro 1359: Recuerdos de un diplomático italiano en Chile (1973–1975)*. Santiago: Atena, 1991.

Zerán Chelech, Faride. *O el asilo contra la opresión: 23 historias para recordar*. Santiago: Paradox, 1991.

# List of Interviews

* All interviews were conducted in Santiago, Chile, unless otherwise noted.
† The interview with Julieta Campusano was conducted between September and November 1991. Our thanks to the interviewer, Germán Palacios.

Ana Laura Cataldo: 6/26/94
Astrid Stoehrel: 6/28/94
María Inés Ruz: 6/29/94
Silvia Quiroga: 6/30/94
Guillermo Meza: 4/20/95, Reno, Nevada
Julio Pérez (anonymous): 5/16/95
Eduardo Montecinos: 7/18/95, San José, Costa Rica
Benjamín Teplizky Lijavetzky: 7/20/95
Anselmo Sule: 7/23/95
Gabriel Fernández (anonymous): 7/28/95
Ximena González: 8/15/95
Ramiro Arriata: 9/22/95
Sergio Buschmann: 2/15/96
Iván Jaksić: 2/17/96, South Bend, Indiana

### OTHER INTERVIEWS

Mario Toro: Oficina Nacional de Retorno, 11/2/93, 6/27/94
Mireya Vera: FASIC, 11/7/93
Ximena Erazo: World University Service, 11/23/93
Isabel Araya: World University Service, 12/1/93
Luis Caro: exile pastor, 6/16/94
Cristián Precht: Archbishopric of Santiago, 6/21/94
Juan Veglia: Organización Internacional para las Migraciones, 6/24/94
Anthony Vassiliadis: Organización Internacional para las Migraciones, 6/28/94
Francisco Orellana: academic and human-rights worker, 6/29/94
Marta Pérez: Comisión Chilena de Derechos Humanos, 6/30/94
Roberto Kozak: Organización Internacional para las Migraciones, 9/10/94

# Index